Proactive Child Protection and Social Work

SAGE was founded in 1965 by Sara Miller McCune to support the dissemination of usable knowledge by publishing innovative and high-quality research and teaching content. Today, we publish over 900 journals, including those of more than 400 learned societies, more than 800 new books per year, and a growing range of library products including archives, data, case studies, reports, and video. SAGE remains majority-owned by our founder, and after Sara's lifetime will become owned by a charitable trust that secures our continued independence.

Los Angeles | London | New Delhi | Singapore | Washington DC | Melbourne

2nd Edition

Proactive Child Protection and Social Work

Liz Davies and Nora Duckett

⑤SAGE | *m* LearningMatters

Series Editors:
Jonathan Parker and Greta Bradley

Learning Matters
An imprint of SAGE Publications Ltd
1 Oliver's Yard
55 City Road
London EC1Y 1SP

SAGE Publications Inc.
2455 Teller Road
Thousand Oaks, California 91320

SAGE Publications India Pvt Ltd
B 1/I 1 Mohan Cooperative Industrial Area
Mathura Road
New Delhi 110 044

SAGE Publications Asia-Pacific Pte Ltd
3 Church Street
#10–04 Samsung Hub
Singapore 049483

© 2016 Liz Davies and Nora Duckett

First published in 2008 by Learning Matters Ltd.
Reprinted in 2009. Reprinted in 2011. Second edition
published in 2016.

Editor: Kate Wharton
Production controller: Chris Marke
Project management by Deer Park Productions
Marketing manager: Tamara Navaratnam
Cover design: Wendy Scott
Typeset by: C&M Digitals (P) Ltd, Chennai, India
Printed and bound by CPI Group (UK) Ltd,
Croydon, CR0 4YY

Library of Congress Control Number: 2016930685

British Library Cataloguing in Publication Data

A CIP record for this book is available from the British
Library.

ISBN 978-0-85725-971-4 (pbk)
ISBN 978-1-4462-5712-8

In memory of Helen Mitchell (1.01.1967–26.01.2014)
social worker and whistleblower

Contents

About the authors

Liz Davies is an Emeritus Reader in Child Protection at London Metropolitan University and a registered social worker. She began her academic post in 2002, and gained her PhD, entitled *Protecting children – a critical contribution to policy and practice development*. Following her work in the 1970s as a mental health social worker, she was team manager in the London Borough of Islington where she exposed wide scale abuse of children within the care system. In the 1990s, as child protection manager and trainer in the London Borough of Harrow, she developed a specialism in conducting serious case reviews as well as in the investigation of organised crime and abuse networks. Liz co-authored the first edition of *Proactive Child Protection and Social Work* (2008) and *Communicating with Children and Their Families* (2013), both widely used as academic texts. She trained police and social workers for over 15 years in Achieving Best Evidence skills and published training manuals in joint investigation and investigative interviewing. As an academic for 13 years, she designed and delivered social work courses on communication in social work, protecting children and children's social policy, and also supervised PhDs. As a regular contributor to television, radio and print media, she has long campaigned to achieve justice for survivors of abuse, most recently working with the WhiteFlowers survivor and whistleblower network. In 2015, she supported the relaunch of the BASW London Forum and contributes to the BASW Children and Families Committee. Her website is www.lizdavies.net

Nora Duckett is a Senior Lecturer in Social Work at Anglia Ruskin University in Chelmsford, Essex and a registered social worker. She began her academic career in 2003 and in 2008 co-authored, with Liz Davies, the first edition of *Proactive Child Protection and Social Work*. Between 2008 and 2011 she contributed to a three-year youth homelessness research project, commissioned by the EU, and she is currently undertaking doctorate level study looking at improving understandings of professional dangerousness in child protection social work education and practice. Prior to her academic role, in the mid-1980s Nora worked in an inner London borough as an unqualified family aide, which led her to complete an access course and obtain a degree and a social work qualification. As well as spending several years working as a social worker in the community and in a hospital setting, she helped pioneer a young women's sexual exploitation service in central London and managed a young runaways strategy project, raising awareness of the risks of running away and coordinating services across London. Her experience of social work with children, young people and families is at the heart of her work as an academic.

Acknowledgements

We acknowledge the contribution of many survivors and whistleblowers, who constantly inform our work, including from the WhiteFlowers campaign. We also remember the children and families in the London Boroughs of Islington and Westminster, and where we worked together in the London Borough of Harrow, as well as young women in the sexual exploitation project *Breaking Free*, all of whose lives we recalled over and over again in writing this second edition. We thank Louise Cooper and Brian Douieb as without their support this book would not have been completed.

Foreword

The revised edition of this book comes at an important time for social workers. Amid the changed and changing political context, which is having such a significant impact on children's present and future circumstances, social workers need courage and integrity to fight for social justice for children. To do so they need to be informed by sound evidence such as this book provides.

I first met Liz in 2004, when she made *Golly in the Cupboard* (Frampton, 2004 – my childhood memoir of growing up as a mixed race boy in children's homes) a key text for social work students. I have since taught many times with both Liz and Nora, contributing my experience and knowledge as a care leaver, survivor and campaigner to social work modules at London Metropolitan University.

The first edition of *Proactive Child Protection and Social Work* became a key text for UK social work courses and reviews praised its practical relevance. This second edition strengthens a children's rights perspective, updates research evidence and focuses in depth on the unmet, neglected protection needs of children in custody, disabled children, young carers and unaccompanied child migrants. The book also draws attention to changes in policy and political and resource reasons for gaps in the social work response as demonstrated by a wide range of case studies.

As co-ordinator of WhiteFlowers, a loose network of campaigners and whistleblowers, I have worked with both authors. Liz, as the whistleblower for children abused in Islington children's homes, has worked for over 25 years to seek justice for survivors. Together we have raised issues in the media and through political channels, including, in 2015, hosting two unprecedented conferences of survivors, whistleblowers, child protection professionals, lawyers and politicians at the House of Commons.

As in this revised edition, WhiteFlowers provides a voice to survivors and draws public attention to the experiences of victims. On the Belgian march of 1996, over 300,000 people carried white flowers in solidarity with parents of the children kidnapped and murdered by a group of child sex abusers connected to powerful people. On 4 October 2014, more than 50 survivors and whistleblowers held a vigil outside 114 Grosvenor Avenue in the London borough of Islington. As it poured with rain, they laid white flowers and spoke about abuse of children in this council home during the 1980s and 1990s.

Nicholas Rabet was a manager at Grosvenor Avenue children's home. He dressed like a cowboy with big boots and a sheriff's badge and owned an amusement arcade in

Sussex. In 1991, Rabet first came to police attention in Cambridge, when photographs were found linking him with a known child sex offender. Later, Sussex police investigated but, despite their best efforts, there was no conviction. Rabet went to Thailand in 1995, was convicted of sexual abuse of 30 boys and then took his own life. Islington survivors say that they were taken by Rabet to Haut de la Garenne, the children's home at the centre of Jersey child abuse.

Many social workers would have visited Grosvenor Avenue just as they visited children in homes across the country where crimes against children are known to have taken place and where children were unprotected. This book is an essential tool for social workers to assist them in hearing the voices of children and noticing the indicators of harm. But as research tells us, hearing and seeing is not enough; children need social work activists and advocates to be courageous in confronting abuse whenever and wherever it happens and pursuing every possible means of keeping children safe. Social workers have a particular duty to children, like those at Grosvenor Avenue, who were in the care of the state. Too many excuses have been made for failings in supporting and protecting young people in care.

In *The Golly in the Cupboard*, I concluded:

> *With all the wealth and knowledge in our society, such children should be looked on as an opportunity to develop fine adults fully contributing to this world rather than future prison fodder. Society pays for its neglect. Children become Adults.*

> (Frampton, 2004)

Protecting young people also involves helping them to develop a strong sense of self-esteem and self-value, and, if society understood and welcomed the real potential of every young person, there would be greater focus on protecting and nurturing every child to achieve that potential. The children's rights approach, presented so consistently throughout this book and grounded in the authors' experience, promotes a sensitive, respectful response to children who have a right to protection from all forms of abuse.

> *Diamonds are not grown in flower nurseries but developed through years of pressure underground. Young people surviving care are diamonds. And diamonds do not appear all polished and shiny. You see a glint and then the task is to polish it. That way you will see the glint turn into a sparkle and the sparkle into a jewel.*

> http://folio4me.co.uk/frampton/showpage.php?page=page6

Phil Frampton www.philframpton.co.uk

Introduction and key themes

A child rights perspective

Children should not be held responsible for reporting their abuse – many will be unable to do so, and feelings of guilt are exacerbated by placing the responsibility for stopping the abuse on their shoulders.

(OCC, 2015, p84)

A rights perspective is fundamental to this book. Protecting children from harm, being proactive in keeping them safe from abuse and crimes perpetrated against them, is a key role for all social workers in the promotion of children's rights. Hearing and responding to children's voices is an essential component of the professional response to abused children. Child abuse is abuse of power and to deny children's voices and fail to protect them constitutes discrimination against children and is an example of how adults misuse their power. *Childism* is the oppression of children and discrimination against them. While racism, ageism, disablism and sexism are rightly part of everyday vocabulary, few have ever heard or thought of *childism*.

The International Federation of Social Workers provides a global definition of social work grounded in human rights:

Social work is a practice-based profession and an academic discipline that promotes social change and development, social cohesion, and the empowerment and libera-tion of people. Principles of social justice, human rights, collective responsibility and respect for diversities are central to social work. Underpinned by theories of social work, social sciences, humanities and indigenous knowledge, social work engages people and structures to address life challenges and enhance wellbeing.

(IFSW, 2014)

An international perspective is essential to a full understanding of social work in the UK and is included wherever relevant in this book, particularly with reference to migration and to varying cultural but abusive practices. Social workers must be aware of world-wide issues affecting the profession or they will not understand the political and social significance of policy and practice changes and the impact on children and families.

The activist Stephan Hessel, a concentration camp survivor who died in 2013, wrote the *Time for Outrage* (2011). His messages are relevant to social work. He stated that:

The worst possible outlook is indifference that says 'I can't do anything about it or I'll get by'. Behaving like that deprives you of one of the essentials of being human:

1

the capacity and the freedom to feel outraged. That freedom is indispensable, as is the political involvement that goes with it. ... The immense gap between the very poor and the very rich never ceases to expand. This alone should arouse our commitment ... They have the nerve to tell us that the state can no longer cover the costs of social programmes. Yet how can the money to continue and extend these as achievements be lacking today when the creation of wealth has grown so enormously? I want each and every one of you to have a reason to be outraged. When something outrages you, as Nazism did me, that is when you become a militant, strong and engaged. You join the movement of history, and the great current of history contin-ues to flow only thanks to each and every one of us. History's direction is towards more justice and more freedom ... When you encounter someone who lacks those [human] rights, have sympathy and help him or her to achieve them.

(pp22–6)

The United Nations Convention on the Rights of the Child (UNCRC) (UN, 1989) is an international treaty and agreement between different governments on a set of rights for children under 18 years. It includes the right to education, the right to play, the right not to be separated from parents unless this is in their best interests, the right to be well cared for if living away from their family, the right to be listened to and to take part in decisions made about their lives, and the right to protection and help from the government. The rights should be implemented without discrimination on grounds such as disability, sex, ethnicity, age, faith or sexual orientation (CRAE, 2014). The UK signed up to this treaty in 1991 and therefore all areas of UK government must do all they can to fulfil children's rights, but the treaty is not part of domestic law. This legislation is referred to throughout this book including reference to where the UK is non-compliant with its principles. The UNCRC includes the following key Articles:

- Article 3: In all actions concerning children, whether undertaken by public or private social welfare institutions, courts of law, administrative authorities or legislative bodies, the best interests of the child shall be the primary consideration.

- Article 19: Parties shall take all appropriate legislative, administrative, social and educational measures to protect the child from all forms of physical or mental violence, injury or abuse, neglect or negligent treatment, maltreatment or exploitation, including sexual abuse, while in the care of parents, legal guardians or any other person who has the care of the child.

- Article 24: All effective and appropriate measures must be taken with a view to abolishing traditional practices prejudicial to the health of children.

- Article 34: Children have a right to protection from sexual abuse.

The Children Acts 1989 and 2004 reflect the principles of the UNCRC (UN, 1989) and state unequivocally that the welfare of children must be the paramount considera-tion. This is sometimes referred to as the paramountcy principle. Child abuse does not simply correlate with social and economic deprivation because all forms of abuse take place within every strata of society. Poor children are more easily visible to the authorities and to the systems assessing their wellbeing and this results in child abuse being seen as situated in that social-economic class. As one example, the *Troubled Families* agenda focused on economically disadvantaged children who were defined as a possible corrosive element in society. Children have received more government attention as potential criminals than as victims requiring protection (Levitas, 2012). A child rights approach applies to all children in society who need protection from harm whether in custody, in care and education institutions, homeless or with their birth or adoptive families.

Statistics of the prevalence rates of child abuse indicate that the professional response is not effective in protecting children from harm. From a study of 6,196 respondents, Radford, et al. (2011, p118) estimated that one in five children aged 11–17 years, one in four aged 18–24 years and one in 17 aged under 11 years in the UK are severely maltreated. Parton (2012) in a critique of Munro (2011) states that the numbers known about and being actively responded to by children's services are considerably lower than those suggested by Radford, et al. (2011). *The potential for the child protection system being overwhelmed if it really did become child centred so that children felt empowered to access help is considerable. In many respects the child protection system acts to control demand and filter cases out of it at various points* (Parton, 2012, p157). He added that although the number of referrals in England was 5 per cent of the child population only 0.31 per cent of children under the age of 18 years were subject to a child protection plan. Children from black and minority ethnic groups are underrepresented in child protection systems and either do not access or receive a poorer quality of support (OCC, 2015, p49; BRAP, 2011). Anti-oppressive practice is integrated throughout this book as it is central to social work. An awareness of and ability to proactively confront and challenge childism, as with racism and other forms of oppression, must be demonstrated throughout all social work practice (HCPC, 2016).

In this book, the rights of all children to be safe are explored and debated. Some children in the UK are particularly oppressed, such as those in custodial settings. Willow, a child rights activist, writes about imprisoned children whose rights are breached in the UK:

> *Imprisoned children inhabit a peculiar world of last resorts. Separation from parents is meant to be a last resort, criminal proceedings are meant to be a last resort, deprivation of liberty is meant to be a last resort, use of force is meant to be a last resort, the removal of clothes is meant to be a last resort, the deliberate infliction of pain as a form of restraint is meant to be a last resort, and personal safety techniques even more of a last resort. In a rich country like ours, with decades of learning about the needs of children – and health, education and child welfare services among the best in the world – it is incongruous that prisons remain a part of the landscape. A roll call of the children who have died in prison since the UK accepted the last resort obligations of the UNCRC stands as a towering memorial of our collective failure.*

(Willow, 2014, p271)

Unaccompanied migrant children are another often unprotected group of children. They are treated unequally by detention and interrogation on entry to the UK, sometimes classified as adults and denied services, and many ruthlessly removed from the UK to unsafe war-torn countries. Some live in poverty in families who have no recourse to public funds, another example of the severe breach of children's rights to be safe from harm. Social workers must oppose all these examples of discrimination and must have the knowledge and skills to be effective in this challenge.

The social work role in protecting children has widened to include *children who are radicalised* as a child protection issue outlined in *Working Together to Safeguard Children* (DfE, 2015, p19). What has become known as the *Prevent* duty became statutory with the implementation of the Counter-Terrorism and Security Act 2015. *Prevent* aims to stop people becoming terrorists by halting the spread of extremist ideology and by mentoring children at risk. Local Safeguarding Children Boards are required to ensure that staff in all agencies are protecting children from the risks associated with radicalisation into extremist activities. Extremism is defined as vocal or active opposition to fundamental British values, including democracy, respect and tolerance of different faiths and beliefs (Home Office, 2015a). *Channel* panels, including the local authority, police and other agencies, must be set up to ensure multi-agency assessment of risk in line with child protection protocols, and children must be considered as potential victims of exploitation (DfE, 2015).

The act of protecting children is political. Children who speak out are silenced, survivors who speak out are silenced and professionals, who speak out for children and survivors, are silenced when they whistleblow on malpractice. Social activism is a core skill of social work. Social workers must comply with ethical codes of practice, work for human rights and social justice, and act with integrity and authenticity. Protecting children is demanding work which can easily overwhelm a social worker. Each of us has to do whatever we can in our corner of practice and sustain a deep awareness of the wider social, economic, cultural and political picture.

Responding to children's voices

The child has a right to express views freely in all matters affecting the child, the views of the child being given due weight in accordance with their age and maturity

(UN, 1989, Article 12)

A thread running throughout all five Ofsted evaluations is the failure to see, listen to or take account of the perspective of the child or children at the centre of a serious case review.

(Brandon, et al., 2013, p18)

Children's voices are represented throughout this book in order to promote their right to be heard and gain protection. *Working Together to Safeguard Children* (DfE, 2015, p11) states that children have expressed their needs as wanting adults to notice what is happening to them and to be heard, understood and seen to be competent within a relationship of trust. They wish to be well informed of procedures and plans as well as about decisions made about them. They ask for support in their own right and to be provided with advocates. Research of 19 children's views of the child protection system provides an insight into children's perceptions of social work:

Twelve children said that the social workers saw them on their own. Older children were more likely than younger children to be seen alone;

Children reported having minimal relationships with their social workers seeing them rarely or only at meetings;

Some found it difficult to talk to their social workers because they felt pressured by the social worker asking questions;

Only 5 children had seen their child protection plans.

(Cossar, et al., 2011, p12)

I could talk to my advocate about any problems and my concerns.

They don't know what I would have said or what I think ... and they wouldn't really know my decisions [without an advocate].

(Laggay and Courtney, 2013, p10).

Independent advocacy must be available to children, empowering and supporting them through child protection processes enabling their full participation. Children need time and space to discuss their situation away from their social worker and family.

Children say that nothing matters more than somebody noticing and caring what happens to them. *She didn't judge me, she understood the kinds of ways I would feel without me telling her ... and gave me space even when my behaviour must have seemed weird and didn't make sense – even to me* (Nelson, 2008a, p35). Social workers often worry that they are too sensitive, feel too much and become over-involved. Yet children, who need protection, are saying that they want social workers, first and foremost, to care about them. Following an abuse referral, children should be seen on their own without alleged or known abusers present. Social workers need to have confidence in ensuring this happens and in entering into the child's world through seeing where they learn, play, eat, sleep and bathe. Ofsted concluded that, a *lesson from the review was that priority needed to be given to providing a safe and trusting environment, away from the carers, for the children to speak about their concerns* (2011a, p7).

Social workers need to be confident to place their feelings in a context of analysis based on knowledge of the subject of child abuse. A comprehensive knowledge base is presented throughout this book to support analysis and challenge dogmatism. Children say they want professionals who are not *rigidly wedded to a narrow understanding of procedures and ... who stick with them over time* (Nelson, 2008a, p31). Yet, in many authorities, an initial referral is passed on to other teams and if the child becomes placed in care there is yet another transfer so that children commonly have three or more social workers within weeks. High staff turnover also results in a lack of continuity, which adds to the abuse children have already experienced, reduces social workers' direct involvement and may lead to mechanistic responses. Working in conveyor-belt systems focused on performance targets relates more to resource limitation than to the needs of children. Social workers need to be creative and persistent in making systems work for the benefit of children. Children especially want to speak about abuse in settings, such as drop-in centres, where they are free to respond away from the abuser. These should be neutral settings away from their home and school where confidentiality is respected, as far as is consistent with the child's safety.

The importance of social workers working closely with police to target child abusers and seek justice for abused children is emphasised in this book because no child will find safety unless either the abuser is removed from their world or the abuser's behaviour is challenged and changed. Proactive protectors, responsible and trusted adults, must be identified and actively engaged in supporting the child. It is not easy for social workers to set aside time for direct work with children. Abused children in particular require sustained and regular contact with social workers to build up trust and to find ways to talk about their distress. *You've got to trust the social worker and she's got to trust you. Otherwise there's no point* (Cossar, et al., 2011, p4). *They didn't have the words, were stuck, paralysed or confused ... If I wanted to tell physically my tongue wouldn't move* (Nelson, 2008a, p11).

- Responding to the needs of children for protection will not be met by the use of tick-box assessment processes but rather through multi-agency working, the implementation of statutory procedures and reaching out to the child through a befriending, unpressurised approach. *The adults praised were honest, thoughtful, empathetic, kind and imaginative in trying to make difficult and humiliating situations easier for children* (Nelson, 2008a, p38). For children to survive abuse takes courage and being heard by even one social worker, survivors tell us, can and does make all the difference.

Overcoming barriers to protecting children

The findings of any next inquiry could reasonably be predicted before it has taken place, we would like to propose that no further public inquiries are commissioned before all training and resource deficiencies identified over the last 30 years have been remedied.

(Reder and Duncan, 2004, p112)

We're seeing children with malnutrition, children who are losing their hair, children who are scavenging in bins. And they are at the bottom of the list. We're snowed under with cases of sexual and physical abuse. Young children battered, shot at, hurled to the wall by drug-addicted parents battling with withdrawal. There are children we don't go near who in order to survive have become drug couriers or drug dealers ... what social worker understands their street language, their criminal network ...

(Keeble and Hollington, 2010, p38)

When protecting children it is important to reflect on the blocks that interfere with good practice, as professionals may unwittingly collude with or maintain the dangerous dynamics of abuse – these pitfalls in practice, included throughout this book, are known as 'professional dangerousness' (Reder, et al., 1993; Reder and Duncan, 1999; Calder, 2008a).

Professional dangerousness

1. **Children and carers unheard**: Child abuse inquiries highlight the central importance of listening to the child. Although children find it hard to speak of abuse, it has been shown that prior to a child's tragic death they have often forewarned someone in authority about the risk. Similarly, prior to fatally harming a child, carers often raise the alarm by telling a professional that they are afraid of hurting the child, or they cannot cope, and also remain unheard.

2. **Rule of optimism**: Professionals tend to want to believe that all is well for the child and even when the indicators of abuse are visible, there is a tendency to be falsely convinced that the child is safe. This form of denial is the most common type of dangerous practice.

3. **Concrete solutions**: This response to abuse is to provide practical solutions such as housing, washing machines or money, rather than investigating allegations of harm.

4. **Assessment paralysis**: Professionals feel helpless, overwhelmed and incapacitated and change is perceived as hard to achieve because the family are seen to have always behaved in that way. Chronic neglect is often ignored because of this approach.

5. **Stereotyping**: Assumptions are made about how families bring up children including cultural stereotypes.

6. **Closure**: Families may shut out professionals and calls go unanswered, appointments are missed, curtains closed and doors locked. Child deaths from abuse are often preceded by closure. This dynamic may also be mirrored by professionals avoiding contact with the family.

7. **Priority given to recent information**: Information which is recent, emotional and vivid may take precedence over the old. Inquiries demonstrate that agencies held a great deal of knowledge and understanding about actual or potential harm to the child but did not give this due weight in their analysis. New information must be examined in the context of prior facts. The importance of chronologies to allow analysis cannot be over-emphasised.

8. **Non-compliance with statutory procedures**: Inquiries commonly report that legislation, policy and practice are sound but that professionals did not comply with their implementation. Children are generally well protected when formal child protection procedures are in place, enabling collation and analysis of available information.

9. **Role confusion**: Professionals may be unclear about tasks and assume that someone else is responsible for protecting the child. In child protection everyone has *prime responsibility* for the safety of the child, and clarity of roles and tasks in decision-making is essential.

10. **Exaggeration of hierarchy**: Adults of low status who report abuse may not be taken seriously even though they may be close to the world of the child, for example neighbours, friends or nursery staff. A psychiatrist, lawyer or paediatrician will often be heard more readily by professional peers.

11. **The Stockholm syndrome**: Hostages begin to identify with their captors as a survival mechanism. This is a common dynamic in child abuse cases. Abusers may be intimidating and critical of professionals leading workers to see the perpetrator's point of view rather than the child's.

12. **Omnipotence**: Professionals believe that they alone know the child's best interests and will not revisit their perceptions in the light of new evidence.

13. **False or disguised compliance**: Professionals may become enmeshed and collusive with the family so they do not see the needs of the child. Parents may convince professionals that they are co-operating where in fact they may be harming a child or failing to protect.

14. **Professional accommodation syndrome**: The worker may mirror the child's retraction of abuse (Summit, 1983), deny the reality and be keen to be persuaded that any allegation by the child must be suppressed. Other possible reasons for the signs of abuse tend to be accepted in preference to considering the possibility that the abuse is real.

Other barriers to protecting children include:

- fear of exposing the child to further abuse or breaking up the family;

- fear of personal reprisals;

- fear of over- or under-reacting;

- assuming one non-abusive adult is able to protect;

- not taking a child's account seriously;

- allowing a temporary improvement in the situation to distract from the child's reality;

- being overwhelmed by the pain of abuse and unable to protect;

- fear of contaminating evidence for legal proceedings.

Equally important is the need to consider what organisational and managerial systems need to be in place to support the social worker in safe practice (Calder, 2008b). Organisational dangerousness refers to deficits in protective systems which are evident in contemporary policy and practice. Of concern is that the Chief Social Worker has introduced a knowledge and skills base for children's social work making no mention of human rights and social justice (DfE, 2014a). Also, the most recent statutory guidance, *Working Together to Safeguard Children* (DfE, 2013; 2015), was significantly reduced by 75 per cent, amounting to deregulation within this sector with an emphasis on localism. Local Safeguarding Children Boards have increased responsibilities in writing procedures and over 200 authorities have commissioned a private company Tri.x to write protocols (www.trixonline.co.uk). In 2015, the Prime Minister announced a child protection taskforce to *transform social work and children's services* and consider *innovative methods of delivery* but it received criticism for a lack of focus on necessary resources and transparency (HM Government, 2015b; Stevenson, 2015a; Jones, 2015a). This development further opened the door to the wholesale privatisation of child protection. Jones states:

> *No other country in the world delegates to the market crucial decisions about the welfare and safety of children, such as initiating court proceedings to have children removed from their families and deciding where they should live. But with the health service, schools, probation, prisons, and welfare benefits assessments open to the market, the direction of travel has been clear for some time.*

(2015b)

In 2014, 70,000 people signed a petition against the privatisation of children's services. A government consultation resulted in over 94 per cent of respondents opposing the proposed policy to privatise and the proposal was withdrawn. However, shortly after, this decision was reversed and a considerable number of child protection services were outsourced (Jones, 2015a). Abused children who need protective responses have been corralled as a marketing opportunity and subjected to the vagaries of the market economy. Social workers working for a private company, offering high salaries and providing a frontline child protection response, have told the authors of their serious ethical concerns. These included cases being closed prematurely and stepped up unnecessarily, unqualified administrative staff making decisions about referrals, social work records being altered, no support before 9.00 am or after 5.00 pm when the office closed, a lack of training or supervision, management from a distant location, working long hours, and unsupported and unsafe decisions being made about children's safety.

A further development is the increased use of the Volunteers in Child Protection scheme (http://volunteeringmatters.org.uk/) promoted by government as a cost-cutting resource. Volunteers, however, lack professional training and accountability in this complex area of work which could compromise children's safety. The private market has also extended into social work education with the introduction of *Frontline*, a fast track programme to recruit Russell Group University graduates into social work (Adler, 2012). In 2015, the British Association of Social Workers (BASW), Social Work Action Network (SWAN), Joint University Council Social Work Education Committee (JUCSWEC), Association of Professors of Social Work (APSW) and representative trade unions, UNISON, the University and College Union (UCU) and the Social Workers Union (SWU) produced a joint statement to outline their critique of government policy and contended that:

> *recent Government policy announcements can be seen as an attempt to privatise social work as part of a wider process of welfare transformation ... Social work, as a helping profession, works alongside some of the most vulnerable and marginalised communities in society. There is an intimate link between how the vulnerable are treated and how social work is perceived. Social workers and service users are stronger when they stand together; it is the job of social work to protect and advocate on behalf of the most vulnerable.*

(BASW, 2015)

This book aims to support social workers in doing just that.

Prevention is integral to protection

Lisa [Arthurworrey] was always clear that as long as the unsafe working conditions she had found herself in persisted and as long as the government continued to pursue the demise of child protection systems there would be further child tragedies and further scapegoats.

(Davies, 2010, p15)

After 2003, children at risk gained a new meaning as children at risk of being a trouble to society which diverted resources from the protection of children from harm to the control of their behaviour.

(Davies, 2008a, p11)

It is apparent that the risks of serious harm had not abated once the plan was discontinued and that these children might have needed a Child Protection plan again, or for longer. These children do seem to have fallen through the net and provide an argument for ensuring continued support and maintenance of safe care for children who have had a plan for neglect. These children should not be overlooked through the emphasis on early intervention.

(Brandon, et al., 2013, p23)

Prevention and protection are commonly presented in policy and practice as an either/or decision. This perspective denies the complexity of child protection work, which requires both prevention and protection as a single protective strategy. Given the known prevalence of child abuse, a prevention strategy would bring to attention far more cases than are currently referred and expose many more perpetrators as members of the community become proactive protectors – effective *eyes and ears* for children (Davies, 2004; Nelson, 2004). The division between policies of prevention and those of protection developed from the mid-1990s to challenge what were thought to be over-zealous professionals, excessive state intrusion into family life, a reactive incident-led forensic approach and financial resources deemed to be wasted on 'unrequired' investigations – a view still unfortunately perpetrated by academics supportive of the so-called moral panic debate. The prevention agenda progressed to mark the demise of child protection systems and a change in language from protection, abuse and risk to safeguarding, concern and need (Munro and Calder, 2005; Davies, 2015), a devaluing of professional investigative skills, and punitive, pathologising approaches to child victims.

Social workers became over-burdened with assessments, and far from being a shift from alleged over-intrusion into the family, practice became the exact opposite, as professionals intervened in family life at a level of concern rather than significant harm. This development led Parton to comment on a reconfiguration of the relationship between the state, professionals, parents and children with regulation and the surveillance of children and parents as a dominating characteristic of children's services

(Parton, 2006). Social work child protection teams became child in need teams and assessment of the child's needs became the dominant mode of intervention minimising proactive child abuse investigation. At a time of severe cutbacks, assessment and non-statutory services were ready-made for privatisation and outsourcing and subsequently many were closed down altogether. The introduction of competitive tendering distracts management time and resources from delivery and the maintenance of practice standards and also creates professional division which contradicts the principles of working together. This book promotes prevention strategies which support proactive child protection such as child safety strategies, working with protective communities and focusing on removing perpetrators from the child's world including through criminal prosecutions and convictions.

Teaching children to remain safe

Abuse stopped in only 16 per cent of cases where a child told a teacher.

(OCC, 2015, p65)

I tried to tell a teacher but she did not believe me and told my mother what I had told her. My mother was the main abuser.

(OCC, 2015, p63)

The school should itself be a safe space where children have a sufficient level of trust in education professionals to disclose sexual abuse.

(OCC, 2015, p83)

Children cannot be expected to solve abuse themselves but do need age-appropriate knowledge of the risks posed by child abusers. Prevention organisations work to raise awareness of child abuse and to empower children to learn to keep themselves safe. This approach is valuable but must be used together with strategies to target perpetrators and implement child protection procedures. Child abusers target children who are most vulnerable and a child's positive sense of self-esteem may well help to keep them safe. The Children's Commissioner recommends that all schools equip children so they know how and who to tell if they are worried about abuse, and that there should be whole-school training because it is clear that young children remain particularly unprotected (OCC, 2015, p10).

Children may not realise what is happening to them emotionally, and therefore may be unable to describe the abuse they are experiencing. In oral evidence to the House of Commons (HC 137:1, 2012–13, p31) the *Railway Children* charity cited research of 100 children living on the streets in 2009 finding that *there was a sense that this is how it is. Some had very few expectations or ideas that life could or should be different and … [children abused in the care system] … had not understood that they were being treated very badly.* Safety training can give children enough information and understanding to keep them safe from abusive or uncomfortable situations and to recognise their entitlement to high standards of care and protection.

Organisations such as Kidscape (www.kidscape.org.uk) raise awareness of abuse and Thinkuknow (www.thinkuknow.co.uk) addresses online abuse. *Chelsea's Choice* is a film used in schools to raise awareness of child sexual abuse (www.alteregocreativesolutions.co.uk/chelseas-choice) as is *Somebody's sister, somebody's daughter* (www.gwtheatre.co.uk). The Magdalene Group delivers awareness training to schools (magdalenegroup.org).

Responsible citizens as proactive protectors

Two attempts were made by members of the public to share their concerns [about Khyra Ishaq], one by a telephone call, the second by a referral in person at a children's social care office in March 2006. This information was not acted upon ... It is alarming because it was clear to us that many people in the community had concerns but did not feel able to share them with the many agencies that are there to help.

(BSCB, 2010)

The community is a source of protection for children which can be taught how to understand the nature of child abuse and the means of reporting it (Nelson and Baldwin, 2002). Numbers of inquiries have demonstrated that neighbours and responsible citizens raise the alarm about children needing protection but often go unheard (Reder, et al., 1993, p75). Local Safeguarding Children Boards have a responsibility to keep children safe in their locality. Through awareness, publicity and training programmes, key citizens can become a local network of protective adults, well informed about the recognition of child abuse and the importance of referral. Both Davies (2004) and Nelson (2004) have developed methodologies for such community awareness strategies that include working with cultural and religious groups to assist understanding about any practices abusive to children. Kane (1998) provides an example of a child who was protected by a responsible member of the local community and of an effective professional response. Neither would have protected the child without the other being in place.

A girl is seen by a woman getting into a car after a man had called out to her. The woman notes the number and calls the police. She approaches the child and offers to walk her home safely. As the car sped away the police identified the number as belonging to a known child sex abuser and proceeded to locate him for questioning.

(p128)

Local Safeguarding Children Boards have a responsibility to inform the public about child abuse and to provide a means of reporting abuse.

Online sources of information and advice to parents to raise awareness of how to protect children from child sexual abuse include Parents Protect (www.parentsprotect. co.uk) and Stop it Now (www.stopitnow.org.uk).

Removing abusers from the child's world through intervention and prosecution

They should have done something to the men, not me.

They did nothing to the men who made me go missing.

I was found in the presence of the men constantly. Why were they not pulled in?

No one spoke to me about the men in London. There were hundreds of them – untouched.

(OSCB, 2015, p14)

Publications addressing investigations into child abuse by entertainer Jimmy Savile, politician Cyril Smith and within the Catholic Church (Gray and Watt, 2012; Danczuk, 2015; Scorer, 2015; Davies, 2015) have highlighted how predatory child sex abusers can function *in plain sight*, their activities well known within the many local communities and organisations where they were prolific perpetrators of abuse.

Children will remain unprotected unless abusers are removed from their world or the behaviour of abusers is changed through intervention. The Multi Agency Public Protection Arrangements (MAPPA) in each authority are responsible for managing adults who present a danger to the community, particularly to children, and the Public Protection Unit police teams implement risk strategies with other professionals. The Violent and Sex Offender Register (ViSOR), managed by the National Crime Agency, is a database of those offenders required to be registered under the Sexual Offences Act 2003. (The Act does not apply to those convicted before 1997, which leaves many known, convicted abusers unmonitored representing a gap in the protective system requiring urgent remedy.) Police officers visit known perpetrators and review their cases regularly, constantly reassessing the level of risk to children. Through multi-agency meetings information is shared, interventions planned and decisions reached about community notification about known abusers. Some high-risk offenders are subject to surveillance, others access treatment programmes and some live in supervised accommodation where they can be monitored, electronically tagged and under curfew.

Information about people who present a risk to children can be given to parents and guardians under the Child Sex Offenders Disclosure Scheme (also known as Sarah's Law). The scheme enables parents, guardians and third parties to enquire whether a person who has access to a child is a registered sex offender and/or places a child at risk.

The policy and practice of assessment conflated with investigation

The social worker did not initiate an immediate child protection investigation ... the error of judgment could have been identified and the case [Gilbert] relabelled as a child protection case.

(Swansea LSCB, 2006, p9; Davies, 2009b)

A referral received by social services which indicated the likelihood of non-accidental injuries to Victoria [Climbié] was labelled from the outset as 'child in need'.

(Reder and Duncan, 2004, p104)

Analysis of risk was limited across agencies. This could have been avoided if information sharing and planning [about Baby O] between all relevant agencies had been consistent throughout, and a comprehensive risk analysis and protection plan drawn up.

(Newcastle LSCB, 2006)

The social worker said her role was to support the family ... but in the Peter Connelly case there were three main indicators: the mother's avoidant behaviour, unexplained serious injuries over time and ... risk posed by other adults in his life. A rigorous child protection investigation was indicated.

(Davies, 2008b, p11)

An opportunity to pick up on concerns about a 13 year old child associating with older men and being sexually active was missed. The team manager should not have signed off the assessment just because a Team Around the Child was in place.

(OSCB, 2015, p44)

Working Together to Safeguard Children (DfES, 2006a: 5.60) stated that the assessment is the means by which a section 47 (Children Act (CA) 1989) enquiry is carried out and the terms *assessment* and *investigation* became conflated from that time. *Working Together to Safeguard Children* (DfE, 2013; 2015) removed the term *joint investigation* altogether, referring to investigation as solely a police activity associated with criminal proceedings. It was Laming (2003, p382; Davies, 2008c) who recommended that police should focus on crime and this represented a shift in their role away from the investigation of significant harm jointly with social workers (Davies, 2008c, p34).There is now a gap in processes whereby social workers focus on the assessment of the child's needs and police focus on investigation of crime. The joint investigation of significant harm has been lost from policy and practice guidance but remains in the Children Act 1989 as section 47. As a single process, assessment does not protect a child from harm – this requires an investigative process, as outlined throughout this book. A vast knowledge base exists derived from hundreds of findings from serious case reviews following the death or serious injury of children. It has been commonly reported in these reviews that there was professional non-compliance with section 47 (CA 1989) procedures. The vulnerable child was generally referred to children's services and defined as a child in need (s17, CA 1989 – to promote the welfare of the child and provide relevant services) rather than a child in need of protection and consequently no protection plan existed. The focus of this book is child protection, considering perpetrators as well as the child and family, and a proactive multi-agency investigative approach carried out by social workers and police working together through joint investigation.

The Common Assessment Framework (CAF), in operation since 2006, is one example of a standardised approach often used as a referral and gate-keeping tool to rationalise resources. The government aim of this protocol was to identify the need for early intervention before problems reached a crisis point (DfE, 2012a, p12). The CAF is described not as a referral process but as a request for services, which might prevent needs escalating to a point where statutory intervention is required. The CAF, in both statutory and non-statutory guidance, is variably presented as a referral tool, the basis for a referral discussion, a request for services, an early help assessment or as supportive of a referral for an assessment. It is very important that the completion of the CAF, does not delay a child protection referral.

The purpose of the book and structure

What is to be done depends on what you think is going on.

(Howe, 1987, p9)

This second edition has a more serious tone than the first quite simply because as social workers we find ourselves in far more serious times. This book emphasises where serious case reviews and inquiries have highlighted gaps in the social work practice response. These gaps are sometimes caused through lack of knowledge and skewed value systems but also as a result of policy shifts, structural changes in services, lack of supervision and training, and deleterious cuts in resources. Good practice is promoted by drawing attention to areas such as children in custodial settings; unaccompanied asylum-seeking children; child victims of faith beliefs, ritual and non-recent abuse; older children's homelessness and issues relating to poverty. As with the first edition, case studies highlight these specific practice areas and children's views are at the forefront to emphasise their voice and perspective.

This book is written primarily for students and qualified social workers who are developing practice skills and understanding in both children's and adults' services. The book seeks to support confident, creative and critical practitioners who always place the child at the centre. The *proactive* element in the title is to inspire action and deep thinking about the issues, engaging critically with knowledge, examining the contexts within which children live and where social workers practise, and strengthening the values of social justice in order to better protect children.

Professionals from agencies represented on Local Safeguarding Children Boards (LSCBs) and multi-agency public protection arrangements (MAPPA), as well as those working in the private and voluntary sector, will find this book a valuable resource. It provides essential and accessible knowledge to services positioned outside the welfare state in the context of the rapid development of social enterprises and private companies within social work, probation, police, education and health provision. Increasingly, unqualified staff are employed to work with children and the book will assist them to understand the limits of their role, the complexities of the task and, most importantly, when it is appropriate to refer to specialist agencies.

Munro suggested that child protection workers should be like detectives making a thorough search for *truth* with an open mind that considers different possibilities and tests conclusions (2002, p170). Social workers need to combine analysis with intuition. Analysis is an intellectual process derived from a knowledge base, whereas intuition is an unconscious process which draws on experience, metaphor, imagination and feelings. Intuitive reasoning can be guided by knowledge and analysis requires intuitive skills in collating and organising information (Munro, 2002, p112). Making decisions to protect children involves making judgements about whether or not an action (commission) or inaction (omission) is abusive and assessing the level of response. Social workers may conclude *false positives* by thinking everything will be fine when it is not, or *false negatives* by thinking everything will not be fine when actually it is. To guard against these possibilities of error, social workers should always scrutinise decisions from the opposite perspective, learn to rigorously examine their judgements and consider what information may be missing from the analysis.

Social workers tend to act on vivid, recent and easily available information whereas inquiries inform us that much highly relevant information is less obvious. It is helpful to always ask: what is the Factor X in this situation, what can I not see, what have I not been told, what information have I not acquired? Evidence would then need to be sought to prove or disprove the hypothesis formed. The use of both intuition and analytical reasoning in reaching sound decisions provides a framework for this book.

The book is structured to address the four main categories of child abuse and to consider legal safeguards and protective processes. Each chapter presents evidence and informed analysis, including definitions, facts, indicators and types of harm relating to each of the four categories – emotional, sexual, neglect and physical – as outlined in *Working Together to Safeguard Children* (DfE, 2015, p92). Children are rarely victims of just one form of abuse. Research with a sample of nearly 500 children found that just eight per cent of physically abused children and five per cent of sexually abused children had these forms as a single type (Manly, 2001, cited in Davies, 2012, p142). The Office of the Children's Commissioner reported that poly-victimisation – the experience of more than one form of abuse – was common in a survivor survey suggesting that concerns about physical abuse and neglect should give rise to concerns about sexual abuse (OCC, 2015, p54).

Indicators of abuse

Statutory services are largely disclosure-led with the burden of responsibility placed on the victim. It is unrealistic to expect victims of child sexual abuse linked to the family to disclose abuse. Disclosure-led approaches are demonstrably failing the majority of victims. Proactive enquiry is necessary to substantiate concerns and activate protection processes. Child sexual abuse may come to the attention of the authorities as a secondary presenting factor leading it to remain unidentified (OCC, 2015, p9). Recognition of indicators of harm is essential to a proactive approach.

Indicators of abuse are included in chapters where they are specific to a particular type of harm. The following indicators apply to all forms of abuse. Although some indicators will be definitive, most will need evaluation through multi-agency debate. Clusters of indicators may point to specific forms of abuse:

- lethargy, listlessness, fatigue, sleep disturbance;
- misuse of alcohol, drugs and/or substances;
- rocking, head banging, other compulsive behaviour;
- not wanting to go home from school or nursery;
- running away, school non-attendance;
- being fearful in the presence of the parent/carer;
- eating disorders, constant hunger;
- begging or stealing;
- over- or under-achieving, lacking concentration;
- being socially isolated;
- having inappropriate responsibilities;
- being fearful of criticism which may lead to lying;
- attempting suicide and/or self-harm;
- constantly trying to please adults;
- behavioural extremes such as being withdrawn or aggressive;
- physical symptoms without obvious cause;
- experiencing painful incidents with little response;

- not turning to a parent for support;

- enuresis (wetting) and/or encopresis (soiling);

- believing themselves deserving of punishment;

- unexplained developmental delays;

- being fearful of physical contact;

- inappropriate clothing;

- reluctance to undress to hide injuries/neglect;

- hiding or flinching away from someone;

- indiscriminately seeking attention.

Practice analysis includes professional dangerousness, assessing parental responses and adults' ability to protect, as well as using practice tools such as chronologies. Wherever possible, reference is made to the concept of *harm* or *crime* against children rather than *abuse*, which can underestimate the impact on the child and adult survivor. Learning from serious case reviews is essential to all child protection work. Many children who have died, or been seriously harmed, did not obtain protection because statutory procedures were not understood or effectively applied. For example, the serious case review following the murder of Daniel Pelka stressed that if professionals had used more inquiring minds and been more focused in their intentions to address concerns, it is likely Daniel would have been better protected (CSCB, 2013).

To enable learning, an example of practice from a child abuse inquiry is included in each chapter. Chapter 2 presents an account of Alex Kelly, who took his own life in a custodial setting where the review raised questions about chronic and systematic emotional neglect. Chapter 3 examines the case of Laura Wilson, a victim of child sexual exploitation in Rotherham, who was murdered. In Chapter 4 the case of Daniel Pelka, who was murdered by his parents, is outlined. Professionals responded to the adults' needs and Daniel became 'unseen'. Chapter 5 looks at the case of three children from Cheshire who were adopted by professionals, experienced years of violent assaults and their repeated attempts to tell went unheard.

In social work it is common for adult agendas to predominate. To counter this tendency, children's voices are highlighted throughout each chapter so that the child is kept in mind and heard at every stage from initial contact, throughout an investigation and during proactive action. Survivors' autobiographical accounts also inform understanding because it is from their experience that there is so much to learn. Excerpts have been included from three books by Keeble, a child protection police officer (Keeble and Hollington, 2010; 2011; 2012) to demonstrate a proactive professional response.

Evidence on key themes of child trafficking, neglect, disabled children, vulnerable older children and thresholds of intervention, emphasised by the House of Commons

Education Committee in *Children First*: *The Child Protection System in England* (HC 137:1; 2, 2012–13), is also included throughout the book. For instance, the ages at which certain forms of abuse are most likely to occur is discussed within each chapter, as is the abuse of disabled children who represent one child in 20 in the UK (Contact a Family, 2011).

Social work practice is increasingly procedural in approach involving the completion of data entry and standardised forms, *luring professionals, or more importantly the children and families with whom they work, onto slippery and sometimes fatally jagged rocks* (White, 2009, p96). In this context, White advocates to enable sound and safe work with children and families professionals should be educated for *uncertainty, compassion, carefulness and wisdom* (2009, p107). Social workers want more emphasis on training with regard to the non-procedural aspects of their work such as direct work with children, multi-agency working and supporting children and families post-disclosure (Brady, et al., 2014, p6). Calder refers to the need to be able to hold and see simultaneously the needs of the parent and the child as it can be difficult to *feel connected to the child's powerlessness to protect themselves* (Calder, 2008c, p69). Practitioners need to recognise the rights of the child and their agency in making choices and yet also steadfastly adhere to the principle of the child's best interests. This will only be achieved through the use of informed professional judgement.

The case diagrams

Case diagrams at the end of each chapter provide an opportunity to consider five responses to a child protection referral and to reflect on judgement. The case diagrams focus on the process of joint police and social work decision making and investigation of actual or likely significant harm and statutory multi-agency meetings and procedures. A number of the procedures are outlined in more depth in Chapter 1.

The case diagrams are:

- mainly non-specific in terms of recognising diversity such as ethnicity and religion;

- presented chronologically, although in practice interventions rarely progress in a linear way;

- designed to promote a confident approach to forming judgements, making decisions and acting to protect;

- usually progressed from a referral to joint/single agency investigation, multi-agency planning and action;

- inclusive of consent issues.

There are five possible responses.

1. A child is not thought to be at any risk of abuse.

2. There is concern about the abuse of a child.

3. There is suspicion of likely or actual significant harm to a child (s47 enquiry, CA 1989).

4. A section 47 (CA 1989) investigation of a child is indicated.

5. Immediate action is needed to protect a child. There is evidence of actual significant harm and/or criminal offence.

The following factors will help the reader in thinking about what influenced their response in each case diagram:

• experiences as a child, as a parent or from observations and interactions with children and families;

• social work experience of a particular case;

• cultural or religious perspectives of family life;

• knowledge of the law, child protection policy, practice guidance and research;

• knowledge of learning from child abuse inquiries;

• attitudes, beliefs and values about the nature of childhood and family life;

• media reporting.

Prompts to support thinking when studying the case diagrams

Referral

What was the nature of the referral and reason for making it?

Who made the referral and what is their relationship to the child?

What is the risk of actual or likely significant harm?

Have immediate protection needs been addressed?

What has been said to whom, by whom and in what context?

What are the views of the parents/carers and are they proactive protectors?

What has been observed?

Was the information provided fact, opinion or hearsay?

Has there been an appropriate response to the needs of disabled children and parents?

How has discrimination and oppression been accounted for?

Have power relations been considered?

Have crimes been reported to police?

Which individuals and agencies have knowledge of the child?

Has a referral been made to the designated lead or agency with responsibility for child protection?

What key information has been reported?

Investigation/child protection enquiry

Has the child and any other children been made safe?

Has the investigation ensured that the child's best interests are paramount?

Have the needs of disabled children been addressed throughout?

Have checks been made with all relevant agencies and individuals?

Have the child's needs in relation to discrimination and oppression been addressed?

Has consent been obtained (where doing so does not place the child at risk of harm)?

Is the case a child in need (s17 CA 1989) or a child in need of protection (s47 CA 1989)?

Is this a single or a joint agency investigation?

Did a strategy discussion take place at the right time for the child to gain protection?

Has there been a strategy meeting and have arrangements to review the decisions been made?

Were the appropriate professionals present at the strategy meeting to ensure the full sharing of relevant information?

Has the child been interviewed alone and their perspective understood?

Has the child been interviewed in a suitable environment and in a child-centred way?

In making the decision about who interviewed the child, was account taken of gender, ethnicity and other relevant factors such as resemblance to the abuser?

Was a visually recorded interview conducted in accordance with the *Achieving Best Evidence* guidance (MoJ, 2011) ?

Have the child's wishes and feelings been taken into account?

Was there a paediatric assessment or medical examination?

What were the consent issues in relation to any interviews and medical examinations?

Was there a home visit? Was entry gained?

Were the child's bedroom, the kitchen and other areas seen?

What was the condition of the fridge, beds/cots and general hygiene?

Was there a need for forensic (relating to crime) evidence and was this obtained?

In agreement with police colleagues was photographic evidence obtained?

What other interviews took place?

Was the parental/carer response evaluated?

Has the alleged or known abuser been excluded from the household?

Was the alleged or known abuser interviewed and/or arrested?

What is the response of the alleged or known abuser?

Has the non-abusive parent's/carer's capacity to protect been evaluated?

Were all the decisions of the strategy meeting carried out as agreed by those with responsibility to do so?

Has a decision been made to convene a child protection conference?

Child protection intervention and planning

What plans have been put in place to protect the child?

What support has been agreed for the family?

What is the child's view of what has been decided?

What civil legal proceedings have been implemented to protect the child?

Has a child protection conference taken place?

Did the family, including the child, participate fully in the conference process?

What type of abuse was decided at the conference as the main category?

What individuals/ agencies have contributed to the protection plan?

Are the arrangements to review the child protection plan in line with local and national guidance?

Has the abuser been arrested/charged/prosecuted/convicted?

Has an application for criminal injuries compensation been considered? (www.gov.uk/claim-compensation-criminal-injury)

Flowchart 0.1 Statutory procedures flowchart

The referral
An allegation or evidence of child abuse

Gathering Information

Social workers must gather information from the referrer, from records relating to the family, relevant children, adults, and all other agencies in order to inform decision making. Information gathering must never delay taking urgent or immediate action to protect a child. Seeking consent from parents, carers and children for these checks is not required if to do so places the child at risk and might lead to the child being pressured to retract an allegation. Social workers should consult children's legal services for advice about legal safeguards.

Immediate Action

Where there is a risk to the life of a child or possibility of immediate significant harm, the social worker must act to protect. This may be achieved through a protective parent or carer, removing the abuser, or the child or children, to a safe place or the abuser agreeing to leave the household. For children needing urgent medical attention this must be arranged through hospital admission and liaison with the child protection paediatrician or forensic medical examiner (via the police). The police may remove the abuser through criminal justice measures. These actions would usually follow a strategy discussion/meeting (DfE, 2015, p31).

The three boxes below refer to key statutory powers social workers could pursue to protect a child at any stage

Emergency Protection Order (EPO) s44 (CA 1989)

The social worker obtains an EPO from a magistrate which gives the applicant shared parental responsibility (PR) for a limited time. The grounds are that the child is likely to suffer significant harm if not removed or if the child does not remain where they are being accommodated or where s47 (CA 1989) enquiries are being frustrated, for example where the social worker is denied access to the child. This is effective for no more than eight days and can be extended for a further seven days. Conditions may be attached for medical or psychiatric examinations, investigative interviews, to exclude somebody from the household or area, to gain powers of entry or regarding contact with parents and carers. Any person can apply. An Interim Care Order (ICO) (s31, CA 1989) may be applied for to extend an EPO.

Recovery Order s50 (CA 1989)

For children who run away, are missing or who have been unlawfully taken away, a Recovery Order can be sought. This enables the police to search and recover a child who is subject to an EPO, a Care Order or Police Powers of Protection.

Police powers of protection

The police may be requested to use police powers of protection to secure the immediate safety of the child by removing the child to suitable accommodation or preventing the removal from a safe place such as a hospital. This lasts for up to 72 hours (s46 (1), CA 1989) and does not require a court order.

Joint agency investigation – police AND children's services. Responding to allegations of actual or likely significant harm and crimes against or involving children.

Single agency investigation – police OR children's services following agreement and keeping the other agency informed. Responding to allegations of actual or likely significant harm and crimes against or involving children.

The child must be safe while the investigation is ongoing. This may be with agreement from adults with PR (s20, CA 1989) or through obtaining an EPO or other legal safeguard. A number of strategy discussions and/or meetings may be required as the investigation progresses to evaluate the evidence and risk to the child.

Strategy discussion

An immediate and formal discussion takes place between the social worker, police and a senior medical professional if relevant, (usually) by telephone to facilitate urgent action to protect a child or to agree the need for a strategy meeting and s47 (CA 1989) enquiries. Discussion follows a referral or at any other time. A record of the decisions, responsibility for actions and timescales should be circulated within one working day. This must not take the place of a strategy meeting and must never be a mechanism for saving time or resources (DfE, 2015, p36).

Strategy meeting

A professionals-only meeting chaired by a social work manager held at a convenient location, about the child, family or alleged perpetrator. A non-professional referrer may attend to provide information but must not be included in the decision making. A record of decisions, responsibility for actions and timescales is to be made immediately for all participants (DfE, 2015, p36). Strategy meetings can be reconvened where necessary.

Achieving best evidence interview (MoJ, 2011)

This is a formal interview, primarily for criminal proceedings but it may be made available for civil proceedings, in the child interview suite. It is visually recorded, planned and conducted jointly by a police officer and social worker trained for the task. The child must consent and the consent of a non-abusive adult with PR must be sought, unless doing so places the child at risk.

Paediatric assessment

This may be required to provide the child with necessary treatment, secure forensic evidence, obtain medical documentation, reassure the child/parent and plan follow up. Only a medical professional can physically examine a child. The social worker must be sensitive to the child's need for privacy during any examination. Following the decision at the strategy discussion/ meeting, the designated child protection doctor will decide, in consultation with the police, which medical specialist is the most appropriate to conduct the examination. The child must consent to any medical examination and if reluctant may be offered an initial consultation. Even a very young child may express that they do not consent to an examination. Seek consent of a non-abusive parent unless to do so places the child at risk (DfE, 2015, p40).

Child protection conference

To be convened within 15 days of the strategy meeting decision to have one, or in response to notification from another authority about a child already subject to a child protection plan. Chaired by an independent social worker, it is attended by the professionals conducting the investigation, by those with knowledge of the child and family, parents/carers, the child as appropriate and advocates. The purpose is to reach a decision about whether or not the child and any other children, in the family or children identified as a result of the investigation, need to be the subject of a child protection plan, and the relevant category/ies of child abuse are identified. The child protection plan outline with actions, timescales and core group membership is agreed (DfE, 2015, p43–4).

Child protection plan

A children's social worker co-ordinates the plan. A core group of professionals and family implement and review the progress of the plan including any necessary legal safeguards. The plan needs to include who has responsibility for the agreed actions within appropriate timescales and how implementation will be monitored. Contingency planning must be in place should the child/ren not be protected. The first review is usually after three months and subsequent reviews at six-monthly intervals until the plan is discontinued when the child/ren are no longer at continuing risk of significant harm, have left the area or have reached the age of 18 (DfE, 2015, p46). A decision about whether to convene a further strategy meeting should take place where there is new information about risk to the child/ren.

Public Law Outline (MoJ, 2008)

This must be considered prior to any care proceedings and must include a record of the strategy discussion(s), a record of the single agency or joint agency materials, a social work chronology, child protection plan, a care plan and any pre-existing care plans.

Interim/Care Order, Interim/Supervision Order (s31, CA 1989) Section 8 Orders

These can be obtained by the local authority which acquires PR for the child. The grounds are that the child is suffering or likely to suffer significant harm, such harm being attributable to the care given to the child not being what it would be reasonable to expect a parent to provide, or likely to be given if the order were not made, or if the child is beyond parental control. Conditions may be attached as with an EPO. It may mean an abuser is removed from the household or from the child's environment. A Prohibitive Steps Order (s8, CA 1989) may be used to prevent a person with PR taking actions with regard to the child, such as removing them from the country. A Specific Issues Order (s8, CA 1989) can help determine any specific question about the way a child is brought up. It might be about schooling, health or religion.

Who will be involved in the core group meetings to implement the conference decisions?

What may prevent the plan from being carried out effectively and how might this be addressed?

As social work is difficult and challenging there is a strong tendency to rely on lists, but the above questions are intended as prompts to form the basis of reflection in the context of supervision, team and inter-agency discussion and training processes. To apply these routinely to individual cases would not necessarily lead to good practice as it denies the complexity of each unique child's situation.

A flowchart (see pages 23–24) provides a guide to child protection procedures from referral, to section 47 (CA 1989) investigation, strategy meeting, child protection conference and action to protect. It includes details of child protection procedures and legislation.

The prime statutory guidance for all professionals working with children is *Working Together to Safeguard Children* (DfE, 2015) and this represents far-reaching changes to prior guidance with extensive practice implications. Social workers and other practitioners should be aware of the context in which statutory practice guidance, represented in *Working Together to Safeguard Children* (DfE, 2015), has been amended and considerably minimised from that of earlier versions. Previous guidance, developed from the findings of research, serious case reviews and inquiry recommendations since the early 1980s, continues to be a strong reference point within this book. A constant criticism of professional practice over these years has been professional non-compliance with child protection procedures. Instead of discarding detailed and complex sections of the guidance, professionals need training and safe working environments to ensure their understanding and application of it.

Social worker and solicitor Norman commented that whereas *Working Together to Safeguard Children* (DCSF, 2010a) stated that the guidance and concepts of abuse were grounded in human rights legislation, this has been eliminated from the 2015 version. He therefore recommends that everyone should continue to keep the 2010 version of *Working Together to Safeguard Children* as a resource *by their elbows* (2013, p.1).

CHAPTER SUMMARY

This chapter presents the theoretical and research framework of this book with explanation about the book structure. There is an emphasis on promoting childrens' rights to protection, listening to children's voices, the importance of prevention as a form of protection and the role of the community as proactive protectors. Effective child protection is explored including the barriers to achieving this. Complex issues of policy and practice are debated. The indicators of abuse that apply to all categories are included as is a statutory procedures flowchart.

FURTHER READING

Children's Rights Alliance for England (2014) *State of children's rights in England*. London: CRAE. This annual report shows key developments in the progress of implementing children's rights.

HC 137:1 (House of Commons Education Committee) (2012–13) *Children first: the child protection system in England. Fourth Report of session 2012–13*. Volumes 1 and 2. London: The Stationery Office. This Select Committee report is based on the testimonies of a wide range of professionals and service users, highlighting contemporary child protection issues.

Office of the Children's Commissioner (OCC, 2015). *Protecting children from harm*. London: OCC. Critical analysis of the scale and nature of child sexual abuse within the family and its network. Includes findings from the largest ever survey of adult survivors of child sexual abuse with 756 respondents.

WEBSITES

www.basw.co.uk
British Association of Social Workers (BASW): the professional organisation for social workers in the UK

www.brap.org.uk/our-ideas/child-protection
Website about equalities and protecting children

www.article39.org.uk
Article 39 UNCRC: Fighting for children's rights in institutional settings

www.gov.uk/claim-compensation-criminal-injury
A compensation scheme for victims of violent crime including sexual crime. There is discretion relating to the timescale of reporting and to payment where the victim has criminal convictions.

Chapter 1
Legal safeguards and protective processes

This chapter will help you to develop the following capabilities, to the appropriate level, from the PCF.

- **Professionalism**
  Represent and be accountable to the profession.
- **Values and ethics**
  Apply social work ethical principles and values to guide professional practice.
- **Diversity**
  Recognise diversity and apply anti-oppressive principles in practice.
- **Knowledge**
  Apply knowledge of social sciences, law and social work practice theory.
- **Critical reflection and analysis**
  Apply critical reflection and analysis to inform and provide a rationale for professional decision making.
- **Intervention and skills**
  Use judgement and authority to intervene with individuals, families and communities to promote independence, provide support and prevent harm, neglect and abuse.
- **Contexts and organisations**
  Engage with, inform and adapt to changing practice contexts and operate effectively within own organisational frameworks and within multi-agency and inter-professional settings.
- **Professional leadership**
  Take responsibility for the professional learning and development of others through supervision, mentoring, assessing, research, teaching, leadership and management.

It will also introduce you to the following academic standards as set out in the social work subject benchmark statements:

5.1.2 The service delivery context
5.1.4 Social work theory
5.5 Problem-solving skills
5.6 Communication skills
5.7 Skills in working with others
7.3 Knowledge and understanding

(www.qaa.ac.uk/en/Publications/Documents/Subject-benchmark-statement-Social-work.pdf)

Work with the family was not sufficiently formalized. Strategy meetings did not properly record individual agency and professional responsibilities and there was a lack of analysis based on accurate chronologies and sharing of information. There was no child protection conference and therefore no forum for multi-agency collation of information and analysis and no child protection plan.

(CSCB, 2013: 6.19)

Responding to an allegation

For 59 per cent of respondents the abuse continued following disclosure. In only 11 per cent of cases did abuse stop at the same time as telling someone.

(OCC, 2015, p65)

On hearing a child's initial disclosure a social worker must find out just enough to inform a referral to the appropriate duty team. This involves asking a few open questions such as: *Tell me more, explain/ describe that further to me* and *how did it happen as I wasn't there?* Such questions do not put words in the child's mouth and will not interfere with any subsequent investigation. The social worker should reassure the child that they are taking what they say seriously rather than say they believe the child at this stage, as whether the statement has validity is a matter for later investigation and possibly a court. They should reassure the child that they are brave to speak and that they are not in any way at fault. Some children may only be able to describe child abuse using crude language. It is important not to prevent the use of such words but to explore what is meant by them with as little interruption to the flow of the account as possible. The child should be informed that in order to keep children safe other social workers and police must be informed and that the disclosure cannot be kept a secret. No false promises and no assumptions should be made about what may have happened. If the child continues to provide a lengthy account, the social worker should listen and not interrupt. A child may say that they do not feel *normal* or they feel *dirty* and it is important to acknowledge the feelings and then explore further what they mean. Saying *of course you aren't dirty* would be to dismiss their feelings. Gaining the child's trust and supporting them sufficiently to help them have the courage to tell a police officer what happened is a very important social work skill.

Recording must be contemporaneous in order to be credible in any civil or criminal proceedings. This means making a record as soon as possible after the interview, even if that means a hand-written report and possibly writing a few phrases down during the interview while checking with the child that you have recorded their words exactly as they meant them. An account of the child's emotional response should be recorded, as well as any repetition and the context of the disclosure being made as these factors may validate the account.

Social workers must act as a bridge between a child and the investigating social workers and police to enable a formal, visually recorded statement to be made. Social workers may avoid direct communication with a child about abuse out of fear, inexperience and concern about not wanting to contaminate evidence. In fact it is essential that social workers do enable children to tell and clearly understand how to do this.

Statutory protocols

Practitioners need to have a clear overview of the law relating to children, particularly the Children Acts 1989 and 2004. It is important to recognise the distinction between criminal law, which targets the perpetrators of crime and where evidence is tested *beyond all reasonable doubt*, and civil law, where children may gain protection on the lower *balance of probabilities* level of proof. In child protection it is difficult to achieve the prosecution of abusers; however, if there is no criminal prosecution, social workers must still protect the child using civil proceedings and support any application for criminal injuries compensation.

Working Together to Safeguard Children (DfE, 2015) states that all professionals must be alert to the risk of harm that abusers may present to children and implement the actions needed to keep the child safe. Sections 10 and 11 (CA 2004) place duties on a range of organisations and individuals to ensure that their services, including those outsourced, lead to effective child protection arrangements. Each local authority must have an LSCB. The membership is outlined in the Children Act 2004 (s13) and includes senior members of all relevant agencies. *Working Together to Safeguard Children* (DfE, 2015) states there must be an independent chairperson and outlines that the LSCBs have responsibility to co-ordinate the work of all the individuals and agencies involved. LSCBs are responsible for policy and practice development in relation to thresholds for intervention, training, recruitment and supervision, investigation of allegations, the resolution of inter-agency conflict and co-operation with neighbouring authorities. Another key responsibility is to conduct serious case reviews when a child has died or been seriously harmed by abuse and where there are concerns about how professionals worked together on the case. These must be published to support learning (DfE, 2015). Each agency has specialist designated child protection leads who act as consultants. Systems relevant to a focus on perpetrators include the MAPPA and Multi Agency Risk Assessment Conference (MARAC) (DCSF, 2010a).

Section 47 (CA 1989) refers to the local authority's duty to investigate when *they have reasonable cause to suspect that a child who lives, or is found, in their area is suffering or is likely to suffer significant harm, that authority shall make or cause to be made, such enquiries as they consider necessary to enable them to decide whether they should take any action to safeguard or promote the child's welfare.* The Children Act (1989) defines harm as *ill-treatment* or the *impairment* of *health* or *development*. The Adoption and Children Act (2002) extended this definition to include impairment suffered from seeing or hearing the ill-treatment of another. *Development* means physical, intellectual, emotional, social or behavioural development; and *health* means physical or mental health. *Ill-treatment* includes sexual abuse and forms of ill treatment which are non-physical. It is a matter for professional judgement as to whether these criteria apply in a particular case, including making comparison with what could reasonably be expected of a similar child. Practitioners strive to reach agreement about the threshold for protective intervention through debate and analysis at multi-agency statutory forums, such as strategy meetings and child protection conferences.

Assessment protocols require consent to be gained from parents and carers for checks to be made but in a section 47 (CA 1989) investigation, the protection of the child is the paramount consideration and consent must be gained only where this is in the best interests of the child and when it does not interfere with any criminal investigation. For instance, conducting an assessment might interfere with police interviews of the parents/carers as suspects or witnesses and the interview of the child might be inappropriate if a visually recorded interview is needed. Decisions about consent to information sharing must be made at a strategy discussion/meeting. Seven golden rules for sharing information are outlined in government guidance (HM Government, 2015a) which specifically emphasises the principles of *necessary, proportionate, relevant, adequate, accurate, timely* and *secure.* Social workers need to be absolutely clear that strategy meetings and child protection conferences have a foundation in law with accountability for all professionals involved and must never be replaced by processes such as network or professionals meetings.

The multi-agency safeguarding hub

Year after year there had been far too many communication breakdowns meaning crucial information was not passed on or acted on when received. Amazingly this problem had been addressed way back when in 1990 in an enlightened experiment, a north London police child protection unit and a team of social workers were housed together in Havering. This made perfect sense to me. We would love to have organised face to face formal and informal meetings, information exchanges and to travel together on visits but for whatever reason it was judged by the powers that be as a failure and was forever forgotten.

(Keeble and Hollington, 2010)

We strongly encourage all local authorities to consider the merits of moving to multi-agency co-location models ... this should include co-location of local police child abuse teams with children's social care.

(Home Office, 2013; Stanley, et al., 2010; HC 137:1, 2013, p68)

Many local authorities now co-ordinate a multi-agency safeguarding hub (MASH) team at the point of referral. The MASH principles are of information sharing across agencies, joint decision making and co-ordinated intervention. Numbers of key agencies are situated together with access to their specific databases, enabling fast checks to be made as to action required following a referral and enabling urgent protective action. Co-operation promotes multi-agency working but team structures must be in place to take those actions forward to continue any subsequent investigation. Parents/carers and children need to consent for family information to be shared within the MASH. Without consent, the MASH manager decides whether or not the threshold of child protection has been reached sufficiently to justify over-riding the parent's/carer's view. All such decisions must be proportionate and balance the risk to the child with family rights to privacy.

Research of MASH functioning (Home Office, 2013) in five local authorities provided positive feedback stating that MASH led to more robust decision making based on sufficient, accurate and timely intelligence resulting in better assessment of when to step up or step down investigations. The approach avoided duplication of process across agencies, reduced the risk of cases slipping through the protection net and there was strong accountability through the LSCB. Also, co-location of agencies led to shared risk assessment and facilitated delivery of joint training.

The strategy discussion/meeting

A strategy discussion involves an immediate communication between social workers and police, usually by telephone, at the initial stages of a referral, or at any other time, as checks are made by both agencies and agreement reached about whether the threshold for a section 47 (CA 1989) is met. On receipt of the referral, the very first consideration must be the child's immediate safety. A strategy discussion must not take the place of a strategy meeting.

At a strategy meeting, knowledge is shared, facts debated, issues, feelings and intuitions raised. Multi-agency decisions are made about how best to investigate the possibility or actuality of harm caused to the child. Importantly, at this stage, as the investigation develops, there may or may not be evidence of crime. Whether or not the child is best protected by means of civil or criminal proceedings, or a combination of both, or by a family support approach, will be clarified.

A strategy discussion/meeting should take place as soon as possible following a referral to children's services unless there is a need for immediate action to protect the child or to preserve forensic evidence. A joint investigation cannot be restricted by timescales. Gaining an abused child's trust and a non-abusive parent's or carer's co-operation, collating evidence about an alleged abuser and having multi-agency debate and analysis of the risk of harm to a child or children cannot be time limited. Investigations must be progressed with integrity and not allowed to drift.

This meeting, chaired by a senior children's services manager, is to share information and plan the section 47 (CA 1989). A single or joint agency investigation may take place and the meeting will agree any immediate action to protect, including legal action if needed. Importantly, it is a professionals only meeting and parents or carers must only be informed about it if this does not place the child at risk. Police, usually from the Child Abuse Investigation Team (CAIT), must attend as well as any professionals with relevant involvement, particularly from health, education and probation. Consideration must be given to including specialist advisors to inform about disability, ethnicity and specific cultural practices and how the child's wishes and feelings will be taken into account.

Decisions must be made about:

- if and how information is to be shared;
- whether non-abusive parents or carers should be informed;
- who should interview whom for what purpose, where and when;

- the need for visually recorded interviews;
- the need for paediatric assessments;
- how to obtain and secure forensic evidence;
- whether to convene a child protection conference;
- actioning legal safeguards;
- the need for review strategy meeting/s;
- the protection needs of other children;
- the assessment in parallel with the section 47 (CA 1989) investigation;
- not convening a child protection conference (this should be approved by a senior children's services manager).

The investigators must collaborate with the MAPPA if the alleged or known perpetrator is thought to pose a risk to others. If the allegation is against a member of staff, following immediate protective action any disciplinary action must await the outcome of the child protection investigation and any criminal proceedings, and the Local Authority Designated Officer (LADO) must be consulted and involved throughout the investigation (DfE, 2015, p54).

When a strategy meeting takes place, consider the following questions.

Who has been invited?

Is a police officer present?

Who is absent? What difference will this make?

Is the chairperson a senior manager?

Is all the key information available at the meeting?

Is it safe to inform the parents/carers and the child about the meeting?

How are the child's views represented?

Is there clarity of tasks between professionals with clear timescales?

Has a review been arranged?

Are the decisions consistent with the child's best interests?

Has there been due consideration of the child's and family's needs and circumstances?

Is there provision for a contemporaneous record of decisions?

Child protection conference

Detailed guidance about conferences is well presented in *Working Together to Safeguard Children* (DCSF, 2010a).The conference must be held within 15 days of a strategy meeting decision to convene one or in response to another authority's concerns about a child in the area. The conference is chaired by an independent senior social worker and is attended by professionals involved in the section 47 (CA 1989) investigation, as well as those working with the child and family. Specialist advisors may need to be included. The child and/or family can attend or be represented by an advocate (Laggay and Courtney, 2013). By agreement with the chairperson, the child may attend for all or part of the conference, may meet with the chairperson beforehand or may contribute by letter, drawing, audio or visual recording. Children who attend should not be exposed to parental conflict or adult language, and professionals must be sensitive to the impact on the child of any contribution. An adult may be identified within the child's world such as a teacher or nursery worker, who the child feels comfortable and confident to talk to. This is to provide effective monitoring of the child's safety.

Children's views about the child protection processes were collated for the Office of the Children's Commissioner (Cossar, et al., 2011).

My advocate comes a couple of days before ... when she comes round I'll tell her what to say at the meeting and she'll write it down and she'll say it the way I put it and erm she's really good

I did go once but it was awful ... they were just all talking and I didn't understand what they were saying.

Every time I went to speak someone interrupted me and that really annoyed me so I was like right I'm going I've got to get to school.

... the questions that they ask, well if I answer them then I am going to like upset you know my mum.

(pp57–62)

Parents and carers are central to processes for keeping children safe. Social workers must help them contribute to the conference unless to do so would place the child at risk or undermine the process. Parents may be excluded if their involvement compromises a police investigation or if there is risk of violence. During the conference, parents, carers and children should never be surprised by the sudden disclosure of sensitive information and there must be recognition of their relative powerlessness. The following parents' views illustrate their experiences of conferences:

I could feel they had power and I had none.

It was difficult to keep track of what was happening.

We had to introduce ourselves and I was asked to go first. I messed up. I couldn't say my name and who I was. That finished it. I didn't come in with much confidence but after that I felt really stupid.

(Peake, 1997, pp32–3)

When working with parents it is important to understand the legal concept of PR Parental Responsibility (CA 1989 s31) and to be clear which adult has PR. PR refers to all the rights, duties, powers, responsibilities and authority which by law a parent of a child has in relation to the child and his/her property. People other than parents can acquire PR. The local authority acquires shared PR if a Care Order or Emergency Protection Order (s31 and s44 CA 1989) is made and this may limit the extent to which PR can be exercised by a parent. If a Residence Order (s8, CA 1989) is made, determining where a child must live, shared PR is awarded to the person looking after the child.

The purpose of the conference is to share and analyse information, particularly the outcome of the section 47 (CA 1989) investigation, to make judgements about the likelihood of a child suffering significant harm and to decide whether the child is at continuing risk based on evidence or research findings. The social worker must provide a report of the investigation and assessment. Any concern about presenting sensitive information must be discussed with the chairperson prior to the conference. Each agency presents background information about the child and family, who contribute and are invited to comment throughout. Following discussion, a decision is reached about whether or not the child (and any other children in the family or children identified as a result of the investigation) needs to be the subject of a child protection plan. The relevant category, (or multiple categories) of child abuse, emotional, sexual, neglect, physical is identified and a judgement made about whether further harm is likely. The chairperson takes into account other professional views but is not bound by them and any dissent must be recorded. A conference must be convened prior to the birth of a child when there is concern that an unborn child may be at future risk of significant harm. A child protection plan must state clearly the purpose of the decisions and the roles and responsibilities of professionals and family members with clear timescales. Contingency plans must be in place should the safety of the child not be achieved. The child protection plan must outline the circumstances which would trigger legal proceedings to protect the child.

The conference designates members of a core group to implement the child protection plan. This group must meet within ten days of the conference. The core group is chaired by a social worker and attended by the family, advocates and professionals closely involved such as health visitors. It is not usual for police, paediatricians and others with in-depth knowledge of the risk factors associated with original allegations and findings to attend. This can result in a loss of focus on child protection strategies and over-identification with the adults' perspective. Whenever a new allegation of harm is made a strategy meeting will need to be convened. The review conference must be brought forward if the child remains unsafe, for instance if there is a significant change in family circumstances or new evidence of harm, a child is born into the household or an adult presenting a risk joins the family.

Legal proceedings will be considered if the child continues to be at risk of significant harm which will involve a local authority legal planning meeting. The *Public Law Outline* (MoJ, 2008) sets out the requirements for the pre-proceedings checklist which must include a social work chronology, a record of the strategy meeting and any single or joint agency materials as well as a child protection and care plan.

Family group conferences

I said, no, I'd speak for myself.

We're a bit closer in understanding each other – well in understanding me.

They didn't make us feel like we had to watch what we said – we could speak how we spoke. It just depended who you get and whether your social worker can be bothered.

(Bell and Wilson, 2006, p676)

Family group conferences (FGCs) are facilitated by children's services as a way of working with families where plans and decisions need to be made. If the child is thought to be at risk of significant harm the FGC must always be held within child protection procedures and must never replace a child protection conference. A child protection conference might include a decision for an FGC to progress the child protection plan.

The FGC has four parts. At the convening stage an independent co-ordinator, meets with the social worker to clarify concerns. They meet the family to define the network to be invited and to agree dates, food and venue. This stage sets the tone and is very significant to the success of the process. At the information-giving stage the social worker presents their concerns. The private family time stage involves the family response and planning how to protect the child. Children should be invited to take part in the FGC with someone of their choosing to act as an advocate. At the agreement stage the family present their plan to be agreed by professionals, together with arrangements for review and evaluation.

Children have reported positively about involvement in FGCs valuing the experience of being heard, and finding them enjoyable in their own right and the means also for resolving family conflicts and developing relationships. Children need to be well prepared and their presence was an important factor in achieving change at least in the short term (Bell and Wilson, 2006). However, research suggested the convenor must control who attends and that what is discussed to prevent the child hearing disturbing content. Children's involvement worked well to assist a single parent or grandparent where family communication had broken down and also where relationships with children's services had become entrenched. Black and minority ethnic families are under-represented in FGCs according to Bain and Dar (2015). They promote the need for practice which includes practitioners having awareness of culture in relation to power, inequalities and discrimination.

Investigative interviewing

Children's social workers should be trained jointly with police in the skills of investigative interviewing according to the Achieving Best Evidence (ABE) guidance (MoJ, 2011; Davies and Townsend, 2008a). This recommends that a child is interviewed by both a police officer and a social worker, usually in a specialist, child-centred interview suite, and that the interview is visually recorded and conducted according to the phased interview approach. This includes an introductory and rapport stage and supporting the child in providing a free narrative account of what happened, prior to non-leading questioning. The process provides a permanent record of the child's statement which can be presented in court, although the child still needs to undergo cross-examination in court. A professional interpreter must be involved in the planning and conduct of the interview if English is not the child's first language and the guidance provides for intermediaries to assist children with communication needs.

The child's statements may be analysed using the principles of statement validity analysis, a technique used to assess the statements of children. The child's free narrative, without prompting or pressure from the interviewer, is the most evidentially credible statement. The most accurate account by a child is the initial report made spontaneously, which is referred to as the *evidence of first complaint* in criminal proceedings and has high evidential value.

If the children's statements include sensory perceptions, such as how something smelt, felt to touch or tasted, this is indicative of an account based on personal experience. Corroborative evidence from witness statements, medical, forensic or photographic sources, assist validity when consistent with the child's statements. A child's behaviour may be supportive of their account, as would their statements if consistently repeated with little alteration. The child's emotional response may support the credibility of the child's statement though children rarely respond predictably. A lack of emotion may indicate a history of repeated abuse and subsequent trauma. During an investigative interview a child may provide detail through drawing or make spontaneous gestures while describing an abusive incident. It is not advisable for interviewers to ask a child to point to a part of the body as this may involve the child replicating abuse. If the child has been photographed or filmed as part of the abuse then the young person may choose to make a written instead of a visually recorded statement.

An OCC (2015, p9) report was critical of the diminished role of social workers in ABE interviews and of a lack of joint training with police. As a police-led process ABE interviews are conducted for criminal proceedings but could also be used for civil proceedings to help gain evidence to protect the child. There are shortages of intermediaries to assist young children and those with a disability. The Commissioner recommended the presence of a psychologist or intermediary in each interview and that the *Barnahus* model of practice should be considered. This practice is well-established and common to Scandanavia where children are visually recorded for both their statement of evidence and cross-examination and therefore do not have to attend court. They also have a therapist to monitor the process as being child-centred (http://lizdavies.net/campaigns-and-topics/child-protection-in-sweden).

Listening and hearing about child abuse

The large number of respondents who cited shame and guilt as a barrier to telling is particularly striking (OCC, 2015, p66). *Children will know if you can hear or not hear* (Nelson, 2008a, p25). Children find their own ways of telling or not telling about abuse. Listening to sexually abused children gives them voice:

They feel they cannot trust anyone to tell.

> *I thought all grown-ups were the same anyway, didn't trust them and … they would hurt me.*

They are threatened by the abuser – the threats may be implicit given abuse of power.

> *I was told people would die if I told.*

> *I feared for my life. I believed my abuser would know if I told. They had such power over me.*

> *My mum told me not to speak.*

They think they are to blame and are afraid of punishment, particularly if they have been made to take part in the abuse.

> *I was so brainwashed into feeling I was bad.*

> *I felt I was responsible for not stopping the abuse.*

They fear loss of family, home or school.

> *If you are different you are targeted – you tell one person and then the whole school finds out.*

They are emotionally and/or physically dependent on the abuser.

> *You don't want to upset people.*

They have a low sense of self-esteem and think no one will believe them.

> *My parents were respected. Everyone admired him … it seemed impossible to me to present people with a different image.*

They think the abuse is normal behaviour.

> *You tell yourself it can't be that bad. 'I'm fine,' you say, 'it doesn't bother me.'*

They feel loyalty to the abuser.

> *I was brought up to respect my elders (in the religious group) – to me I was doing what I was told.*

> *I used to comfort my abuser who cried after abusing me.*

They think that they will not obtain justice.

We did the feeling Yes, feeling No thing, at school. I knew I was getting the No feeling but I believed it wouldn't matter what I said.

They lack the communication skills.

First you don't know it's wrong; then when you find out you're stuck and trapped;

I couldn't say the words but I began writing darker and darker poetry.

(Nelson, 2008a, pp11–14)

RESEARCH SUMMARY

In Allnock and Miller's (2013) study, No one noticed, no one heard, *60 men and women who had experienced sexual abuse and family violence were asked about disclosure and if they had sought help. For 90 per cent the experience of disclosure was negative and characterised by a lack of support and protective action.*

The majority disclosed abuse to at least one person; 86 per cent of those sexually abused disclosed during childhood and 66 per cent tried to disclose while the abuse was happening. Of 203 disclosures made in childhood, 58 per cent were acted on. For children sexually abused, the younger they were when the abuse began, the longer the delay in disclosing – an average of eight years. The reason for disclosure was for the abuse to stop but also to protect others, seek justice and receive emotional support. Many told their friends, who importantly provided physical protection, emotional and practical support. Of mothers who were told, 30 per cent took action to stop the abuse but 17 per cent ignored the disclosure or denied it was true. A quarter of initial disclosures were made to teachers and some provided helpful responses. Initial disclosures were not made to social workers, even where they were known to the families. Some said they might have disclosed if social workers had seen them alone, shown more interest and asked directly about abuse. Children said they were made to meet perpetrators and others complicit in the abuse, often leading to allegations being withdrawn and abuse continuing. The researchers were in little doubt that seeing children with the family present led to retractions.

Further barriers to disclosure existed when there were multiple perpetrators, when families had parental mental health problems, substance misuse or where there was violence. My mum's quite ill and I was conscious of not wanting to upset her *(p25). For many the abuse began before they had the words to describe what was happening.* It was just one of those things you couldn't really explain *(p25). Children were threatened with actual violence or told they, or someone else, would be killed if they told. Abusers said the abuse was a secret, no-one else's business and it was normal. Some children were too ashamed, embarrassed or afraid of being called liars. Others believed that professionals and parents should have noticed.* I never went and asked for help but no one ever asked me *(p25). Sometimes when I was talking to my Mam I tried to leave hints ... (p30).*

Positive responses included finding a safe place to speak, using age appropriate language, keeping them informed and speaking to them not just to the adults. Positive responses included being believed, protected and emotionally supported. Some children's contact with police was positive, he talked to me like a young person not a stupid little kid, but others found the process overwhelming and felt out of control (p42).

The National Association for People Abused in Childhood (www.napac.org.uk) states that most survivors speak about abuse for the first time as adults. A study of Bangladeshi young women showed that the issue of izzat (honour) keeps socially unacceptable behaviour such as sexual activity hidden, making it difficult for professionals to hear abuse allegations (Ward and Patel, 2006). In the context of child sexual exploitation, disclosure is unlikely because of the fear of those exploiting them, loyalty to perpetrators, a lack of understanding that they are being exploited and a negative view of authority figures (OSCB, 2015, p41).

Over time children may develop a pattern of adjustment to abuse as a form of survival. The child abuse accommodation syndrome assists understanding of children's responses (Summit, 1983). As part of this syndrome following disclosure, the child is commonly met with adult denial and disbelief from their family, friends and local community. The child will be in crisis because of anxiety caused by the telling of the secret. They will be in fear of the authorities' response and the impact on their lives. They will also carry responsibility for the possible destruction of the family unit by telling and the child is under pressure to lie that nothing harmful has happened. Adults then suppress the allegation and in the absence of support, and fearing the offender, the child may retract, withdraw or minimise the disclosure. Retractions should always prompt questions about the reasons for the child changing their account.

Direct work

Ten respondents said they tried to tell through drawing pictures and 4 through playing with dolls in a particular way ... adults generally detected the abnormal behaviour but did not act upon it.

As a child I play acted out what happened to me. I did it with my dolls. I used to rip their arms and legs and heads off.

(OCC, 2015, p64)

Children need a safe space to talk about abuse.

(OCC, 2015, p35)

In order to provide children with opportunities to tell about abuse, toys, drawing materials and resource books are essential. The *Anti-colouring book* (Striker and Kimmel, 2012) enables the social worker to enter into the child's world by facilitating the child's view without prejudging or imposing interpretations. Children can express their worst nightmare, how they visualise their future or their feelings about friends and family. An excellent resource to assess the child's feelings about *Yes* and *No* touches, particularly when there is high suspicion of harm with no forensic evidence or disclosure, is *My Book, My Body* (Peake and Rouf, 1989). This book does not introduce concepts of abuse or contaminate the evidence of the child. The *Bear Cards* and *Kids' Need* cards are methods for exploring children's feelings (Veeken, 2012; Hamer, 2007). *Creative Therapy: Activities with children and adolescents* (Hobday and Ollier, 1998) provides many activities for work with children, such as how to create a wall of hope or build a first-aid kit to assist healing. The timing in using these resources is important and should be discussed within the context of the investigation.

A helpful resource is storytelling which allows children to gain healing (Sunderland, 2001). Nancy Davis provides stories for children in a wide range of circumstances to promote empowerment (Davis, 1999). The child absorbs the message contained within the story and relates this to their unique situation. For instance, a story for children who have not disclosed trauma, *The burned tree* is about a tree which has been struck by lightning which receives assistance from a beaver to remove the burnt branches and to be nurtured and achieve regrowth (*www.therapeutic-stories.com/therapeutic/ example_of_stories.html?panelno*). It is each social worker's responsibility to make use of a range of practice resources to assist communication with children, to prioritise one-to-one contact and to make sure emotionally responsive supervision is accessed.

Investigation of organised abuse

Organised abuse involves one or more abusers and a number of children. The abusers concerned may be acting in concert to abuse children, sometimes acting in isolation, or may be using an institutional framework or position of authority to recruit children for abuse.

(DCSF, 2010a, 6.10)

42 per cent of 756 survivor respondents said they were abused by more than one person and of these 74 per cent said their abusers knew each other.

(OCC, 2015, p8)

Child sexual exploitation and abuse (CSEA) represents one of the highest serious and organised crime risks. Although we may never know the full extent of the problem, law enforcement operations and high-profile cases have given us a much better insight into the scale and the challenges it presents. CSEA remains a particularly significant threat, with every UK policing region reporting cases of contact child sexual abuse in 2014; the proliferation of indecent images of children and online child sexual exploitation continue to subject children to risk. We have also seen a continuation of offending overseas by British nationals.

(NCA, 2015, p13)

While police have defined child sexual exploitation and abuse as a strategic threat and are increasing resources to protect children and prosecute perpetrators, social workers have been largely removed from this form of investigation by policy changes and restructuring. Two high profile government reviews focused solely on abuse within families omitting all mention of abuse in an organised context (Munro, 2011; Laming, 2009). In the UK, there is no national multi-agency, child protection investigation team and very few local joint police and social work teams. Police cannot do this work alone; they hold knowledge about perpetrators but social work and other agencies have contact with and knowledge of child victims.

Organised abuse protocols are the appropriate multi-agency response to organised crime that targets children. The global industry of child abuse includes the illegal adoption trade, trafficking of children for domestic servitude and for sexual exploitation, online abuse – abusive images of children but also live-streaming of sexual assaults – the illegal organ trade, forced marriage, *honour* violence crimes and child sexual exploitation. Global crime requires a global law enforcement response.

After much public pressure, specifically survivor campaigns, a statutory and Independent Inquiry into Child Sexual Abuse (www.iicsa.org.uk) was established in 2014. The aims of the inquiry include considering *the extent to which State and non-State institutions have failed in their duty of care to protect children from sexual abuse and exploitation.* This followed the Savile Inquiry and high profile arrests made by Operation Yewtree with regard to abuse of children within the entertainment industry (Gray and Watt, 2012). There were also serious allegations regarding a Westminster network of child sex offenders (Watson, 2012a; 2012b; see also Mann, 2015). Yet, the definition of organised abuse and all reference to the means of investigating it were removed from *Working Together to Safeguard Children* (DfE, 2013; 2015) leaving professionals with no practice guidance. This led to a worrying situation as public outcry increasingly demands justice for survivors and has led to some members of the public seeking their own solutions such as conducting their own entrapment of online perpetrators (www.stinsonhunter.com) or, through social media campaigns, acting as judge and jury where it is believed insufficient action has been taken by statutory bodies. This reaction in itself may have an impact on police investigation including supporting or hindering prosecutions and may undermine or contaminate child and survivor testimony. There is also an online database of convicted and cautioned child abusers (theukdatabase.com/).

The following organised abuse protocols are largely based on the *London Child Protection Procedures* (LSCB, 2015) in the absence of national guidance. Each investigation of organised abuse will be different according to the number of places and people involved, sometimes over long timescales. The investigation requires specialist skills from both police and social workers working in dedicated teams and the setting up of a specialist investigation management group to lead the investigation, agree staffing, resources, legal services and media management. A victim support strategy and protocol must be established at the outset to ensure support and protection for victims throughout the investigation and subsequent legal proceedings.

An initial strategy meeting involving senior managers from children's services and police should be convened which will involve other senior staff from health, education, probation and other agencies as required and must ensure co-ordination across local authority boundaries. The meeting will undertake an initial mapping exercise to determine the scale of the investigation and assess information about child and adult victims and possible perpetrators. It will make decisions about the immediate safety of children and adult survivors, arrange investigative interviews of alleged victims and corroborative witnesses and consider the need for medical consultations, forensic retrieval, search of premises and securing evidence. Each individual child will require their own child protection plan following section 47 (CA 1989) procedures.

The meeting will appoint a strategic management group to oversee the investigation chaired by a senior children's services manager. This group will make operational decisions and bring together teams of skilled investigative practitioners. It will ensure that appropriate resources are made available to support the work of the operational teams and consider the interests of staff in terms of their safety and support needs. This group should also provide a means of safe reporting for whistleblowers. Information is collated about alleged or known perpetrators including previous allegations/suspicions, inspection reports/complaints and employment records. Patterns of abuse are mapped, including venues, methods of offending and grooming behaviours. The team liaises with the Crown Prosecution Service to enable exchange of information and to implement strategy on a daily basis. The strategic management group will review the outcome of the operational team and consider, in sequence:

1. child protection investigation/s by children's services;

2. police investigations of alleged or known criminal offences;

3. consideration by an employer of disciplinary action in respect of the alleged or known perpetrator/s.

The employers responsible for disciplinary action should await the outcome of the child protection investigation and police action, before progressing to disciplinary proceedings. This does not prevent the employee being suspended pending the outcome of the investigations.

CASE STUDY

Kingfisher Team, Oxford (www.oxfordshire.gov.uk/saferchildren)

This multi-agency, co-located team was set up in 2012, following Operation Bullfinch, which resulted in seven men being imprisoned for sexual crimes against six girls. A serious case review reported that over 300 children had been sexually exploited over a period of eight years.

The abuse included vaginal, anal and oral rape and also involved the use of a variety of objects such as knives, meat cleavers, baseball bats, sex toys ... it was often accompanied by humiliating and degrading conduct such as biting, scratching, acts of urinating, being suffocated, tied up ... they were also beaten and burnt. The sexual activity was often carried out by groups of men, sometimes it would go on for days on end ... the girls were guarded so they could not escape.

(OSCB, 2015, p9)

One parent criticised social workers for only working with one model of abuse – intra-familial – and wanted police and social workers to work together, not passing the buck (p16).

The team consisted of over 20 staff from police and social work. In two years it identified more than 200 children at risk of child sexual exploitation (CSE). The emphasis is proactive protection. One police officer said, *if you look properly you will find it...we have realized the power of sharing even the smallest piece of information with the rest of the team. That's how you start putting together the jigsaw* (Hill, 2015a). The staff have small caseloads and the social workers remain in contact with children until after a court case has concluded and the child has settled. The team work according to the child's timescale. If a child is identified as at risk then it may take months before they disclose. In 2015, six men were convicted as a result of Operation Reportage, which was the culmination of months of work by the Kingfisher Team, which proactively sought to identify child victims to support them while pursuing the prosecution of the exploitative adults. The children, aged between 12 and 16, were targeted between 2009 and 2014 and groomed via social media. Once befriended, sexual relationships were established before the girls were exploited. A number of tactics were deployed to ensure compliance, namely the use of power, evoking of guilt and threats or use of violence.

Social work integrity and accountability

Victoria's parents have noted that social workers blame doctors, front line staff blame management, managers blame the council, the councils blame the Government for lack of funding. Typical responses to failings have been 'I am poorly managed', 'we did not have the resources' or 'it was not my job'.

(Laming, 2003, p97)

Every child protection professional is responsible and individually accountable. They must follow guidance in working with other professionals, challenging them where necessary and making sure conflict is addressed and resolved. Social workers must act with professional integrity. This means practising according to accepted professional guidelines and ethical codes. It is a professional value linked to accountability in the International Federation of Social Work's *Statement of Ethical Principles*:

... social workers should act with integrity. This includes not abusing the relationship of trust with the people using their services, recognising the boundaries between personal and professional life, and not abusing their position for personal benefit or gain. Social workers should be prepared to state the reasons for their decisions based on ethical considerations, and be accountable for their choices and actions.

(IFSW, 2012)

The concept of integrity is also central to the BASW's *Code of Ethics* (2012a: 2.3): *Social workers should be prepared to account for and justify their judgments and actions to people who use their services, to employers and to the general public.*

Accountability means literally to be called upon to give an account of what one has done or not done. Social workers may be held to account by their employer and the regulatory body the Health and Care Professions Council (HCPC). Recent case decisions can be viewed on the HCPC website (www.hpc-uk.org/complaints/hearings/archive). Social workers should be aware that they are expected to behave professionally outside the work environment which has implications for social activity and the use of social media. Social workers have a duty of care to service users and must use best evidence and current knowledge to inform practice based on research, policy, theory, practice experience and service user perspectives. They must understand and weigh up the legal options, powers and duties that apply to specific cases, promote human rights, counteract discrimination and not accept work beyond their competence. Social workers must take action when services are inadequate and notify appropriate managers and/or regulatory bodies of concerns that standards are not being met (Kline and Preston-Shoot, 2012). These principles are represented throughout this book.

There are often dilemmas for social workers when managing the interface between accountability to an employer and accountability to a professional organisation. A survey of social workers in the UK concluded that high caseloads, excessive administrative demands, inadequate supervision, high vacancy rates, bullying cultures and low morale were putting service users at risk. Of the 1,100 social workers contacted, 77 per cent said that caseloads were unmanageable and 88 per cent believed that lives were at risk because of cuts to services. Social workers also said that they had less time to do direct work (BASW, 2012b). Two-thirds of children's social workers responding to a Community Care survey said they had been threatened by service users in the last six months. Many had been victims of multiple threats. Over half said they had received no training in how to respond to intimidation and hostility (Cooper, 2011). These serious findings were the subject of an All Party Parliamentary Group *Inquiry into the State of Social Work* (BASW, 2013). Six local authorities reported difficulties in recruiting experienced social workers leaving gaps in staff being able to work in child protection and conduct investigative interviews (Brady, et al., 2014). A survey of 1,000 social workers revealed that 70 per cent did not feel they had enough resources to protect children and 43 per cent felt pressured to reclassify child protection cases as children in need (Stevenson, 2015b). Comments included:

> *Managers want to process cases speedily to meet targets. Unless there are SERIOUS child protection concerns, no social work involvement is likely.*

> *Cases can be downgraded to children in need so more child protection cases can be allocated.*

> *Every case on my allocation is a case of money over protection.*

Unmanageable caseloads create a culture where the focus is on justifying doing nothing.

There is pressure to close cases before they should be closed.

All experienced child protection social workers are leaving the profession and newly qualified social workers are undertaking most of the work.

(Stevenson, 2015b)

Compliance with professional codes is commonly included in contracts of employment for social workers. If a social worker considers they have been asked by an employer to act in a manner which breaches their professional codes then this should be questioned as unreasonable and if necessary the social worker should refuse to comply. Local authorities are ultimately accountable to the electorate. However, when services are privatised accountability becomes obscure. For instance, when private providers of children's homes found they were not making a profit, they closed homes forcing many children to be moved (Wood, 2007). The role of the statutory sector has been narrowed with privatisation of social work tasks and a reduction in social work posts. The employment of unqualified staff saves money and facilitates the transfer of services to the private sector. This development has led to an emphasis on individual professional accountability as social workers are employed in a wide range of settings often managed by non-social work managers.

In order to proactively protect children, social workers need to work within safe working environments and require reflective supervision and quality training. There is no statutory requirement for qualified children's social workers to receive regular supervision but it is recognised as good practice to provide regular uninterrupted supervision with an experienced practitioner. Social workers report they have supervision which lacks *reflective support which is really needed when workers are dealing with cases which are really horrific … because of the tendency to be target and process driven* (Brady, et al., 2014, p23).

Working Together to Safeguard Children (DCSF, 2010a, p127) provided statutory guidance on all levels of child protection training including advanced skills for police and social workers in the investigation of abuse and interviewing of children (Davies and Townsend, 2008b). However, subsequent versions of *Working Together to Safeguard Children* (DfE, 2013; 2015) removed all guidance on training and development leaving responsibility with LSCBs. Social workers reported, *on-the-job training amongst social workers was variable in terms of availability, access to training, focus of the training, format, quality and relevance to practice* (Brady, et al., 2014, p12). The ABE guidance requires a child-centred interview to be conducted collaboratively by police and social workers (MoJ, 2011:2.22). However, with no statutory requirement on police or local authorities to conduct this training, few social workers are now trained in these skills and it is not uncommon for police to conduct child interviews without social work involvement.

ACTIVITY 1.1

A child tells you that they are physically punished. Your manager directs that the case is defined as child in need (s17, CA 1989) and recommends that the parents attend a parenting programme. Think about whether you would:

- *follow your manager's instructions, carry out an assessment and arrange the parenting programme, while feeling unsure about the child's safety and being afraid that you might be mistaken; or*

- *analyse the case, informed by knowledge of research and inquiry reports, and wish to convene a section 47 (CA 1989) strategy meeting because, in your judgement, you consider the child to be at risk of significant harm and requiring multi-agency child protection procedures.*

Child abuse inquiries provide us with a list of 'if only' reflections. How would you make sure you were not left with these 'if onlys' and were empowered to protect the child?

If only:

- *the child had been heard;*
- *the adults concerned about the child had been heard;*
- *signs had been recognised;*
- *someone had called children's services or police;*
- *emails had been followed up;*
- *workers had safe working conditions;*
- *suspicions were checked;*
- *someone had blown the whistle;*
- *budgets hadn't been cut and services hadn't been restructured;*
- *quality training, supervision and management had been in place.*

Whistleblowing

Working Together to Safeguard Children states the need for, *clear whistleblowing procedures, codes of conduct, and a culture that enables issues about safeguarding and promoting the welfare of children to be addressed.*

(DfE 2015, p53)

Whistleblowing is the disclosure by an individual or group to the public or to those in authority of mismanagement, corruption, illegality or some other form of wrong-doing in the workplace (HCPC, 2015; HCPC, 2016: 7).

Investigating child abuse requires social workers to be courageous in practice and to know how to fully represent the child's voice. The professional child abuse accommodation syndrome, (see page 8), may lead to a social worker being met with disbelief and denial, which mirrors the probable adult response to the child. They may find themselves unheard, unsupported or even prohibited from acting to protect. If children's voices are to be heard, then professional voices must also be heard when they are carrying the child's message. Powerful adults abuse children and networks of perpetrators extend to the highest levels of society. It can be difficult and frightening to carry the message forward to protect children. It may require individuals, organisations or processes to be challenged in order to break the secrecy and silence that perpetuates abuse.

Speaking out on behalf of abused children is supported by legislation and statutory guidance. The Public Interest Disclosure Act 1998 provides statutory protection to workers who speak out against corruption and malpractice at work and who experience victimisation and dismissal. The law states that a disclosure must be *reasonable* and statutory protection requires the making of a *protected disclosure* in good faith and not for personal gain. It is expected that a professional will first raise issues through the usual channels provided by management such as informing a team manager (unless the complaint implicates this manager), child protection specialist or a member of the LSCB. This would usually involve social workers clarifying and gathering evidence, setting it out in writing, raising the concerns collectively with colleagues, and using internal means such as supervision, team meetings, grievance procedures and consultation processes. Any difference of view between a practitioner and manager must be recorded on the service user file and in supervision notes for future reference. Advice and representation can be sought through membership of a trade union and clear records of all actions must be kept.

The charity Public Concern at Work (www.pcaw.org.uk) provides advice to whistleblowers in confidence. If all internal mechanisms have been implemented without resolution, then the concerns may be escalated externally, which would usually be to the HCPC or a relevant inspection agency such as Ofsted. The HCPC advises that, only in very serious circumstances should concerns be made public. The law on whistleblowing is complex. To raise serious issues with the media, on social media or through accessing political processes is also complex and legal advice must always be sought for the protection of service users and professionals. As an example, social workers can be open to prosecution for taking documentary evidence from their employer or held in contempt of court for keeping court documents (Davies, 2014).

Following much political and media pressure from survivor and whistleblower campaign groups, The Independent Inquiry on Child Sexual Abuse made an undertaking to provide strong legal protection for whistleblowers. Consistent with the requirements of the public interest, it stated that *no document or evidence provided to the Inquiry will result in, or be used in, any prosecution under the Official Secrets Act 1989 or any prosecution for unlawful possession of the evidence in question.* (www.iicsa.org.uk/news/attorney-general-grants-protection-whistleblowers)

CASE STUDY

Nevres Kemal, social worker – *we are good people doing a good job*

In 2007, Nevres Kemal, then a social worker in the London Borough of Haringey, alerted management to flaws in the child protection system for sexually abused children. She wrote to the Department of Health informing them that Haringey children were at risk. Six months later Peter Connelly, aged 17 months, died from abuse *(HSCB, 2009)*. *Nobody bothered writing back. No one was interested. Then it came out in the press. There was no feeling of vindication. It doesn't matter if I was wrong or right: it didn't save that kid's life, it didn't save me and my family four and a half years of hell.* She also said, *I never regretted speaking up for the children who needed protection. I never thought, even when I was at my most scared, why did I not keep my mouth shut? You can take everything from me; my home, my job, my good name, but you cannot strip me of my integrity* (Cooper, 2013; Fairweather, 2008).

C H A P T E R   S U M M A R Y

This chapter provides a comprehensive outline of child protection legislation, guidance and protocols. Methods of investigation of organised abuse are included. Responding to children who disclose abuse is a particular focus, as is direct work with children and how to be heard as a professional striving to protect children. In this context social work accountability and whistleblowing are addressed in some depth.

FURTHER READING

Calder, M and Hackett, S (eds) (2013) *Assessment in child care*. Lyme Regis: Russell House.
A critical analysis of current practice and policy initiatives enabling an informed approach to assessment.

Kline, R and Preston-Shoot, M (2012*) Professional accountability in social care and health.* London: Learning Matters.
A practical guide to accountability and safe working in health and social work.

WEBSITES

napac.org.uk
National Association for People Abused in Childhood – a charity supporting adult recovery from child abuse.

www.paceuk.info
Parents against child sexual exploitation – supports families of sexually exploited children.

www.pcaw.org.uk
Public Concern at Work – an independent authority which provides advice to whistleblowers and aims to ensure that concerns about malpractice are addressed in the workplace.

voicesforchildren.blogspot.com
Website of Jersey survivors.

Brynalynvictims.blogspot.com
Website of North Wales children's home survivors

www.survivorsni.org
Survivors of institutional abuse in Northern Ireland

Chapter 2
Emotional abuse

Introduction

I love you mum and dad. I'm sorry I just can't cope. Don't be sad. It's no one's fault. I just can't go on. None of it was any of your fault. Love you and family, Joe. I tried telling them and they just don't listen.

Joseph Schole, 16 years, wrote this letter to his parents in 2002. He was found hanging in his cell in Stoke Heath young offender institution in Shropshire. He died just nine days after being admitted to prison for street robbery. *He's in a cell, he's stripped naked, he's got a horse-blanket-like garment on fastened with Velcro. It's filthy and squalid ... He's on a concrete plinth with a thin plastic mat. He had told his mother he would make a suicide attempt to try and be moved from prison to a children's home* (Willow, 2014, p49).

No person reading the lengthy section devoted to Victoria [Climbié] herself could fail to realise that as well as being tortured and battered to death, she endured an emotional and psychological hell (O'Hagan, 2006, p10).

I've been bad for years and years (Written on the wall of a cellar in Haut de la Garenne children's home in Jersey) (Batty, 2008).

This chapter focuses on the protection of children from emotional abuse with children and survivor perspectives at the forefront. It presents this category of abuse in a range of contexts including children in custody, 'honour'-based violence, bullying, institutional abuse and other areas where serious case reviews and inquiries have drawn attention to gaps in practice. Research summaries, activities and case studies provide a basis for sound decision making. The chapter concludes with case diagrams about emotional abuse involving children whose parent or carer has mental health problems and an investigative process is escalated through five levels of social work intervention to support in-depth analysis.

Definition of emotional abuse

Emotional abuse is defined as the persistent emotional maltreatment of a child such as to cause severe and persistent adverse effects on the child's emotional development. It may involve conveying to children that they are worthless or unloved, inadequate, or valued only insofar as they meet the needs of another person. It may include not giving the child opportunities to express their views, deliberately silencing them or 'making fun' of what they say or how they communicate. It may feature age or developmentally inappropriate expectations being imposed on children. These may include interactions that are beyond the child's developmental capability, as well as overprotection and limitation of exploration and learning, or preventing the child participating in normal social interaction. It may involve seeing or hearing the ill-treatment of another. It may involve serious bullying (including cyber bullying), causing children frequently to feel frightened or in danger, or the exploitation or corruption of children. Some level of emotional abuse is involved in all types of maltreatment of a child, though it may occur alone.

(DfE, 2015, p92)

Learning about emotional abuse

ACTIVITY 2.1

The definition suggests that emotional abuse is harmful only when persistent. Do you agree with this definition or do you think emotional harm can be caused through a one-off incident?

COMMENT

Maltreated children are more likely to be suicidal, suffer mental health problems, self-harm and show delinquent behaviour. They are also more likely to be bullied by other children, siblings or adults. Bullied children, in turn, are more likely to have poorer emotional wellbeing. The more types of maltreatment and victimisation children experience, the greater their trauma.

(Radford, et al., 2011, p16)

The inclusion of persistent *in the definition is significant. It recognises that potentially emotionally abusive behaviours can feature in children's lives from time to time, for example when an overtired or stressed adult, because of an experience such as bereavement, may temporarily be unable to prioritise the child's emotional needs. While survivor accounts convey that even a single act can be harmful, such as witnessing a violent act on television, the persistent nature of emotional abuse is a key characteristic. Beckett maintains that any kind of neglect, physical abuse or sexual abuse conveys to a child a negative message about their worth and this is why emotional abuse is present in all forms of child abuse and is therefore the primary form of abuse (Beckett, 2007, p70). The abuse may be by commission such as acts of verbal abuse, or omission such as by ignoring a child's achievements.*

Defining a child as in need of a child protection plan under the category of emotional abuse only takes place if it is the sole or main category. Child protection systems are mainly triggered by incidents and ongoing emotional abuse does not always gain a protective response leading to significant delay in decisions about the threshold of significant harm being reached. There may be no obvious cut-off between abusive and non-abusive parenting (Barlow and Schrader McMillan, 2010, p42).

Definitions often involve lists of abusive behaviours, for example parents or carers being critical, undermining and/or verbally abusive, and these can be experienced by almost every child at some point without a child necessarily being emotionally or psychologically abused. O'Hagan states that definitions of emotional abuse should refer to context, duration and consequence *(2006, p39) and that social workers should distinguish between emotional (feelings) and psychological (thoughts) abuse.*

Inequality and poverty as causes of parental stress impact children's emotional wellbeing over time. Parents and carers living in poverty may experience increased stress through

(Continued)

concerns about debt, housing, health and wellbeing. Children in poor families are nearly three times more likely to have mental health problems than those in high-income families and babies growing up in low-income areas have been shown to be at greater risk of displaying high levels of chronic stress. Children are often keenly aware of their parents' experience and worry about their parents not having enough money to pay for essentials, such as food and energy bills (Kothari, et al., 2014, p5).

Emotional abuse – the evidence

- The number of children made the subject of a child protection plan in England because of emotional abuse increased from 6,000 in 2006 to 15,860 in 2014 (DfE, 2014b). Evidence from self-reports suggests a much higher prevalence than is indicated by the number of children subject to child protection plans (Barlow and Schrader McMillan, 2010, p25; Parton, 2012). For example, nine per cent of women and four per cent of men reported exposure to emotional abuse in childhood (Gilbert, et al., 2009).

- During childhood 3.6 per cent of under 11s, 6.8 per cent of 11–17s and 6.9 per cent of 18–24s had been emotionally abused, while during one year 1.8 per cent of under 11s and three per cent of 11–17s had been emotionally abused by a parent or guardian in the UK. One in 14 young adults and the same number of children have experienced emotional abuse (Radford, et al., 2011).

- Over 100 children were moved from long-term placements when more than 65 children's homes and 14 schools for children with complex needs were closed because one company went into liquidation (Meghji, 2007, p1).

- There were 171 suicides of 15–19 year olds in 2013 in the UK. Data for under 18s is not readily available (Jutte, et al., 2015, p22). ChildLine reported 17,782 children reported suicidal feelings or felt actively suicidal in a period of one year to March 2015 (NSPCC, 2015).

- Employment, occupation and class are not clear indicators of emotional abuse. Of a sample of children registered under the category emotional abuse, 17 per cent were from social classes 1 and 2 (Doyle, 2013, p256). Radford, et al., (2011) showed that the numbers of children experiencing regular, verbal harsh treatment were significantly higher in lower social economic groups and among children whose parents had separated.

- Rayns, et al., (2011, p4) estimated that in the UK, 93,500 babies (79,000 under 1s in England) lived with a parent who was a problem ('hazardous' or 'harmful') drinker.

- Chamberlain, et al., (2010) in a survey of the views of 253,755 children in school Years 6, 8 and 10, estimated that 46 per cent have been bullied and an Ofsted (2012a) schools study further supported this figure.

- In the year 2014–15, ChildLine was contacted by 25,736 children who said that bullying was their main concern, while 3,306 children called ChildLine about emotional abuse (NSPCC, 2015).

- In 2013, the HM Government's Forced Marriage Unit (2014b) gave advice or support related to a possible forced marriage in 1,302 cases which were mainly girls and women. Fifteen per cent of victims were below 16 years, 97 cases involved disabled victims and 12 involved children identifying as lesbian, gay, bisexual or transgender.

- In a snapshot survey by CAFCASS (2012) over 60 per cent of cases which led to care applications between 11 and 30 November 2011 involved a parent who had been the victim of domestic violence.

- Radford, et al., (2011) found 12 per cent of under 11s, 18 per cent of 11–17s and 24 per cent of 18–24s had been exposed to domestic violence during childhood.

- A study of 139 serious case reviews in England (2009–2011) found 63 per cent had domestic abuse as a risk factor (Brandon, et al., 2012a). Domestic violence accounts for 14 per cent of all violent crime (ONS, 2013).

CASE STUDY

Alex Kelly – extremely vulnerable and utterly failed

What [Alex] needed was good quality therapeutic support in the community that could have addressed the many problems that had resulted in him offending in the first place. He was extremely vulnerable. He was in prison for non-violent offences. He was crying out for help and he was utterly failed.

(Coles, 2015)

A few weeks before his release from Cookham Wood young offender detention centre, Alex Kelly, aged 15 years, died from brain injury after hanging himself with laces from a pair of trainers. This act took place in the 15 minutes gap between observations by prison staff. Alex was of mixed heritage, black African and white British, and was a child in care in the London Borough of Tower Hamlets (LBTH), from 2002 until the time of his death. Alex had been sentenced to a ten-month Detention and Treatment Order (DTO), five months spent in custody and five months in the community, for minor offences including burglary and theft from a vehicle. Alex and his three siblings were taken into care, when Alex was aged 6 years, due to neglect, emotional abuse and medical evidence confirming Alex had been repeatedly raped, allegedly by a family member. No criminal case was brought against the alleged perpetrator. Alex was placed with a white family outside of his home borough and, while he considered himself white, he was treated as black in the largely white community where he and his foster family lived.

(Continued)

When Alex was 12 years old, he was diagnosed with Attention Deficit Hyperactivity Disorder (ADHD) and for a while treated with medication. Contact with his family was sporadic; however, his father maintained regular contact with him between 2002 and 2010. After this time, the local authority did not keep Alex's parents informed about developments in his life. Alex had eight different social workers from 2002 until he died in 2012, and had no allocated social worker for more than a year before he died. He had no forensic psychiatric assessment prior to sentencing, nor while in detention. The Youth Offending Team (YOT) did not make it known to the court when Alex was being sentenced that he was a vulnerable child or recommend that he be placed in a Secure Training Centre (STC). Had that happened, Alex might have been sentenced to a STC, which tend to be smaller and have a higher ratio of staff to children. Alex's behaviour became increasingly unstable in the time before his death, including acts of self-harm, blocking his cell observation panel, drawing pictures of figures hanging, practising making nooses with his shoelaces and attaching them to his locker. He placed notes on the observation panel of his cell saying he was going to *string up*. He was placed on an open Assessment, Care in Custody and Teamwork (ACCT) plan and observed five times per hour. On the night of his death, he told a prison officer about the sexual abuse he had experienced.

The inquest found that there was a systemic failure by the local authority to allocate a named social worker, which impeded inter-agency communication, the ability to address ongoing concerns about his mental health and continuity of care, and led to an inadequate level of support. Additionally, the inquest found that LBTH failed to address where he would live on release and his repeated wish to see his grandmother. During a period when Alex was in the young offender institution, no one from LBTH monitored his welfare or responded to his deteriorating mental health. The serious case review (THSCB, 2013) made 47 recommendations and found the local authority had failed in its duty to Alex during his detention and in the nine years prior. Specifically, after October 2011, Alex's case remained unallocated for over three months and the supervision of the social worker responsible for Alex from October 2011 was inadequate with records of only two supervision discussions about Alex in 11 months. The local authority failed in its commitment to promote Alex's educational needs, contact with his family or, where contact was not taking place, to help Alex to understand why and how this was happening.

Disabled children and emotional abuse

I feel like I've been left out a lot. Like having fun outside in the park and I get very tired and I can't stand up for long.

I've had people calling me names, really bad names.

Sometimes you get beat up you know. I've been beaten up.

When you're in public, people stare at you.

They think that if you are disabled physically then you are disabled mentally.

(What do you think about disability?
http://disability-studies.leeds.ac.uk/files/2011/10/kidsnews.pdf)

It is estimated that disabled children are nearly four times more likely to be emotionally abused than non-disabled children (Jones, et al., 2012). Experiencing multiple types of abuse is associated with disability and special educational needs (Radford, et al., 2011). Negative attitudes towards disability mean that disabled children are more vulnerable to bullying and to abuse, and the internalisation of oppression can result in compliant victims who may see themselves as deserving of abuse. One of the main barriers faced by disabled children is that they are commonly defined as their impairment. Their unique individuality becomes subsumed into this one-dimensional labelling.

Children with visible impairment are particularly likely to meet with patronising, hostile or demeaning comments (OCC, 2006; Mepham, 2010). In a survey of 1,024 children using social networking sites, 11 per cent identified themselves as disabled. Of these, 43 described experiences of unwanted sexual messages, homophobia, sexism, encouragement to self-harm and cyberstalking (Miller and Brown, 2014, p24). *Safeguarding Disabled Children Practice Guidance* emphasised the importance of communication with disabled children to enable them to make known their wishes and feelings in respect of their care and treatment (Murray and Osborne, 2009, p36).

A Mencap campaign entitled *Don't Stick It Stop It* aims to prevent the bullying of learning disabled children (www.mencap.org.uk/sites/default/files/documents/2008-03/Bullying%20wrecks%20lives.pdf).

RESEARCH SUMMARY

Shakespeare, et al., (1999) asked 300 disabled children aged between 11 and 16 years for their views and found their disability was dominant whereas other aspects of their identity such as gender and ethnicity were secondary. The children felt compelled to adopt behaviour and ways of speaking and walking which most closely approximated those of non-disabled children. This discrimination is compounded for disabled children from minority ethnic groups through racism and a lack of support for their families (Chamba, et al., 1999; Miller and Brown, 2014, p26). Shakespeare, et al. found that all the children got picked on and they experienced physical, emotional and verbal bullying, for example being called names such as 'spastic', being excluded from peer groups, or being kicked and hit [and that] even those who had not actually experienced bullying personally were aware of the possibility, and it therefore shaped their sense of self and their social relationships (1999, p18).

Emotional abuse of children at different ages

Social workers sometimes think that children are more vulnerable to abuse at particular ages. Why is it important to take age into account?

COMMENT

There is some evidence derived from analysis of serious case reviews which indicates that emotional abuse may begin pre-birth (Reder, et al., 1993, p40). Parents may not want to develop an emotional connection with the baby if they have had ambivalent attitudes to being pregnant, became pregnant as a means of leaving home, through unplanned sexual contact, or as a result of rape. A disinterest in the unborn baby may manifest as lack of access to antenatal care, wanting the baby adopted and changing their mind at the last minute, making no material preparations, only wanting a child of a specific gender or referring to the unborn child negatively. Sometimes a termination of pregnancy was desired but did not go ahead.

A level of awareness of typical child development for individual children is essential when assessing the impact of emotional abuse. An analysis of six serious case review findings suggested that if allocated social workers had been more inquisitive about why the child's behaviour was so difficult and if they had been more curious about the research behind neglect, attachment and child development, outcomes may have been different (Brandon, et al., 2012b). This research also found a pattern in professional failure to recognise children's emotional development and problems in children's relationship with caregivers where there were concerns about faltering growth (2012b, pp8–10).

In recent years the findings of neuroscience have been increasingly cited in policy debates to strengthen the case of early identification of and intervention with children at risk of maltreatment *(Munro and Musholt, 2013, p.18). Neuroscience tells us that the brain grows rapidly during the first three years of life and that enrichment is most effective and deprivation most damaging during these critical years. In his book* The Myth of the First Three Years, *Bruer suggests that the brain is, in fact, highly plastic throughout life and he expresses concern that neuroscientific theory can be misused to justify the provision of fewer resources to those who begin life at a disadvantage, because the theory allows little hope for change following early deprivation. If we take the Myth to heart, it seems to follow that if we can't help children by age 3, then we can't help them at all (1999, p205). Bruer calls for critical questioning of the neuroscientific approach as the brain, childhood and human development are far more complex than the theory allows for (Wastell and White, 2012, p409). Munro and Musholt (2013) describe the risks of this reductionist theory which ignores the complexities of the social world, arguing that it should be integrated with the broader social sciences. Scanning children's brains for non-therapeutic research reasons is in itself an ethical issue and media images of such scans have a strong emotional impact. This has been much used to justify early intervention policies such as fast track adoption. If maltreatment did cause permanent damage to the brain, it does not follow that the policy should be to remove children quickly from neglectful parents but could instead indicate the need for increasing support services for disadvantaged families (Munro and Musholt, 2013).*

Many influential social work educational texts looking at child development (for example, Bee, 1992; Sheridan, 1992) pay little attention (if any, in the case of Sheridan) to emotional development (O'Hagan, 2006, p29). Attachment theory provides a framework of ideas about how babies and their caregivers bond together to ensure the baby's survival. Bowlby describes attachment as a lasting psychological connectedness between human beings *(Bowlby, 1969, p194). Where this attachment relationship is deficient or disorganised and the parent does not or is unable to respond sensitively to the child's attachment-generating behaviours. For example, a lack of response to a child's eye contact, smiling and crying, leaves the child feeling emotionally insecure and anxious. The child conveys this through any series of identifiable behaviours such as withdrawal, avoidance of contact, ambivalence, frustration, anger or suppression of anger, over-vigilance, over-compliance and frozen watchfulness (Ainsworth and Bell, 1970). Emotional harm may also impact on physical development leading to faltering growth. This may be the result of feeding patterns fraught with tension and emotional neglect (Barlow and Schrader McMillan, 2010, p30).*

The House of Commons Education Committee addressing the child protection system focused on older children stating that young people are not being identified as at risk by professionals and are less likely to receive a child protection response from Children's Social Care, they are more likely to receive an assessment through a child in need referral … [they are] … often perceived as more resilient or able to cope with situations compared to younger children. *Professionals may assume young people are making choices without considering that they may be functioning at a younger emotional or developmental age (HC 137:1, 2012–13, p32-38).*

An analysis of serious case reviews also emphasised focusing on the needs of older children. Nearly all the reviews of those over 16 years were because a child had died as a result of suicide:

> … most of the teenage children had grown up in climates of significant adversity. The deaths of older adolescents show the consequences of the failure to address trauma. A trauma perspective would acknowledge the cumulative stresses to which these older young people had been exposed through their lives. When trauma is not addressed there are risks for school failure, anxiety, depression, substance misuse and engaging in violence.
>
> *(Brandon, et al., 2008, p109)*

Brandon, et al. (2012b, p10), in a further serious case review analysis, made key findings about professional failures in relation to the abuse of older children. These included:

(Continued)

COMMENT *continued*

- *not making a relationship, or getting to know or speaking to the child;*

- *not taking account of what the child has to say to make sense of them as a person or of the impact of their experiences;*

- *allowing parents' voices to dominate, especially if they are volatile and difficult to confront;*

- *seeing the disability not the child;*

- *accepting lower standards of parenting for a disabled child;*

- *that pockets of good development in maltreated young people do not necessarily signal resilience.*

Emotional abuse – specific forms and contexts

Children emotionally abused by their carers

In thinking about types of emotional abuse, it may be useful to think in terms of dimensions as opposed to categories because emotional abuse is essentially repetitive and sustained. Glaser's (2002) headings describe aspects of emotional abuse and survivors' accounts provide added perspective.

Emotional unavailability, unresponsiveness and neglect

Adults are preoccupied with their own mental health problems, substance misuse or overwhelming work commitments.

> *There was no bonding in relationships at home and I got no kissing or cuddling whatsoever ... Even if I fell down or had an accident. I think they generally regarded me as a nuisance and did not want to spend money or time on me.*

(Fyfe, 2007, p162)

Negative attributions and misattributions to the child

Adults perceive the child negatively and as deserving of maltreatment and the children internalise this hostility. This may include humiliation, threats of abandonment or singling out one child for inferior treatment.

> *When I was nine or ten, I wouldn't come home until very late at night or ... at all and no one would bat an eyelid. But when I broke a plate, insult after insult was screamed at me. If I apologised I'd be told off for saying sorry. They'd tell me that if I was really sorry then I wouldn't have been evil in the first place. No matter what I did within the walls of that house, whether it was good or bad, nothing made any difference.*

(Fyfe, 2007, p196)

I did not want anyone near me. I felt so disgusting and dirty. I didn't want to exist. It did not matter how much people said they hated me – I hated myself much much more. I absorbed the words and the voices around me all the time and held onto their every word.

(Fyfe, 2007, p212)

Developmentally inappropriate or inconsistent interactions with the child

Adults expect more than the child can achieve developmentally. They may be overprotective and this may include pressurising the child educationally. The child is exposed inappropriately to emotionally harmful events such as domestic violence and self-harm. Interactions with children are often misguided and unintentional, based on their own poor childhood experiences, leading to a chaotic environment. There may be role reversal with the child taking on the parental role.

Living at home was like living under a lightning storm, you never knew when you might get struck. There were no firm boundaries and I never knew where I stood. I would behave in a crazy or bizarre way or be very naughty as a cry for help to get attention and no one cared or listened. So I would hide in my room.

(Fyfe, 2007, p196)

Following the death of Aaron Gilbert, aged 13 months, a neighbour reported to the court that she had seen the mother's partner hold Aaron by the ankles and spin him in circles as he screamed and cried. The partner was alleged to have told the neighbour *this will toughen him up. I want him to be hard* (BBC, 2006a; Davies, 2009b).

Failure to recognise or acknowledge the child's individuality and psychological boundary

Children are used as pawns in relationship conflict or as a means of gaining attention through fabricated illness. The adult does not distinguish between their distorted sense of reality and that of the child.

Mum loathed everything about me ... I just remember the constant rage and screaming. I was very very good so that I could be as sure as possible of not doing anything wrong. I also tried to keep still and quiet – again so that I wouldn't do anything worth the blame. I was equally afraid of tongue lashing and physical violence. I was just afraid all the time.

(Fyfe, 2007, p138)

My father had this strange habit of never using my name. I found this odd but could never work it out. Once at my grandmother's house my father said, ask him what he wants to eat ... He'd never say ask John what he wants to eat. He always called me you or him.

(Fyfe, 2007, p162)

Failing to promote the child's social adaptation

This involves corrupting children, such as by involvement in criminal acts, and can involve grooming and access to adult activities such as illegal substances. The adult may harm or threaten to harm a treasured pet or toy. The adult may not encourage the child's social and cognitive development.

> *When I went to stroke the head of the older girl she jerked her head away ...'My mamma said I mustn't let you touch me. She said that you're sick and have diseases and that you're dirty'. Now even the children were treating me like an animal. Worse than an animal as even dogs were patted and stroked.*

> (Nazer and Lewis, 2004, p141)

ACTIVITY **2.3**

Making reference to the above descriptions of emotional abuse, think about the following examples and whether the children are being emotionally harmed:

- *An aunt shouts racist abuse at a bus driver and encourages a child to join in.*
- *A grandfather tells a child about distressing war experiences.*
- *Parents do not tell a child that he is adopted.*
- *Parents insist that a child sees the body of a dead relative before the funeral.*
- *A child accesses the internet unsupervised.*
- *A child is not allowed to speak to anyone about her mother's suicide.*
- *Parents take a child to religious services to hear sermons about hell.*
- *A foster carer tells a child that their birth father is a wicked man.*

Children caring for their parents, siblings and extended family

> *I could never speak to anyone about the problems at home because I thought I'd be judged. All my friends seemed to have perfect families and lives and I couldn't be different. In the end I had a breakdown because of keeping everything covered up.*

> *I don't talk to friends because their lack of understanding is frustrating. Especially when somebody has a problem that cannot be seen by people.*

> *My school attendance started to drop at a time when my dad was really poorly in and out of hospital and I daren't leave him because I was too scared.*

People were asking what was wrong with my parent and I had a set story I would tell which was a complete lie because I was so ashamed it was to do with drugs and alcohol.

(Main, 2013)

The children reported often hiding the extent of their caring role for fear of professional interference or a punitive approach to their non-school attendance or educational underachievement and some did not recognise what they were doing as unusual. They said they wanted ongoing support including information about the illness and prognosis, recognition of their role in the family, practical and domestic help, a contact person in the event of a crisis and someone to talk to (Main, 2013). Caring may come at a developmental price as child carers bring themselves up and often care for adults' emotional wellbeing.

In 2011, 166,363 children in England were officially recognised as caring for their parents, siblings and extended family members. Some child carers are as young as 5 years old (ONS, 2011). However, one survey estimated that there are four times as many young carers in the UK than stated in the census statistics (BBC, 2010a). Ofsted interviewed 37 young carers from eight local authorities and found that those caring for parents with drug- and alcohol-related and mental health problems were a challenge to identify and therefore were often a hidden group (Ofsted, 2009). Children have a wide range of caring roles including housework, healthcare, intimate personal care and managing the family budget. They mainly care for adults with mental and physical health problems and learning difficulties and spend from between three and 30 hours a week caring. About two-thirds of young carers care for their parents.

Young carers are more likely than their peers to live in poverty, have special educational needs, be disabled, come from black and minority ethnic families and miss out on social life and education. The Children's Society (2013) reported a weak relationship between young carers and their contact with sources of support such as children's services and police, and also that benefit changes introduced by the Welfare Reform Act 2012 had severe negative effects on young carers.

Children tell us about how, as young carers, they wish to be treated:

Introduce yourself. Tell us who you are and what your job is.

Give us as much information as you can.

Tell us what is wrong with our parent.

Talk to us and listen to us. We are not aliens.

Ask us what we know and what we think. We live with our parents. We know how they have been behaving.

Tell us it's not our fault. We can feel guilty if our mum or dad is ill. We need to know we are not to blame.

Please don't ignore us.

Tell us if there is anyone we can talk to. Maybe it could be you.

(Wardale, 2007; see www.barnardos.org.uk/
news/media_centre/press_releases.htm?ref=31905)

Often services focus on the adult without thinking through the implications of the disability, mental illness or substance misuse problem for the children in the family. Sometimes the label *young carer* is perceived as a stigma and it is important that the child's role is respected as they commonly value their caring roles and are proud of their contribution. However, they may assume a level of responsibility that no child should be expected to take on. Disclosure of abuse is difficult for young carers and there is concern that it mainly happens at crisis points. They worry about the family being split up and that they may be taken into care, as well as not always understanding that their caring role is different from most of their peers (ADASS and ADCS, 2011).

Ofsted identified barriers to young carers receiving support. Only 3 out of 37 young carers they interviewed said their views had been sought or included in parental assessments (Ofsted, 2009, p5). Social workers must be informed of the legal rights of young carers as well as relevant policies and protocols in order to best advocate for them.

The Children and Families Act 2014, following extensive lobbying by the National Young Carer Coalition, gave young carers a right to assessment and to have their needs met. The Care Act 2014 and the Children and Families Act 2014 together should provide a framework to ensure whole family needs are met and inappropriate caring by children is prevented or reduced. The Carers Trust (2015) provides a guide to young carers' rights.

While taking into account the child's views, social workers will need to prioritise the child's best interests in circumstances where a child's caring role is defined as abusive and multi-agency child protection procedures must be applied. A report, *Big Bruv, Little Sis,* about children caring for siblings to prevent them going into the care system, highlighted the lack of support they received (Roth, et al., 2011).

Bullying

Bullying is of particular concern to children and, as discussed at the start of this chapter, disabled children are twice as likely as their peers to be targets of bullying behaviour with a devastating impact on their lives (Shakespeare, et al., 1999; OCC, 2006). A UK survey of 500 children aged 8–19 years found that eight out of ten with a learning disability had experienced bullying (Mencap, 2005). Kovic, et al. (2009) identified ways in which deaf children are bullied, such as by making up signs to humiliate them or turning away to exclude them on purpose.

Bullying can be defined as any hostile or offensive action commonly based on perceived difference usually repeated over time where it is difficult for those bullied to defend themselves. There are three main types:

- physical: hitting, kicking, theft, stabbing and setting alight, and being filmed with mobile phones;

- verbal: racial and homophobic remarks, threats, name-calling, making fun of customs, music, accent or dress, offensive graffiti, online and mobile phone messaging abuse;

- emotional: humiliating, excluding, tormenting, ridiculing, threatening.

For all children, verbal abuse is at least as damaging as physical bullying, in particular where associated with feeling left out of friendship groups. The focus of bullying can be about a child's appearance and about lies and rumours (Benton, 2011, p10).

Bullying is included in the definition of emotional abuse in *Working Together to Safeguard Children* (DfE, 2015). Bullying can rapidly escalate into serious harm. Where bullying involves an allegation of crime (for example, assault, theft, harassment), a referral must be made immediately to police, and child protection procedures must be implemented where bullying constitutes suspected or actual significant harm. The Anti-bullying Alliance (www.anti-bullyingalliance.org.uk) works to stop bullying and create safe environments for children.

Children have legal rights to be protected from bullying, including in educational settings. The Equality Act 2010 makes it illegal to discriminate on the grounds of age, disability, sex and sexual orientation, race, religion or belief. Faith schools are exempt from this requirement and children in these schools may therefore be more isolated and vulnerable to abuse.

RESEARCH SUMMARY

Racist bullying

In 2007–08, ChildLine found 406 child callers (five per cent of all calls on bullying) talked about bullying where they were called racist names and told to go back to where they came from. One girl said:

I am being bullied at school. They are calling me names. They take the Mickey out of my religion. Nobody cares. I don't want to live in this country. I don't eat. I am having suicidal thoughts.

(NSPCC, 2008:3.6.1)

A girl of 9 years, who wore a headscarf, reported daily bullying where children would shout verbal abuse and call her a terrorist.

I was so depressed and I lost weight because I just stopped eating, because I just didn't feel hungry. I wanted to go to bed to get each day over with since there was

(Continued)

nothing to look forward to, not even coming home, since I would have to go to school the next day.

(Talwar, 2012, p1)

A report about Roma, Gypsy and Traveller children in England cited bullying as the main reason for children leaving school prior to secondary stage. Of those interviewed, 85 per cent said they had experienced racial abuse and 63 per cent had been bullied or physically attacked. One young person said:

Yes, I went until some girls poured water all over me because I was a 'dirty traveller'. My Mam went up to school and asked them what they were going to do about it but they did nothing so Mam said I wasn't going again 'cos it was disrespectful to ignore her complaints

(Ureche and Franks, 2007, p33)

A London report found that black, Asian and refugee children were three times more likely to be attacked in the street than white children. Of those interviewed, ten per cent had been physically attacked, 80 per cent had been racially abused or threatened and more than a third had direct experience of crime in the past year (GLA, 2003). Racism is recurrent and may be accepted by children as an inevitable part of life rather than as an abusive activity.

RESEARCH SUMMARY

Homophobic bullying

A Stonewall survey of over 1,600 pupils aged between 11 and 19 years found that more than 55 per cent of lesbian, gay and bisexual young people have experienced homophobic bullying. Of these, more than half were subjected to verbal bullying, a quarter to cyber-bullying, one in six to physical abuse, and six per cent had received death threats. In addition, while school responses were improving, the survey found around 60 per cent of those bullied said that teachers who witnessed the bullying did not intervene (Guasp, 2012).

The following quotes are from children interviewed for the research.

I hear 'dyke' and 'homo' nearly every lesson.

I hate it when students use homophobic words like 'gay' or 'faggot', it's horrible. I always tell them it's wrong but only a few of the teachers ever say anything.

People in the year above give me strange looks and whisper about me. I know it's because of the way I dress. It hurts knowing that these people walk past me every day and can't see me for anything but a lesbian.

I experienced a lot of bullying at school. I contemplated suicide and attempted it enough to get me referred to the Child and Adolescent Mental Health Service.

(Guasp, 2012, pp5–22)

RESEARCH SUMMARY

Cyberbullying

Cyberbullying is when technology such as the internet or a mobile phone is used to deliberately hurt, humiliate, harass, intimidate or threaten someone. Tarapdar and Kellett (2011, p14) explain that it is controlled remotely, anonymously and repetitively and has a potentially large audience creating infinite and often unintentional consequences in publicising the abuse. Up to 34 per cent of children in the UK have been victims of cyberbullying (DfE, 2011a). Fear of bullies makes some children reluctant to go to school; they do not feel safe as the perpetrators remain invisible with little fear of reprisal. Adults have little grasp of the problem and children sometimes see the behaviour as acceptable within their peer group.

Children state:

When you walk to school, even with mates they do it. You can't see them and you can't get away from it.

I wouldn't go to the police as they're gonna tell you to deactivate your account. But what if you don't want to?

Cyberbullying is without saying it to your face, but targeting someone and sending you pictures and messages of rude people doing rude things – mentally or sexually.

(Tarapdar and Kellett, 2011, pp21–6)

While cyberbullying, as an act on its own, is not a specific criminal offence in UK law, it is subject to laws governing cyber-stalking and menacing and threatening communications. Also schools have extended powers to identify, prevent and tackle all forms of bullying including powers relating to students being off the school site (DfE, 2011b).

Sexting, in the context of peer to peer abuse, is when someone sends or receives a sexually explicit text, image or video on their mobile phone, usually in a text message. It is illegal to

(Continued)

take, possess or share 'indecent images' of anyone under 18 years and if the picture includes naked images, genitals or sex acts, including masturbation, then it will be defined as indecent. Children posting explicit images online has become normalised behaviour leaving children open to exploitation and blackmail. One boy, after sending a naked photo of himself to a girlfriend, had no idea this could result in him being on a police file for ten years (BBC, 2015c). The Home Office has introduced guidance to allow more professional judgement about sexting in a consensual context between young people (BBC, 2016) to avoid criminalising them.

Domestic violence

There was a lot of arguing but I didn't understand what was happening.

It was the worst part of my life constantly being shouted at frightened, living in fear. You will never know what it is like thinking every day will be your last day.

I used to think it was my fault because I was in the middle of it a couple of times.

If I was brave enough I would have gone and told him to stop.

(Mullender, et al., 2003a, pp6–43).

The Adoption and Children Act 2002 extended the definition of significant harm to include impairment suffered from seeing or hearing the ill treatment of others which is included in the definition of emotional abuse in *Working Together to Safeguard Children* (DfE, 2015, p93). In 2013, the UK government definition of domestic violence was extended to include those aged 16–17 years. The cross-government definition of domestic violence and abuse is:

... any incident or pattern of incidents of controlling, coercive, threatening behaviour, violence or abuse between those aged 16 or over who are, or have been, intimate partners or family members regardless of gender or sexuality. The abuse can encompass, but is not limited to: psychological; physical; sexual; financial; emotional. Controlling behaviour is a range of acts designed to make a person subordinate and/or dependent by isolating them from sources of support, exploiting their resources and capacities for personal gain, depriving them of the means needed for independence, resistance and escape and regulating their everyday behaviour. Coercive behaviour is an act or a pattern of acts of assault, threats, humiliation and intimidation or other abuse that is used to harm, punish, or frighten their victim.

(Home Office, 2015b)

The Serious Crime Act 2015 (sections 76/77) extended the Children and Young Persons Act 1933. It includes non-physical abuse and repeated or continuous coercive or controlling behaviour perpetrated against a family member or intimate partner which has a serious effect on the victim causing them to feel fear, alarm or distress.

Evidence presented to the House of Commons Education Committee stated that 75,000 children every year witness domestic violence and it is a feature of the lives of 75 per cent of children who are the subject of child protection plans. Two women are killed each week in the context of domestic violence and children discover 30 per cent of these women. Forty per cent of young people are in abusive relationships and 70 per cent are young parents. Domestic violence is largely defined as an adult issue and children's voices are not heard, especially as thresholds increase, and many children are at risk of falling through the gaps in services. Concern was raised about young people between 15 and 18 years, living with domestic violence, who did not receive a child protection response or access mainstream services (HC 137:2, 2012–13). Stanley, et al. (2010) recommend that the police response to domestic violence incidents should include giving information leaflets to children. Violence may increase during pregnancy and childbirth and this indicates the need for a pre-birth conference to ensure a protection plan for when the child is born.

It is essential that non-abusive parents and carers should feel confident to report the violence to statutory services without fear. However, parents who are victims of domestic violence may become physically and mentally exhausted, in some cases leading to neglect of their children. In cases of domestic violence,

> *there should be no assumption that an abused parent cannot be a good parent. Wherever possible the focus should be on supporting that parent and helping them to protect their children rather than removing the children. But the interests of the children must come first.*

> (HC 137:1, 2012–13, p30)

To understand the impact of emotional abuse as a result of domestic violence, the following should be considered:

- Has the child witnessed or overheard the violence and/or been directly harmed?
- Is the abusive parent or carer encouraging the child to take sides?
- What is the severity, frequency and duration of the abuse as experienced by the non-abusive parent/carer and children?
- Is the child being singled out?
- What are the child's own coping strategies?
- Has the child disclosed? Are they being heard? Is a child protection plan in place?
- Is the non-abusive parent/carer protective?
- Is domestic violence tolerated within the child's wider community?

> (Calder and Hackett, 2013, p139)

Witnessing domestic violence may cause symptoms of post-traumatic stress disorder such as: numbness, anxiety, fear, panic attacks, disturbed sleep, nightmares, flashbacks, impaired concentration and memory, and hypervigilance. Children may also show higher rates of psychological problems and be at higher risk of injury, eating disorders and self-harm even when they are not themselves victims of the violence (Barlow and Shrader McMillan, 2010, p28). They may also experience disruption to their lives of having to leave their family, school, friends and protective communities. Exposure to domestic violence can have a significant impact on babies leading to poor health, interrupted sleep patterns, excessive crying and attachment problems (Barlow and Schrader McMillan, 2010, p29). There is evidence to suggest that the provision of a safe and secure environment, free from post-separation violence, enables many children to recover and heal (Mullender, et al., 2003b).

ACTIVITY 2.4

Children consistently report that they want to be actively involved in decision making (Mullender, et al., 2003b). A young person's safety plan is included below and should be used as part of child protection planning and never as a way to place sole responsibility on children to protect themselves. Think about how you might use this plan with a child who is witnessing domestic violence and how you might adapt it for different ages.

A Child's Safety Plan

I can't stop the violence and it is not my fault but I can do these things to keep safe.

This plan records how to keep .... [child's name] ....safe.

- I have a right to be safe and cared for in a safe place.
- Violent words and actions at home are not my fault.

To protect myself I can say NO, shout, kick and scream if I need help, also: ....
....
....

The best thing I can do when there is violence at home is get out of the way.

To be safe I can do these things:

1. Get out of the room where the violence is occurring.

    The room/place in my house where I feel safe is ....

    There is a lock on the door   yes   no

2. The nearest telephone is ....

    If it is safe I can telephone 999 and ask for police. I will need to say:

    my full name ....

my home address ....

what's happening ....

3. People I can trust in an emergency are: ....

   A code word so they know I need help is ....

4. My brothers and sisters:

   have a safety plan too, that I know   yes   no

   know my safety plan   yes   no

5. If we leave the house I would like to go to (name of safe relative/friend's house) ....
   ....

   I have a bag of things that are important to me at ....
   ....

6. If I am hurt I will tell (including phone numbers) ....

   If my parent/carer is hurt I will tell (including phone numbers) ....

7. I can talk about how I feel with (including phone numbers) ....

8. The people who know this plan are:

   Safe carer ....

   Safe relative/friend ....

   Teacher ....

   Social worker ....

   Others ....

   Signed ....Date ....

   Social worker ....Date ....

This plan should not be kept by the child or in a place where it might be accessible to the perpetrator. This is adapted from *Safeguarding Children Abused through Domestic Violence* (LSCB, 2015, Part B:27).

Forced marriage

Why were your brothers looking for you?

Because once I finished my GCSEs they were going to fly me to Afghanistan to marry a man twenty years older than me ... I was going to spend a lifetime being raped by someone old enough to be my dad in the middle of nowhere. I wanted to be a doctor, fall in love and marry whoever I wanted.

Did you tell your family this?

Yes! My brothers punched me in the face. They said I should never speak to them like that, that if I did not do what they said then I was ruining the family honour and they would be forced to kill me and that nobody would find out.

(Keeble and Hollington, 2012, p9)

Forced marriage can involve emotional coercion, forced imprisonment, violence and murder. In 2004, the government's definition of domestic violence was extended to include forced marriage and 'honour' crimes perpetrated by extended family members and intimate partners.

A forced marriage is where one or both people, men and women, do not (in the case of some people with learning or physical disabilities, cannot) consent to the marriage and pressure or abuse is used. There is no justification for forced marriage. The pressure put on people to marry against their will can be physical (including threats, actual physical violence and sexual violence) or emotional and psychological (for example, when someone is made to feel they are bringing shame on their family). Financial abuse can also be a factor. There is a clear distinction between forced and arranged marriage. The latter is one in which both people consent to the union. Many victims of reported 'honour'-based violence and forced marriage in the UK are under 18 years of age and there is significant under-reporting. Karma Nirvana, a charity supporting victims of 'honour' crimes and forced marriages, reported 3,000 calls from children between 2008 and 2010 (HC 137:1, p46). In 2014, the Forced Marriage Unit responded to 1,267 cases of which 22 per cent victims were under age 17 years (HM Government, Forced Marriage Unit, 2014b).

Forced marriage may involve children being removed from the country for the ceremony and sexual abuse, while refusals to marry are sometimes linked to 'honour' killings. Forced marriages have involved children from South Asia, East Asia, the Middle East, Europe and Africa. Some marriages take place in the UK while others may involve a partner coming from other countries.

Some key motives include to:

- control unwanted behaviour and sexuality, and sexual orientation;
- prevent relationships which challenge cultural norms;
- maintain family 'honour' or *izzat;*
- strengthen family links and fulfil commitments;
- achieve financial gain, debt repayment or alleviation of poverty;
- ensure land, property and wealth remain within the family;
- assist claims for UK residence and citizenship;
- appease aggrieved family members;
- marry disabled children considered unlikely to find marriage partners (HM Government, Forced Marriage Unit, 2014a; LSCB, 2015, Part B:23; HC 137:2, p42).

In 2004, the government's definition of domestic violence was extended to include acts perpetrated by extended family members as well as intimate partners. Consequently, forced marriage and 'honour' crimes (which can include abduction and homicide) come under the definition of domestic violence and are a breach of human rights. The Anti-Social Behaviour Crime and Policing Act 2014 made it a criminal offence to force someone to marry including taking them overseas to force them to marry whether or not forced marriage actually takes place.

Since 2008, anyone threatened with forced marriage can apply for a Forced Marriage (Civil Protection) Protection Order through the family courts. With the leave of the court, third parties, such as relatives and friends, can also apply for an order to prevent a forced marriage from taking place or to offer protection if one has happened. The court can make orders such as to prevent someone being taken abroad and can attach a power of arrest for the protection of children. *Working Together to Safeguard Children* (DfE, 2015) recommends compliance with the statutory multi-agency practice guidance (HM Government, Forced Marriage Unit, 2014a).

Social workers need knowledge of the indicators of forced marriage which may include:

- a child indicating fear of being taken abroad;
- extended absence from education, parental restriction such as being locked indoors, a history of siblings forced to marry;
- depression, self-harm, attempted suicide, eating disorders, substance misuse;
- family conflict, domestic violence;
- running away.

One chance rule

Specialist advice is required as approaching children and families, family mediation or family group conferences may place children at risk of harm, including the possibility of murder. Social workers should consult child protection procedures and ensure that contact with the Forced Marriage Unit (www.gov.uk/forced-marriage) is made for guidance (HM Government 2014a; HC 137:2, p43). Children should be seen immediately, on their own in a secure, safe place. During the interview, as much information as possible must be gathered about the plans to force the child to marry because there may be no other opportunity to contact the victim again. An emergency safety plan can be devised with the child including where they can access immediate help, even if outside the country, leave identification documents with a trusted friend or professional and have access to a pre-paid telephone card. This plan is referred to as the *one chance rule*. If the child does not want intervention then protective action must be taken. Record keeping must be restricted to named staff over and above the usual confidentiality and extreme caution must be applied not to use members of the community as interpreters.

The Home Office has produced a card, 'Marriage: It's YOUR choice', to be given to young people thought to be at risk (www.gov.uk/government/publications/forced-marriage-it-s-your-choice-card).

A film published by the Forced Marriage Unit demonstrates well the impact of forced marriage (www.gov.uk/government/news/new-video-shows-the-devastating-impact-of-forced-marriage).

'Honour'-based violence

My family treated me with disgust, as if I had shamed them. My father, mother, even my young brother, beat me on a daily basis. My body was covered in bruises.

I wasn't given any food for days on end, and I tried to take an overdose on several occasions. I just used to sit on my bed from morning to night. Prison would have been a better place.

After around a month, they let me go out to the doctor. Terrified, I sat in the toilet and called a solicitors' firm. I've not seen my family since that day. A wonderful solicitor got me a place at a refuge and a forced marriage protection order.

But I'm still constantly paranoid: I'm always looking over my shoulder. I've lost everything. And I'm scared of what will happen if they find me.

(Williams, 2011)

Honour-based violence is the term used to describe murders in the name of so-called honour, sometimes called *honour killings*. These are murders in which predominantly women and girls are killed for perceived immoral behaviour, deemed to have breached the honour code of a family or community, causing shame. A child who is at risk of honour-based violence is at significant risk of physical harm, neglect and emotional abuse.

A child wearing make-up or types of dress, having a boyfriend, kissing in public, rejecting a forced marriage, becoming pregnant, being raped or having an inter-faith relationship have all been cited by perpetrators as justifications for this crime (LSCB, 2015, Part B:22).

The Crown Prosecution Service (CPS) website provides information about this type of abuse (www.cps.gov.uk/legal/h_to_k/honour_based_violence_and_forced_marriage).

Children who self-harm

Some people do it for attention ... that doesn't mean they should be ignored ... And if someone's crying for help, you should give them it, not stand there and judge the way they're asking for it.

People often link self-harm to suicide but for me it was something very different; it was my alternative to suicide; my way of coping.

The one thing that always helps if I'm feeling really bad is to be around someone that I trust ... just being around someone who doesn't question my odd behaviour and lets me be around them without talking or expectations helps.

(Richardson, 2006, pp 8–15)

It is estimated that one in twelve children self-harm. In 2014, 38,000 children were admitted to hospital because of their injuries as a result of self-harm (www.youngminds. org.uk/about/our_campaigns/cello_self-harm).

The phrase 'self-harm' is used to describe a wide range of behaviours. Self-harm is often understood to be a physical response to an emotional pain, can become a pattern and is often carried out in secrecy. There are many ways to self-harm including cutting, burning, swallowing poisonous substances or objects and pinching, misuse of drugs and alcohol or having an eating disorder. Some groups of children are particularly vulnerable such as those in residential and custodial settings, those with learning disabilities and children exploring their sexual orientation.

CASE STUDY

Mary Stroman – failure of agencies to respond

In January 2014, shortly before her seventeenth birthday, Mary took her own life on a railway line in Wiltshire. She had self-harmed and attempted suicide since early adolescence. She cut herself, banged her head, tried to strangle herself and had ingested cleaning fluid, batteries and screws. She was known to mental health services and had been placed in residential care, but there had been no involvement of the police Child Abuse Investigation team. Following concern about child sexual exploitation, police had been involved, but were criticised by the serious case review for not appreciating child protection concerns. There had been no formal child protection investigation including no conference or reference to statutory guidance. Assessments were slow and did not involve the family or consultation with the child. Mary spoke many times about having been sexually abused, but her allegations relating to men outside the family were not substantiated. The serious case review stated that police had failed to respond or investigate adequately and concluded that *we still have no clearly evidenced understanding of how Child O came to be so troubled and why she so resolutely maintained a position of never fully sharing her worries with any professional* (HSCB, 2015, p65; Clarke-Billings, 2015).

Institutional abuse

He was a very snidey kind of person, he had a way of trying to slide into your personal fears ... he operated on a personal level, arm on shoulder, very touchy feely. He had a way of twisting words. He knew how to play with your emotions and your mind.

Beck shouted at the children, reminded them of their worst experiences of their young lives. One girl in Beck's care, for instance, was told ... that her mother had never wanted her. 'It must be something about you, she did not want you back'.

(D'Arcy and Gosling, 1998, pp47 and 83)

Some children only disclosed persistent sexual and/or emotional abuse after they had left the placement. It is essential that social workers see children alone on a regular basis and are alert to the possibility of abuse in foster placements.

(Biehal, et al., 2014, p13)

This investigation is massive and a testimony to how the attitude to victims is changing, how those who have been victims have previously felt unable to come forward or have done so but not been believed, but now have confidence that they will be believed and listened to.

(NPCC, 2015, p1)

The Pindown Report (Staffordshire, 1991) showed that solitary confinement and sensory deprivation had been used to control children's behaviour; 132 children, as young as 9 years, were kept in indoor clothing and made to stay silent. It was a regime of sensory deprivation and torture which the manager of the homes justified in order to re-establish control of the children.

A more recent example of such abuse is called 'holding therapy' (invisibleengland2. wordpress.com). Practised since the 1990s and still used in some private children's homes, this abusive practice involves the child being held down and forced to engage in prolonged eye-to-eye contact inducing rage and leading to emotional breakdown. The 'therapist' then shows 'warmth'. The procedure ends after a number of hours when the child submits.

In the end I was so drained and broken and scared ... another time I was wrapped in a blanket, pinned down and held so tight all I could feel was fright so I responded again with aggression ... looking back this is what they wanted, break you down to comply.

(Chaika, 2013, p30).

RESEARCH SUMMARY

Biehal, et al. (2014) researched the extent and nature of confirmed abuse and neglect in foster and residential care by examining incidents that occurred within placements in 156 local authorities between 2009 and 2012. They found approximately 2,500 allegations per year in foster care with about one-quarter confirmed as abuse or neglect. The total substantiated across the UK per year was approximately 550. Where allegations were substantiated, over half the children were removed from placements permanently and, even when unsubstantiated, about 16 per cent were removed. About half the unsubstantiated allegations could not be proved or disproved through lack of evidence. All forms of harm were evident and of substantiated cases 43 per cent of foster carers had been the subject of prior allegations. Early warning signs of abuse were missed for children in long-term placements and in a very few cases the carers should never have been recruited. The vast majority of substantiated allegations led to no action against the foster carers concerned.

Between 1,110 and 2,500 allegations per year in residential care were identified and the total substantiated estimated at 300 per year. At least 75 per cent of allegations were unsubstantiated. Unlike foster care, fewer than one-fifth of the substantiated cases led to the child being removed from placement. Some allegations were in the context of a secure unit and abuse by excessive restraint procedures. Looked After Reviews to assess care planning needs were rarely held, in most respects life went on much as before (p16). Some staff had their employment terminated but others did not; the reasons for the distinction were unclear. Little is known about historic abuse in children's homes and the extent of allegations against foster carers, as well as about institutional abuse at a national level (Biehal, et al., 2014).

Simon Bailey, National Police Chiefs' Council Lead for Child Abuse Investigation, has provided an update on Operation Hydrant, which was overseeing the investigation of allegations of non-recent child sexual abuse within institutions or by people of public prominence.

Between 2012 and the first quarter of 2015, figures from reports of child sexual abuse from 12 police forces showed that recent cases had risen by 31 per cent and non-recent cases by 165 per cent. Bailey (NPCC, 2015, p1) said, *the figures are stark. They indicate the scale of child abuse police are dealing with.*

Operation Hydrant had in one year received reports of:

- 2,016 suspects (some deceased and including 287 people of public prominence). Of these:
  - 145 are from the world of TV, film or radio;
  - 89 are listed politicians;
  - 38 are from the music industry;
  - 15 are from the world of sport;
  - 372 are from a religious context;
  - 289 are teachers;
  - 157 are care workers.
- 676 institutions which have been identified within the scope of the operation. Of these:
  - 271 are schools;
  - 181 are children's homes;
  - 31 are medical establishments;
  - 76 are religious institutions;
  - 11 are community institutions such as youth clubs;
  - 9 are prisons or young offender institutions;
  - 9 are sports venues;
  - 28 are other, including military establishments (NPCC, 2015).

CASE STUDY

Medomsley detention centre, Durham

This institution for young offenders aged 17 to 21 years is the subject of an investigation into physical, sexual, emotional abuse and neglect during the 1970s and 1980s, with unprecedented numbers of over 1,240 victims having come forward to police. Those abused had often been in care with no family to visit them. In 2014, Detective Superintendent Goundry, senior officer for Operation Seabrook, said that, *from the statements, there is growing evidence to suggest there was an organised paedophile ring operating in Medomsley. This will form a major part of our operation* (Allison and Hattenstone, 2014).

Neville Husband, a prison officer at Medomsley, was arrested in 1969, prior to his appointment, for possession of abusive images of boys but was not prosecuted. He said he was researching a book on homosexuality. In 1977, Kevin Young, after his release from Medomsley, reported being raped by Husband to police.

> *I showed him the marks on my neck where I'd been ligatured the night before. I was told it was a criminal offence to make such allegations against a prison officer .... They were basically threatening to take me back to Medomsley, so I scattered pretty quick ... I knew Husband was one of the most prolific sex abusers this country has seen. Despite all the alarm bells, he was allowed to abuse boys throughout his whole career as a prison officer.*

> (Allison and Hattenstone, 2014)

There had also been two deaths of young people. In 1981, Ian Shackleton, aged 18 years, who had diabetes, died following a mix-up over access to his insulin and in 1982, David Caldwell, aged 17 years, died following an asthma attack. Caldwell's sister told the Inquest that, *the bruises on his legs were caused by him being kicked around by prison officers. He said when they were scrubbing floors if they didn't say 'sir' it would happen* (Engelbrecht, 2014). A Home Office Inquiry concluded that there was no maltreatment at the institution.

In 1985, storeman Leslie Johnson was arrested at Medomsley and pornographic material and sex aids were found in Husband's locker. Husband was transferred to work at Frankland prison and no action was taken against him. By 2005, both Johnson and Husband, now deceased, were convicted of sexual offences against boys. In 2007, the CPS decided it was not in the public interest to proceed with charges that Husband abused a boy at Deerbolt youth offender institution.

Young described:

> *being raped repeatedly, tied up and ligatured [around the neck]. It was the worst of the worst ... I thought I was going to be killed ... I was told by Husband that you*

could easily be found hanged at Medomsley, and that year, six boys had already hanged themselves ... He took me out of the prison against my will and to his private house. He was married with one child. In his house I was blindfolded, ligatured and made to lie on the stairs. Then three or four others raped me as well. I could see them from the bottom of the blindfold. A rope was put round my neck and turned till I passed out. Husband was an expert at it. He was a big, stocky, powerful man.

(Allison and Hattenstone, 2012)

A survivor said he was thrashed across the bare chest with a studded belt and that fellow inmates would attempt to break their own arms and legs to be sent to hospital away from Medomsley. Survivors speak of boys forced to bunny-hop, crouching down into a squat then jumping along a corridor, often at night. Anyone collapsing with exhaustion was kicked until they continued (Engelbrecht, 2014).

Husband had raped boys on a daily basis for 15 years while other staff allegedly did not notice. Survivor, Richard Hall, said he found it devastating that there were staff at Medomsley who did not act on their suspicions. *Some of them are still employed by the state, others are drawing their pensions. Do they not feel any shame?* (Allison and Hattenstone, 2012).

A collation of press coverage about Medomsley can be found at: https://theneedleblog. wordpress.com/operation-greenlight/north-east-england/durham/medomsley-detention-centre/

Children in custody

Our prisons are filled with the poorest, most disadvantaged children who often have considerable mental health and learning difficulties. Even before they begin the admissions process which involves being given a number, removing clothes and answering questions about suicidal thoughts and substance misuse, the lives of most child prisoners will have told them they are worthless – certainly worth less than other children.

(Willow, 2014, p10)

Few parents of children in custody receive home visits and less than half the reports presented to court provided analysis of the child's vulnerability or safeguarding matters. The numbers of children in custody who have learning difficulties, English not as a first language, poor education history, mental health problems and severe trauma raises specific questions about their ability to pursue complaints or legal processes in pursuit of their rights (Willow, 2014, p36).

RESEARCH SUMMARY

An annual survey of 960 boys in secure training centres and young offender institutions in England and Wales, aged 12–18 years, and their perceptions about being in custody, between 2013 and 2014, confirmed their level of need and drew attention to a lack of appropriate welfare services:

- *31 per cent had been in local authority care;*
- *93 per cent had been excluded from school;*
- *23 per cent said they had an emotional or mental health problem;*
- *8 per cent said they had an alcohol problem;*
- *37 per cent said they had a problem with drugs (Prime, 2014).*

About one-quarter of children in custody have a learning disability compared with two per cent of the general population, and a study of over 1,000 children in custody found one in five had learning difficulties (OCC, 2012; Gyateng, et al., 2013).

Nearly half the children in custody had been abused and 38 per cent had witnessed domestic violence (Barnardo's, et al., 2006).

Children in care are four times more likely to be convicted than other children (DfE, 2014c).

Bereavement and loss were factors in a number of cases of the 33 children who had died in prison since 1990 (Willow, 2014, p68).

Strip searching of children in custody

> When I had my first full search I was 14, it was horrible as I have been sexually abused and I didn't feel comfortable showing my body as this bought back memories.

> They look at you like you're a dog, making you strip is bang out of order, makes me angry it really does.

(Willow, 2014, pp79 and 87)

The use of strip searching as a matter of routine in children's prisons was brought to an end in 2014. This was a huge step forward for children's rights (CRAE, 2014). However, it remains mandatory where children are defined as a security risk and *decisions about strip searching are made within the prison walls with no independent external oversight. The barbaric practice of cutting off children's clothes under restraint is still allowed* (Willow, 2014, p96).

Children who had been strip searched reported feeling:

embarrassed, degraded and uncomfortable. One girl told me about being strip searched during her period; she had to pass her sanitary towel to staff for inspection ... Children in young offender institutions have reported being made to squat in front of officers without their underwear.

(Willow, 2014, p13)

The Carlile Report (2006) described strip searching as *inherently coercive*, found no evidence that it was necessary for security reasons and considered that, if imposed by force, any trust between staff and the young person would be irrecoverable.

Children of prisoners

Up to 200,000 children are affected by parental imprisonment in England and Wales. They are at increased risk of having poor mental health and low educational achievement. Separation can be sudden and may impact on the stability of the family financially and emotionally. Social workers need to check if a child wishes to visit a parent and take account of their views. A prisoner's parental status is not routinely considered during arrest, trial, sentencing or on release, therefore social workers need to be proactive in assessing the child's best interests in all forms of contact with their parent (CRAE, 2014, p35; Barnardo's, 2014).

Parental alcohol and substance misuse

A dirty hungry child is a big financial barrier and physical inconvenience to scoring drugs. Trying to satisfy their own insatiable cravings takes a first priority; the child's care and safety is put on the back burner. A hungry child will pick up and eat drugs that have been left lying around. A bored child, its parents zonked out, will start playing with whatever's close to hand, whether it be a whisky bottle or matches and lighters.

(Keeble and Hollington, 2010, p73)

The parent never took up the support she was offered to bring her use of alcohol under control. There was an absence of any recognition of the impact this was having on her child's welfare. She continued to drink and to neglect child Y. This was entirely predictable though the incident could not in itself have been predicted.

There was a tendency for professionals to concentrate on one feature of drug misuse (heroin) without an understanding of the more complex effects of chaotic or polydrug/alcohol misuse – likely to induce drowsiness/deep sleeping and impair parenting capacity.

(Brandon, et al., 2013, pp 58 and 62)

RESEARCH SUMMARY

Children who called ChildLine (Mariathasan and Hutchinson, 2010, pp1–22) about the experience of living with parents who misuse alcohol and/or drugs said the following.

Fear of violence

They are drinking all the time I can't tell anyone because I am scared my mum and dad might do something and hit me.

My dad is smoking weed and gets angry. When I come home from school, there is no food for me. He has threatened to hit me and locked me in a cupboard. I am scared to tell anyone.

Exposure to parental conflict

My dad drinks regularly. My mum suffers from depression. There are also money problems.

My mum is an alcoholic. I need to stop mum and dad arguing … swearing and kicking doors downstairs. This is always happening.

Being left alone and unsupervised (exposed to risk from abusive adults)

My mum left home around 6pm last night after having an argument … I am feeling scared, lonely and hungry. She's not back yet.

My mum and dad are drinking all night. They also had friends over for drinking … My dad's friend took off my pyjamas but I don't know what happened. My body … is hurting down below.

Inappropriate caring responsibilities

My mum makes tea and then smokes drugs. I feed my baby sister.

Mum goes out drinking she doesn't come back till morning. I am left to babysit my little brother and sister.

Disrupted education

My dad locks himself in his room and ignores everyone. I think he has started taking drugs again … I am worried. I can't concentrate on my work.

Loss through separation and bereavement

My mum committed suicide. My dad is drinking a lot. I miss mum and want to talk about her.

I am upset I have been in foster care these few months but I don't like it. I want to be with mum but she is an alcoholic and drug addict … I can only go with mum if she can stop taking drugs.

Running away and homelessness, self-harm and suicidal feelings

I want to run away from home. Both my parents use drugs and alcohol. They fight. I did try to get away with my sister.

I cut myself when I am upset … My mum died when I was four. Dad drinks a lot and is always horrible to me. I feel sad but I haven't told anyone about this.

Mum shouts and hits me she is worse on a Friday. I don't want to feel pain I want to die.

ChildLine counsellors stated:

Children keep bottling it all up. Sometimes they become almost like the carer, mopping up Mum's sick, putting Mum to bed, picking her up off the floor, sometimes cooking the tea, looking after the house.

These children never know what they have to face. One of the biggest issues is fear of what to expect when they come home from school or when parents return home from drinking or taking drugs.

They think it's normal. They think it's happening to everybody. They don't know how bad it is. They just accept it.

(NSPCC, 2010)

About 2.6 million children in the UK live with parents who are hazardous drinkers (Turning Point, 2011) and around 104,000 children were living with adults in drug treatment during 2011–12 (NTA, 2012). In 2011 in England and Wales, 19,500 babies under 1 year lived with a parent who used Class A drugs and 93,000 babies lived with a parent who was a problem drinker (Cuthbert, et al., 2011). Following the death of a baby while sharing the parent's bed, a serious case review drew attention to a disproportionate professional focus on the parent's misuse of substances rather than the care of the children. The risks posed by excessive alcohol and drug misuse were not recognised (WSCB, 2013).

Divorce and separation are twice as likely where one or more partner misuses alcohol (Calder and Hackett, 2013, p266). Forrester and Harwin (2006) reported that parental substance misuse accounted for 62 per cent of all children subject to care proceedings and 40 per cent of those defined as needing protection. A study of 184 serious case reviews between 2009 and 2011 found that 42 per cent included a parent who misused substances, and in one-fifth of all cases substance misuse was linked with mental health problems and domestic violence. This combination is referred to as the 'toxic trio' (Brandon, et al., 2012a). Deaths from child abuse typically occur when the parent is in an acute phase of a mental illness.

Department of Health (2016) advice states that men and women who drink regularly should consume no more than 14 units per week, the equivalent of six pints of beer and seven glasses of wine. Alcohol-free days are recommended.

It is a criminal offence to be found drunk in charge of a child under the age of 7 years in a public place or to be driving under the influence of alcohol or drugs. A parent or carer who presents a risk to a child because of drug or alcohol misuse could also be prosecuted. The Serious Crime Act 2015 (Part 5, s66) added non-physical cruelty to the offence of cruelty and neglect. The offence covers conduct which is likely to cause psychological suffering or injury as well as physical harm. Social workers have a duty to report allegations of crime to police.

Both drugs and alcohol are mind-altering substances. A parent's behaviour may appear confusing and frightening to the child. Dawe and Harnett (2007) found that the adverse parenting outcomes associated with substance misuse were related to multiple difficulties experienced by parents, such as mental health problems, family relationships and socio-economic factors, rather than the substance misuse itself. Parents' lifestyles may be chaotic and centred around their own needs and there may be numerous lengthy separations while the parent is in prison, hospital or residential treatment. Children may also witness frightening events such as police raids of their home and feel acute embarrassment and shame (Barlow and Schrader McMillan, 2010).

RESEARCH SUMMARY

A study of 100 parents using alcohol services between 2010 and 2011 included 48 pregnant women:

- *Over half allowed children under 16 years to drink alcohol and six per cent of these were under 10 years.*
- *32 per cent said their children took on the role of carers.*
- *Over a quarter said children often missed school and were at risk of anti-social behaviour.*
- *52 per cent said they could not provide adequate care and 45 per cent were often away from the children (Turning Point, 2011).*

Some addicted mothers who appear to 'recover' after losing their child, develop something professionals call 'start again' syndrome where a new pregnancy is seen to present a fresh start, or as a way of filling the emotional vacuum. Incredibly, in some cases this was naively encouraged by poorly trained social workers who thought a new baby would set them on the path to recovery.

(Keeble and Hollington, 2010, p75)

The start again syndrome is a form of professional dangerousness where professionals put aside knowledge of past complex family histories and take an over-optimistic view of the parent's capacity to care for the child. This can be a factor for children being returned home prematurely before the parent has addressed their substance misuse (Brandon, et al., 2008). Ofsted (2013) noted that the best case records include details about children's contact with substance misusing adults within and outside of the household (specifically overnight), alternative care arrangements, pregnancy, and where and when substance misuse takes place.

Pre-birth, a child protection conference must be convened to examine the risk of harm to the baby (DfE, 2015, p43). The impact of opiate withdrawal may lead to the baby being removed from their mother for medical attention over several weeks impacting on attachment. Babies of substance-misusing parents, such as those who misuse alcohol, may be born with physiological damage such as low birth weight, distinctive facial characteristics, learning difficulties and hyperactivity. Babies born to drug-misusing mothers are likely to be premature and have low birth weight. The baby may have symptoms such as irritability, hyperactivity, abnormal sensitivity to touch, shivering, fever, diarrhoea, vomiting and convulsions. They may also have brain damage and poor motor co-ordination. The baby may be born with an addiction and have withdrawal symptoms during the first weeks of life.

Although some practice improvement has been noted (Ofsted, 2013), the organisation Adfam (2013) comment that, although the impact of parental substance misuse on children is well documented, in the context of cuts to public services, there has been little service development and child protection in this context has remained on the periphery of discussion. The Family Drug and Alcohol Court (FDAC) based at the Inner London Family Proceedings Court, which was launched in 2008, has improved outcomes for children by tackling substance misuse of parents at an early stage of care proceedings and fewer children have been taken into care. Families see the same judge throughout and meet them every fortnight as well as gaining support from a multi-disciplinary team (Bamburgh, et al., 2014). This scheme is now being extended across the country.

Parents with mental health problems

They have seen the effects of me cutting. How I have harmed myself – left mental scars. Mainly on the oldest one. He doesn't talk about it. Even when he was in care he used to come home from school to see how I was. Felt responsible for me. He grew up too soon. At first it was scaring my kids – they didn't know what I would say next.

(Stanley, et al., 2003, p64)

They say things like, 'we only work with your Mum' but my Mum lives with me so it's all connected

Can you hear me, can you see me? Then why did you ignore me?

(ADASS and ADCS, 2011, p19)

Often children in special circumstances are invisible to the system because they live in the shadow of their parents' problems.

(Stanley and Cox, 2008, p70)

When someone is ill it can be scary. When it is someone you love it can be very, very upsetting and maybe you feel very sad inside. If it's the person who looks after you most you may feel angry with them. You may feel so cross that you want to shout or stamp or break something. If it is your Mummy or Daddy or another special person in your life you may even think they don't love you anymore.

(Falkov, 1998, p183)

Reder, et al. (1993) point out that parental behaviour is more important to assess than the diagnosis or psychiatric label. Out of 35 perpetrators of fatal child abuse, 40 per cent had a mental health problem and in about half of these cases there was also substance misuse. Sometimes there was no clear psychiatric diagnosis despite a history of violent threats to others and irrational behaviour where the impact on the child was missed by professionals. *I have encountered situations where a multitude of support services have been provided, but where these serve to mask the absence of a viable parent–child relationship with a result that children are left for long periods in harmful emotional environments* (Beckett, 2007, p139).

The following facts show the impact on children of parental mental health problems.

- Across the UK, 144,000 children aged under 1 year lived with a parent who had mental health problems (Radford, et al., 2011).

- Lovejoy, et al. (2000) in a meta-analysis found that depression was associated with the mother's negative behaviour and disengagement from the child.

- Parental mental health problems were identified as a factor in over half of a sample of 33 serious case reviews in England from 2009 to 2010. The children were killed, seriously injured or neglected by a parent with depressive mental illness or a severe psychotic episode (Brandon, et al., 2011).

- Maternal depression is associated with negative behaviours towards older children but is most harmful to children when it affects the first five years of life (Foster, et al., 2008).

- In a survey of 100 child deaths, 32 contained evidence of parental mental ill health. The most common method of killing was asphyxia followed by use of implements and poisoning (Falkov, 1995, p8).

CASE STUDY

Faith Lovemore, died aged six weeks

In 2009 near Cambridge, Julia Lovemore, aged 41 years, killed her daughter by stuffing her mouth with paper, dousing her with flammable liquid and jumping on her body. A

CASE STUDY *continued*

community psychiatric nurse and health visitor went to the home and found the father praying *to take the devil out of Julia*. He later went to the doctor's surgery with an older child, also doused in flammable liquid, and with the dead baby. Lovemore had been diagnosed with mental health problems since her twenties and both the baby and the older child were the subject of child protection plans for physical abuse. There were concerns about extreme religious beliefs leading to isolation and refusal of support services. The judge concluded that too much professional time had been spent determining whether the family's religious views were a sign of mental illness rather than considering the risk to the children. The structural division of adult and children's services can be a block to good practice and any conflict between the agencies must be resolved at managerial level with issues taken to the LSCB for resolution (CSCB, 2010; BBC, 2010b).

RESEARCH SUMMARY

Ofsted (2013), drawing on the views of children, parents, carers, practitioners and managers from nine local authorities and partner agencies, found:

- *thinking about the impact on children was more embedded in drug and alcohol services than in mental health services;*

- *young carers were not well identified;*

- *questions about children were included in adult services recording systems but inconsistently;*

- *risk to children was not identified and referrals were not made at an early stage;*

- *adult services often made repeated referrals before children's services took action and the lack of response often went unchallenged;*

- *assessment was not routinely approached as a shared activity between children's and mental health services in order to draw on each other's expertise;*

- *when parents were admitted to hospital, joint working was poor in ensuring discharge plans took the children's needs into account and as a result, some children were returned prematurely and were unsafe;*

- *when in place, child protection protocols mainly led to better protection but for some children their lives were not improved;*

- *where long-term care was required there was often a history of opening and closing cases providing intermittent support, raising questions about the sustainability of change and robustness of planning;*

(Continued)

- *the practice of joint supervision across agencies was not evident;*

- *learning from serious case reviews was evident in children's services but less well under-stood among adult service practitioners;*

- *there are no national requirements to gather information and report on the numbers of parents with serious mental health problems.*

ACTIVITY **2.5**

About 50,000 children are caring for a family member with mental health problems, which in a class of 26 school children includes about six (SCIE, 2011).

Use the following questions to think about how you might seek a young carer's point of view and inform your understanding of a child's perspective on their parent's mental health.

- *Do they know about their parent's mental health problem and how do they think it was caused? Do they see it getting better or worse?*

- *Are they worried about getting ill themselves or about who will look after them?*

- *How do they feel about their domestic responsibilities?*

- *What happens in an acute phase of the parent's illness?*

- *How does life change for them when the parent is well?*

COMMENT

When a parent is emotionally unavailable, it can be devastating and frightening. Poor parental care may expose the child to danger or extreme parental exhaustion may lead to an inability to perform the usual responsibilities such as taking a child to school or pre-paring meals. A parent with depression may provide unpredictable responses to a child who does not understand what to expect from their parent. A parent may be emotionally unavailable through delusional ideas, irrational anxieties or even from the effects of psy-chiatric medication (Beckett, 2007, p133). A parent's delusions may not affect parenting, but could be terrifying for a child if, for example, the parent thinks their food is poisoned, or the child is evil or hates them. A child who is exposed to traumatic emergency situa-tions will be affected, not only through the absence of the parent, but also through the chaotic and unpredictable home environment. Few children can visit their parent in hospi-tal because the setting is often unsuitable. Even if the mental health problem is episodic, the impact on the child's emotional wellbeing may be serious because the child struggles with uncertainty and fear about the future, and even in remission, a parent may not be able to respond to the child's needs.

Support must be in place for the parent and the child. Stanley, et al. (2003) identified that where abuse is suspected, parents with mental health problems most needed support with child care, practical and financial help, development of parenting skills, emotional support and help for their mental health problems, particularly talking therapies. They want professionals to be respectful of them. Strengthening informal friendships was of particular assistance (Newton, 2013).

Investigating allegations about a child emotionally abused whose main carer has mental health problems and deciding the threshold for intervention

The following case diagrams are designed to promote a questioning approach as they progress from no ongoing concerns to immediate protective action. You should be informed by the list of prompts in the Introductory Chapter (see page 20). Continue to add your own questions and consider the implications and barriers to safe practice in each case.

Case diagram 2.1

- A mother tells a midwife she does not feel affection for her newly born child, thinks she cannot be a parent, feels depressed, has a sense of failure and did not expect to feel this way.
- Both parents had wanted and prepared for the baby.
- The mother is a child psychotherapist.
- There are no concerns about the baby's physical health.

- The father, an IT consultant, is supportive and anxious. He is willing to seek professional advice.
- Maternal grandparents move in with the family. Paternal grandparents also assist with the baby's and mother's care and reassure the midwife that they can cope as a family.

Referral of a child for possible emotional abuse and not thought to be at continuing risk of abuse

- Children's services SW closes the case.
- Family continue to gain support from the health visitor and GP.
- Health visitor confirms that she has observed the mother being more responsive to the baby and the baby is achieving her milestones.
- Mother continues to attend the support group and NCT meetings.

- Midwife refers to the Community Mental Health Team (CMHT).
- Mother has no history of depression and has good family support. Two weeks after childbirth, she is reluctantly continuing to breastfeed, is not caring for herself and feels guilty about her lack of affection for the baby.
- CMHT social worker (SW) makes a referral to children's services and realises that the mother has very high expectations of herself as a new parent.
- In the first six weeks after childbirth the mother attends an outpatient appointment, the psychiatrist diagnoses post-natal depression and because of breastfeeding no medication is prescribed.

- Children's services SW completes an assessment and, with mother's agreement, observes the child and mother together, makes checks with the midwife, general practitioner (GP) and CMHT.
- The SW convenes a professionals meeting to assess the risk of emotional harm to the baby, which is attended by the midwife, health visitor, GP, adult psychiatrist and mental health SW.
- Given the family support network, mother's willingness to work with professionals and her lack of a history of depression, the assessment concludes that this is a child in need (s17, CA 1989) case.
- Decisions are made to review in one month, refer the family to a local support group and the National Childbirth Trust (NCT) and for the CMHT to continue to monitor.

- Review meeting is held in one month.
- Maternal grandparents have returned to their home but continue to visit each weekend.
- Father has taken extended leave to be the main carer.
- Mother slowly improves, engages more with the baby, attends outpatient appointments with the CMHT and a local support group, and finds the NCT visits helpful.

Case diagram 2.2

- The girl continues to be monitored at school and through child in need (s17, CA 1989) review meetings.
- Her parents take advice not to enter their daughter for the independent school examination which is in line with her wishes to go to the local secondary school and remain in her friendship group. She no longer attends the eating disorder clinic but continues to see the psychotherapist at CAMHS.
- The family continue attending family therapy sessions.

- A ten-year-old girl, preparing for secondary school entrance examinations, is noticed by her teacher to have lost weight and appears anxious. The girl tells the teacher that if she is successful her parents will buy her a horse.
- Her parents want her to go to an independent school. They tell the teacher their daughter is not very intelligent, needs extra homework and has private tuition most evenings.
- The teacher discusses her concerns with the school's designated safeguarding lead.

- The designated safeguarding lead has also had reports from another teacher regarding how thin the girl has become and seeing her throw away a packed lunch.
- The form tutor speaks with the girl about nutrition and the girl denies there is a problem, saying she just wants to lose weight to look like a well-known celebrity. The teacher explains her worries to the girl and the school decide to speak with the parents.

- The family attend CAMHS and begin to work towards more realistic expectations of the daughter, respond to her individual needs and accept the difference between her and their sons.
- Her weight is regularly monitored and she maintains, but does not increase, her body weight.
- The mother accesses adult psychiatric services for help in managing her OCD symptoms and to understand the impact of her behaviour on the daughter. The father arranges to spend more time at home with the family.

Concern about a child emotionally abused

- The parents attend a meeting at the school, agree their daughter has lost weight and say this is because she has had a sudden growth spurt. They say she eats a balanced diet, is naturally slim and is working hard for her examinations. They describe her as a worrier and say that she finds school work difficult.
- The teacher expresses her concerns and tells the parents she will refer to children's services.
- The parents are upset about this but give their consent.

- Children's services SW arranges a home visit with the parents, and sees the girl separately. The SW obtains permission for checks to be made to complete an assessment.
- The girl tells the SW she is anxious about failing her exams and disappointing her family and that her mother is constantly cleaning and preoccupied with hygiene and her father is rarely at home. The girl is worried that if she fails her exams her mother will become ill and her parents might split up.
- Agency checks confirm no known concerns about two older brothers who board at a public school. The brothers tell the SW they would like to see more of their father when they return home during the holidays and some weekends.
- The SW notes that the parents have very high expectations of their daughter and the father works away from home on a regular basis. The SW refers the family to the Child and Adolescent Mental Health Service (CAMHS) for family therapy and individual therapeutic support for the girl. The GP confirms that the mother has accessed help from adult psychiatry in the past for an obsessive compulsive disorder (OCD). Adult psychiatry agree to liaise with CAMHS. Children's services define the case as child in need (s17, CA 1989).
- The family accept services and although the girl responds to the services offered, a strategy meeting (s47, CA 1989) will be convened if she continues to lose weight. This is monitored by the school and the GP.

- The school nurse contacts the GP after seeing the girl at school fall asleep in the classroom and because of concerns about her weight loss.
- The GP invites the parents to the surgery. The mother and daughter attend. The father is working away from home. The girl tells the GP that she has stopped eating.
- The GP is concerned about emotional abuse and makes a referral to children's services and to the eating disorder clinic.

Case diagram 2.3

- A careful decision must be made at a further stage as to whether or when to confront the mother with the medical facts while ensuring the child's safety. The child and mother are monitored by the school, GP and SW.

- A seven-year-old boy, after arriving at a new school, tells his teacher he has haemophilia and wears a bracelet to alert others to this.
- The teacher is surprised not to have been informed about this before and discusses it with the school nurse.

- School nurse contacts the boy's mother who confirms he has haemophilia and provides emergency contact details.
- The mother gives permission to check any records, tells the nurse she is a single parent, that the boy is her only child and that he is not in contact with his father.
- The boy tells the school nurse he might bleed to death if he falls over in the playground or during sports activities.

- A follow-up strategy meeting at the hospital agrees on-going s47 (CA 1989) enquiries, with very clear timescales, to ensure the child protection plan is carried out.
- A SW is allocated and is to set up meetings with the mother. The strategy meeting is to be reviewed in one month. The SW, school and paediatrician agree to develop a supportive relationship with the boy and the mother.
- Agreement not to proceed to a child protection conference as it is important not to alert the mother at this stage.
- The child is discharged home.

Suspicion of actual or likely significant harm to a child emotionally abused, s47 (CA 1989) enquiry

- After a fall in the playground, where the boy sustains a leg injury, the school call an ambulance which takes the boy to the local hospital accident and emergency department. The mother confirms that the boy has haemophilia.
- The doctor carries out blood tests which show no evidence of haemophilia and subsequently contacts the child protection paediatrician.
- The boy tells the doctor he is frightened he is going to die.
- The wound is dressed, the boy is admitted onto the children's ward for further tests and a second medical opinion is sought.
- The paediatrician is concerned about fabricated illness and makes a referral to children's services but does not inform the boy's mother that this is happening because doing so may increase risk of harm to the child.

- Children's services convene a strategy meeting for the following day at the hospital, attended by the police CAIT, child protection paediatrician, GP, school nurse, children's services solicitor, SW and SW team manager.
- Further tests confirm that there are no clinical signs of haemophilia, the wound is healing well, the mother has visited regularly and appears caring in her interactions with the boy.
- The meeting agree there is evidence of emotional abuse, the boy needs to be reassured about his health and this must be balanced with the need to work with the mother. The paediatrician explains that the child is not at risk of physical harm apart from through unnecessary medical interventions.
- Paediatrician and SW speak to the mother together to explore her belief that the child has haemophilia. This is done with sensitivity, without alerting the mother at this stage to their knowledge that this is not the case as this may increase risk of harm to the child.
- SW to make checks with previous schools, GPs and hospitals. The child to remain in hospital while checks are made to gain a clear understanding of the mother's beliefs and assess risk to the child.

- A strategy discussion takes place between children's services and the police Child Abuse Investigation Team (CAIT) who agree a single agency response as part of s47 (CA 1989) enquiries.

Case diagram 2.4

- Checks show a police referral form was received by children's services two months ago as the father threatened to set fire to a shed. The police calmed the family and there was no further action.
- Housing reported the family had recently been burgled because the father had left the front door open; neighbours were also complaining about noise at night.
- The GP is concerned about the father who is known to adult psychiatry due to a diagnosis of bipolar affective disorder (a mood disturbance with episodes of mania and depression). He often refuses to take his medication and will not meet with the community psychiatric nurse (CPN).
- The school report both children are often exhausted, unable to concentrate and recently they have been late for school and absent a few times without explanation.

- A mother tells a children's services duty SW that her two children aged six and eight years cannot sleep as their father is up all night making noise, disturbing the family, cooking food and leaving the gas on.
- The SW arranges to speak with the children and with the mother's consent makes checks.

- At the six-month review the children are no longer thought to be in need of a CP plan, their mother is an effective protector and the agencies continue to work together, monitoring the father's mental health and the impact on the family.
- The case is now defined as s17 (CA 1989) children in need.

S47 (CA 1989) investigation of a child emotionally abused

- The SW interviews both children at school individually. They speak of continual noise through the night, their father plays loud music, sings while he cooks and expects them to join in. They are embarrassed because the neighbours are also disturbed by the noise. The children are worried about their mother who tries to care for him as he is mentally ill and she has to stay up to watch him all night. They want him to be a nice dad again and get help.
- The SW makes a referral to the police CAIT, conducts a s47 (CA 1989) strategy discussion, agrees a strategy meeting and informs the mother of this.

- A review conference takes place after three months and both children are reported to be more settled at school and no longer tired. Their attendance has improved although they miss occasional days through visiting their father.
- The CP plan remains in place to be reviewed in six months to ensure that the protection of the children is sustained and to have a clear structure for multi-agency planning and co-ordination.

- The SW team manager chairs the strategy meeting which is attended by the police CAIT, school, housing, GP, SW and CMHT SW.
- It is agreed that the children are experiencing emotional abuse as a result of their father's mental ill health. An urgent mental health assessment is planned as well as a SW assessment of the children's needs (S17, CA 1989).

- Following discharge from hospital, the CPN visits the father in his new home and he attends outpatient appointments regularly.
- The CMHT liaise with children's services to monitor and agree the nature and frequency of contact between the father and the children. This is ongoing as the father's mental health is unpredictable.
- The mother and children are no longer exposed to this distress but when he is well they maintain contact with him.

- A child protection (CP) conference is convened. The assessment is completed and the children made subject of CP plans under the category of emotional abuse. CP plans for both children include a referral to CAMHS for therapy and a core group is agreed including the children's SW, mother, mental health SW, GP and teacher.
- The MAPPA panel monitor the risk posed by the father to his family and within the community.
- The housing officer on the MAPPA agrees to seek to rehouse the father within the locality, in line with the mother's and children's wishes to continue to have contact with him.

- The mental health assessment confirms the mother's and children's account of the father's behaviour. He is not taking medication and is compulsorily admitted to a psychiatric unit under Section 2 of the Mental Health Act (1983).
- The mother tells the SW she wishes to leave her husband. For the first time in months the mother and children sleep well at home.

- With treatment, the father's mental health improves and the children enjoy positive visits with him.
- The children's SW attends Care Programme Approach (CPA) meetings for the father and the mental health SW attends the core group to implement the decisions of the plan as a result of the CP conference. With good liaison between these services the CP is assured.
- The mother is recognised to be a proactive protector of the children.

Case diagram 2.5

- Children's services receive a referral from a family therapist in CAMHS about a boy of 14 years who is threatening to take his own life.
- The therapist asks for a strategy meeting because of concerns about emotional abuse and that the boy will carry out the threat, as he has thought carefully about it and planned to jump off the top of a multi-storey car park.
- The therapist arranges a mental health assessment with a psychiatrist and admission to an adolescent psychiatric unit.
- The boy is in foster care under s20 (CA1989) because his mother is an inpatient in a psychiatric hospital as she experiences paranoia and delusions. She has attempted suicide in the past. The boy's father died four years ago from a heroin overdose.

Immediate action to protect a child emotionally abused

- After an assessment of the paternal uncle and aunt the boy is placed in their care.
- The boy continues to have periods of depression but is no longer suicidal. He has begun to engage more in school work. He begins to enjoy childhood games and activities that he had not previously experienced.
- Contact with his mother continues to be well managed by his carers.

- Following a strategy discussion and agreement with the police CAIT to proceed single agency, children's services arrange a professionals' meeting at the adolescent psychiatric unit attended by adult and child psychiatrists, adolescent mental health worker, children's services SW, CAMHS and school.
- The foster carer has been concerned for some time about the boy as he is very quiet and stays in his room for long periods of time. He makes regular visits to his mother in hospital and to his home and his mother sometimes arrives to see him unannounced as she is worried he is smoking cannabis and using heroin. The foster carer does not think this is true, as there is no evidence.
- The boy is extremely anxious about his mother who has a difficult and long history of repeated hospital admissions and chaotic patterns of caring for him leading to repeated emergency foster care placements.
- The school are worried about the deterioration of his school work.
- CAMHS say he is preoccupied with his father's death, believing his mother will also die and sees no point in living.

- The conference agrees a child protection plan. A Care Order (s31, CA 1989) is to be applied for and a permanent placement sought either with the boy's foster carer or paternal uncle and aunt.
- All contact with his mother is now well managed and supervised.
- CAMHS provide therapeutic support for the boy to help him understand the impact on his childhood of his mother's delusional beliefs, as well as to talk about the death of his father.
- The school provide one-to-one learning support and a strategy to assist the boy's sense of self-esteem and increase his confidence.

- The SW makes checks with police who report they have had several calls from the boy's mother saying he is using heroin.
- The SW identifies a paternal uncle and aunt who are willing to consider caring for the boy on a permanent basis and applying for a residence order (s8 CA1989).
- The hospital report that the boy continues to be depressed and self-harming.
- Safe and supervised contact arrangements with his mother are facilitated by the SW and co-ordinated with adult psychiatric services.
- Contact with the boy's paternal uncle and aunt is also facilitated. Children's services attend Care Programme Approach (CPA) meetings for the boy's mother.
- A child protection conference is convened to take place in 15 days.

C H A P T E R   S U M M A R Y

A range of types of emotional abuse are examined in this chapter, demonstrating that intervention to protect children from emotional harm is complex and difficult to evidence. Children and survivor accounts provide essential knowledge about the experience and impact of this form of abuse, particularly in contexts of abuse outside of the family, where children have received little social work involvement. This has indicated a need for social workers to extend awareness to the emotional needs of all children and to ensure that they become more visible within child protection processes.

FURTHER READING

Tuck, C (2013) *Through the eyes of a child.* London: Filament.
One survivor's account of her experience of child abuse including emotional harm.

Morrison, T (2006) *Staff supervision in social care: Making a real difference for staff and service users.* Brighton: Pavilion.
A comprehensive resource for gaining emotional and practical support through supervision.

WEBSITES

www.jagsfoundation.org
A mother's campaign to stop gun and knife crimes.

babble.carers.org
Online support and advice for young carers.

www.youngminds.org.uk
Promotes child and adolescent mental health and mental health services.

Chapter 3
Sexual abuse

Introduction

26 per cent of respondents did not become aware that they had been sexually abused until they were an adult.

(OCC, 2015, p58)

How did the abuse make you feel?

I was never a child, always grown up. I always felt an outsider.

(Nelson, 2008a, p2)

We watch a little girl sitting with her nursery class around the dinner table. She can move, but she doesn't; she can eat but she doesn't – unless you put the spoon in her hand and move it to her mouth; she doesn't play; she doesn't appear to listen or to speak. It's as if she doesn't want to exist. She's one of the children who bring the staff close to tears. She arrives every day with a red, raw, vulva. Doctors have looked at it, worried about it, worried about her ... there are children who we are convinced are being sexually abused. It's not any one thing that makes us think it. You know children pretty well when you work with them every day and they can't always tell us in words, but they can tell you in pictures, in body posture, sometimes it's physical symptoms, sometimes they don't want you to touch them, sometimes they walk around wringing their hands, unable to tell what is wrong.

(Campbell, 1997, p196)

This chapter focuses on the protection of children from sexual abuse. The evidence presented focusses on the voices of sexually abused children and survivors as well as providing insight into perpetrators and the scale and nature of their criminal activity. Case studies provide further contextual detail including in relation to disabled children. The chapter concludes with case diagrams of child sexual abuse involving child sexual exploitation to support decision making on a spectrum from concern to immediate protective action.

Definition of sexual abuse

Sexual abuse involves forcing or enticing a child or young person to take part in sexual activities, not necessarily involving a high level of violence, whether or not the child is aware of what is happening. The activities may involve physical contact, including assault by penetration (for example rape or oral sex) or non-penetrative acts such as masturbation, kissing, rubbing and touching outside of clothing. They may include non-contact activities, such as involving children in looking at, or in the production of, sexual images, watching sexual activities, encouraging children to behave in sexually inappropriate ways, or grooming a child in preparation for abuse (including via the internet). Sexual abuse is not solely perpetuated by adult males. Women can also commit acts of sexual abuse, as can other children.

(DfE, 2015, p93)

Learning about sexual abuse

ACTIVITY **3.1**

Child sexual abuse is essentially abuse of power. What do you think abuse of power means in the context of child sexual abuse?

COMMENT

Sexual abuse and exploitation of a child involves an abuse of power. The social worker should identify possible power imbalances in the relationship. These can result from differences in size, age, material wealth and/or psychological, social and physical development. In addition, gender, sexuality, race and levels of sexual knowledge can be used to exert power. Whilst a large age differential could be an indicator (e.g. a 15 year old girl and a 20 year old man), social workers should be aware that a 14 year old boy, supported by peers might exert pressure on a girl of the same age or older. The sexual abuser might also be a woman or girl and the victim a boy. Power may be exerted through group pressure or peer bullying (LSCB, 2016:9.3).

Children may be sexually abused at all ages, within all cultures and religions, by adult men and women child sex abusers as well as by young people themselves. Children are abused by those they know, who are supposed to nurture them within their families and care systems, as well as by strangers. Disabled children are particularly vulnerable, as are children with few protective adults in their lives such as homeless and unaccompanied migrant children. Child sexual abuse does not occur only in low-income families. A growing number of studies have reported weak or no association between measures of family socio-economic status and risks of child sexual abuse (Fergusson and Mullen, 1999, pp37–8).

Child sexual abuse may be opportunistic or highly planned. Children have become commodities in a global sexual industry and sexual crime against children is recorded and distributed across the world while law enforcement systems struggle in being sufficiently resourced to protect children. There are reports of children sexually abused by people of public prominence such as religious leaders, sports coaches, music tutors, teachers, social workers, lawyers, judges and politicians. Sexual abuse can take place within large institutions and organisations where the power of the abuser is amplified through control of the child isolated from their protective family and community network.

Children are abused by people who call themselves paedophiles, which literally means 'lovers of children', some of whom justify their crimes asserting that it is a child's right to have sexual relations with adults as long as it is what they define as within a 'loving' and 'consensual' context. It is important to use the accurate term child sex abuser/offender which reflects the serious nature of the crime. In the 1970s, the Paedophile Information Exchange (PIE) was set up to promote their view that it was a right of adults to have sex with children and they campaigned, unsuccessfully, to abolish the age of consent. Although some members of PIE were convicted of sexual crimes against children, some continued to promote their views including within academia and still publish their views online. A history of PIE is available online (http://spotlightonabuse.wordpress.com). It is important to know that the Sexual Offences Act 2003 clarified issues of consensual and non-consensual offences against children. Children under 13 years cannot consent to any form of sexual activity and all penetrative sex of such children is automatically classified as rape. Sexual activity with a child under 16 is also an offence. Where it is consensual, it may be less serious than if the child were under 13, but may nevertheless have serious consequences for the welfare of the young person. Consideration should be given in every case of sexual activity involving a child aged 13-15 as to discussion with other agencies and whether child protection procedures are required. For children of all ages, it is also an offence to pay for the sexual 'services' of a child which include vaginal, anal or oral penetration and sexual grooming is an offence. For children under age 18 years it is an offence for a person to have a sexual relationship with them if the adult is in a position of trust or authority in relation to them. The Act abolished the defence of a belief that the child was over the age of 18 years although such a belief can be considered in mitigation.

Only one in eight victims of childhood abuse come to the attention of statutory authorities, *the scale of child sexual abuse is therefore much larger than is currently being dealt with by both statutory and non-statutory services* (OCC, 2015, p8). Social workers must have knowledge about the vast extent of sexual abuse of children and listen to children's voices (Davies, 2007).

- *I cried all the time when I was nine. You are just waiting for one person to ask that question.*
- *We cut and we didn't know why.*
- *I tried to kill myself at 4 and 10.*
- *Eating paper gave some sort of relief. Tore the covers off books and ate them.*
- *He (the abuser) encouraged me to antagonize other people. I became very angry.*

- *I was quiet anyway and became even quieter. I was trying so hard to hide it.*

- *I was not present mentally, I was falling asleep...*

- *I went from being a cheeky, loud and popular girl to a quiet, withdrawn, very tearful girl* (Nelson, 2008a, p18).

A referral to children's services may be based on a child or adult statement, observation of a child's behaviour, medical, forensic or photographic evidence, adult witness testimony, police or other intelligence or an abuser's admission. Whatever the route of referral, social workers must work with police to make sense of the information and to proactively investigate significant harm even if it is unclear initially whether or not a crime has been committed. Collating small clues and working together with other professionals to evaluate their significance is key to identifying and bringing perpetrators to justice.

Unless the professional focus is also on detailed analysis of information about known or alleged perpetrators, children will not gain protection. Protecting one child may well mean protecting many because offenders often abuse more than one child. Seeking justice by gaining the prosecution and conviction of the abuser is very important for a child's healing. Female survivors of child sexual abuse *felt strongly that they should have been protected at an early age and that the perpetrators should have faced justice many years before* (Nelson, 2001, p111). Survivor networks, such as NAPAC, are growing in numbers and demand justice and support services.

Convicted child sex abusers commonly have a previous history of abuse which did not lead to investigation or prosecution. Kelly (2004) examined 13 cases of sexually abusive incidents in the Huntley case and said, *even this is almost certainly not a complete list of the young women.* Huntley was convicted for the murder of Holly Wells and Jessica Chapman, both aged 10 years. Knowledge gained from child sex abusers assists professional understanding of sexual crime; they are often related or known to the child and may abuse many children. Abusers may be isolated individuals or may network with others using international criminal organisations. While many abusers have experienced some form of abuse, in the majority of cases, survivors of child sexual abuse do not go on to become abusers. One study found that 12 per cent of male victims of child sexual abuse subsequently abused children themselves (Salter, et al., 2003). However, it is inaccurate and insulting to survivors to suggest that experiencing abuse makes them more likely to become an abuser. They are often the most proactive protectors of children.

There is a spectrum of abuse including contact and non-contact and varying levels of physical and psychological violence. A child may be exposed to sexual language, abusive images or to seeing or hearing sexual acts. An adult may deliberately expose, or make a child touch, the adult's genitalia or touch a child's genitalia. The adult might put objects or body parts (for example, fingers, tongue, penis) inside the vagina, mouth or anus of a child or inappropriately watch a child undress, use the toilet or bathroom and/or film a child being abused. The adult might orally, vaginally or anally rape a child. Animals may be included in the abuse and groups of adults may be involved. Abusers may coerce children to abuse other children. The abuse may include *physical violence such as beatings, burning, scalding, torture with electrodes, use of weapons, tying of wrists or ankles, isolation, drugging and deprivation of sleep, food or drink* (Nelson, 2008b, p9).

Nelson compared physical disorders to survivors' accounts of child sexual abuse, and made comparisons with the physical impact of torture and child marriage. She referred to violent repeated assaults on developing bodies, untreated through lack of care or the desire to conceal evidence, and drew attention to the impact on a child's back or pelvis of being crushed by a large adult, and throat rape leading to infections and difficulty in swallowing (2002, p52).

Possible physical signs of sexual abuse may include forensic findings such as semen in the vagina, anus or mouth or on other parts of the body, items of clothing or bedding. Other physical signs include: sexually transmitted infections; genital, anal or oral pain; bleeding; injury or soreness; vaginal or penile discharge; urine infections; bruising to inner thighs, breasts, or genital area; genital warts; bite marks; carpet burns to back; symmetrical bruising or marks; constant unexplained sore throat; abdominal pain; difficulty walking or sitting; skin reaction to semen. Yet many sexually abused children show no physical signs because healing takes place rapidly and scarring is uncommon. With the exception of pregnancy or where there is forensic evidence, it is unusual to find medically proven evidence of sexual abuse. The response of the paediatrician will often be that medical findings are consistent with an account of child sexual abuse but do not prove it took place. The forensic window is the time when it is possible to retrieve evidence of physical signs of sexual abuse and is generally around seven days after the abuse has happened (OCC, 2015, p40).

Behavioural indicators of child sexual abuse include:

* sexual knowledge beyond age and developmental stage;

* obsessive behaviour such as constant cleaning or showering;

* arson;

* reluctance to take part in sports or to remove clothing;

* fear of dentists and medical examinations.

It is important to recognise that over-perfect behaviour may be indicative of a child too frightened to draw attention to themselves. Please refer back to other indicators listed on page 17.

Sexual abuse – the evidence

- One in three sexually abused children, aged 11–17 years, did not tell anyone (Radford, et al., 2011).

- 1.3 million children in England will be victims of child sexual abuse before the age of 18 years (OCC, 2015, p27).

- In 2014, there were 2,210 children in England who were the subject of a child protection plan under the category of sexual abuse (DfE, 2014b).

- 90 per cent of sexually abused children are abused by someone they know (Radford, et al., 2011).

- Young adult women reported the highest rates of sexual abuse from a parent or guardian. Of 11–17 year olds in the UK, 16.5 per cent reported sexual abuse by an adult or peer (Radford, et al., 2011).

- 11,398 children called ChildLine about sexual abuse in the year 2014–15, an increase of 124 per cent since 2013–14; 42 per cent of the abuse was within the family and the vast majority of perpetrators were male (91 per cent) (NSPCC, 2015).

- The majority of online child abusers are white men aged 36–45 years including many professionals. Almost all have no sexual abuse convictions and the victims are often their own children (Townsend, 2008).

- Children between the ages of 11 and 17 years who experience physical violence by a parent are four times more likely to experience sexual abuse than other children (Jutte, et al., 2015, p33).

- There were about 30,000 registered child sex offenders in England and Wales in 2012 (NSPCC, 2012a). The number of sex offences against children recorded in 2014 was 36,000 (Jutte, et al., 2015). Those offenders convicted before 1997 are not required to register.

- In the UK, the number of recorded sexual offences against children increased by up to 39 per cent in 2013–14, thought to be due to extensive media coverage (Jutte, et al., 2015, p6).

- A police report showed that between 2008–9 and 2013–14 allegations of rape of children, either currently or non-recent, rose 52 per cent in London. There was a 68 per cent rise in allegations of sexual assault. There was a dramatic increase of allegations of the rape of children in the year before 2014 (GLA, 2014).

- In 2013, there were 602 child victims of trafficking according to National Crime Agency statistics (Jutte, et al., 2015, p74).

- Most children preferred to tell a friend about sexual abuse but often told them to keep it secret (Nelson, 2008a, p26).

- 38 out of 44 children disclosed sexual abuse while they were children, 66 per cent attempted to disclose while abuse was happening. The younger the abused child, the longer the delay in disclosing (Allnock and Miller, 2013, p6).

- Child Sexual Exploitation (CSE) in Rochdale involved 47 victims and led to nine convictions in 2012. CSE in Derby involved 15 victims leading to 12 convictions in 2012–13. In Oxford six victims were involved which led to seven convictions in 2013. In Peterborough five victims were involved, leading to five convictions in 2013. CSE in Rotherham involved 1,400 victims over a 16-year period, leading to five convictions in 2010 and six convictions in 2016 with other prosecutions pending (CRAE, 2014 p37).

CASE STUDY

Laura Wilson – a child with a child

Laura was murdered aged 17 years by Ashtiaq Asghar, also aged 17 years. Her body was removed from a canal in Rotherham and there were over forty stab wounds mainly to her head. Laura had a four-month-old daughter with Ashtiaq's friend, Ishaq Hussain. Ashtiaq, who had a relationship with Laura, killed her just days after she revealed her relationships with both young men to their families. The judge said he believed Ashtiaq treated white girls as sexual targets and not like human beings. Over Laura's life, 15 care agencies were involved but her needs were never met. There was a lack of authoritative intervention as care proceedings were not considered. There was also a lack of a *child centred approach which would have enabled her to choose, make connections and communicate. Laura was not seen by any agency as the highly vulnerable child she was* (RSCB, 2012, p9).

Laura had a learning disability with an IQ of 56, which was not considered by any agency. She experienced bullying at school and could not read or write independently. She self-harmed, misused substances and alcohol, and was sexually active from age 13 years. She presented as angry and unhappy and as not engaging with professionals. In 2005, her name was on the child protection register under the categories of sexual and physical abuse. She was identified as a child in need for just over two years but there was a lack of intervention to protect her despite serious concerns. In 2007, she was known to be meeting with older men and drinking alcohol and was referred to a child sexual exploitation project. There had been no risk assessment and no child protection investigation.

In 2009, Laura was referred to children's services by the project but a confused address led to no action. When Laura was pregnant, aged 16 years, the midwife referred her to children's services because she had a boyfriend, aged 19 years, who was in prison for kidnapping. An assessment concluded that Laura was no longer involved with this man and suggested a parenting assessment and *keep safe* work.

An unqualified family support worker saw Laura five times before closing the case. The serious case review (RSCB, 2012) commented that this complex case would have been challenging for an experienced social worker. The support worker had not confirmed the father's identity or assessed his involvement. In 2009/10, Laura was identified by police as one of 18 victims of men aged 20–29 years alleged to have committed serious

(Continued)

sexual offences against girls aged 13–16 years and five men were found guilty in 2010. The serious case review concluded that a combination of factors including organisational, systems, workforce, cultural and individual deficient practice impacted on the care of Laura. It concluded that children's services had not focussed on her needs stating that, *she was almost invisible to some services* (RSCB, 2012, p8). The review concluded that most agencies knew the history of the family but there was no co-ordinated protection plan.

The *Independent Inquiry into Child Sexual Exploitation in Rotherham* (RSCB, 2014), which included analysis of the murder of Laura Wilson, stated that the true scale of abuse was unknown.

> *One third of the cases were known to services because of a history of child abuse and neglect. The children were raped by multiple perpetrators, trafficked to other towns, abducted, beaten and intimidated. There were examples of children who had been doused in petrol and threatened with being set alight, threatened with guns, made to witness brutally violent rapes and threatened they would be next if they told anyone. Girls as young as 11 were raped by large numbers of male perpetrators. The abuse is not confined to the past and continues to this day.*

(RSCB, 2014, p1)

Disabled children and sexual abuse

I didn't understand. Every day he came straight to me. I suppose it was because none of my family came to see me. I was deaf and I couldn't talk.

I remember the attacks as if it was yesterday, the room, his disgusting smell and beard. He has ruined my life.

Because we can't speak we are at the bottom of the pile. When it comes to justice, you know as soon as they give you the label 'deaf' you are not going to get a fair deal.

One boy wrote 'man rude' on a paper aeroplane and threw it over the school fence hoping to gain attention.

(BBC, 2015a)

The above are the voices of children abused at Woodford School for the deaf.

Professional dangerousness – what false assumptions are made about disabled children and sexual abuse?

COMMENT

- *It is wrongly assumed that children who do not understand abuse are less distressed by it and that child sex abusers would not target a disabled child.*

- *Signs and symptoms of sexual abuse, such as masturbation, are often wrongly attributed to the disability (Kennedy, 1996).*

- *There may be reluctance to pursue prosecution although there is rarely any reason in principle why disabled children should not take part in video-recorded interviews (MoJ, 2011, p172).*

- *Therapeutic services for children who have been sexually abused are often not accessible to disabled children with mental health or learning difficulties (Allnock, et al., 2009).*

- *Abusers may think abusing disabled children means they are less likely to be prosecuted because children may be unable to escape or communicate their experiences (Kennedy, 1996).*

Disabled children are three times more likely to be sexually abused than non-disabled children (Jones, et al., 2012). Increased risk of sexual abuse has been associated with children who have more severe or multiple disabilities (Hershkowitz, et al., 2007; DCSF, 2010a:6.44). However, sexually abused disabled children are the subject of very little research to the point of being dismissed (Higgins and Swain, 2010, p55; Miller and Brown, 2014, p28). Triangle Services provide an online image vocabulary for children about feelings, rights and safety, personal care and sexuality (www.triangle.org.uk/files/2015-11/how-it-is-2002-an-image-vocabulary-for-children.pdf).

CASE STUDY

Abuse of deaf children

Between 1958 and 1970 many children were sexually abused and physically assaulted by the head teacher's husband at Woodford School, a specialist school in East London. He was allowed to work at the school though he had pleaded guilty to nine child sex offences in 1964. In 2004, 22 former pupils tried to bring a prosecution but the judge said the case was too long ago, some witnesses had died, the building had been demolished, there was no surviving documentary evidence and the alleged abuser was too unwell and frail to stand trial. Some former pupils pursued and won criminal injuries claims. Children were assaulted in his vehicles, office or bedroom. Pupils blamed themselves and were threatened by perpetrators if they spoke of the abuse. The children's isolation was compounded because sign language was not allowed, an oppressive but not uncommon practice at the time (Barnet, 2005; BBC, 2015a).

Sexual abuse of children at different ages

It can take years to disclose child sexual abuse … 47 per cent of survivors told one person, 32 per cent told under five people and 20 per cent told more than five people.

(OCC, 2015, p62)

ACTIVITY 3.3

Social workers sometimes think that children are more vulnerable to abuse at particular ages. At what age do you think children are more likely to experience sexual abuse?

COMMENT

Children may experience sexual abuse at any age from birth to age 18 years. In 2006, the Internet Watch Foundation reported a fourfold increase in abusive images depicting the most severe forms of sexual abuse of children, with 91 per cent of children under age 12 years (http://mobile.reuters.com/article/idUSL1648174520070417).

Although children as young as 3 years may be formally interviewed, few of these cases reach court. The age of most victims who come to the attention of the authorities is 12 years. Younger children may not be able to describe the abuse, may not understand it to be harmful and have fewer opportunities to disclose. Yet 60 per cent of survivors said their abuse began before the age of 9 years. The needs of young children are not being met by existing systems (OCC, 2015, p45). Child sex abusers sometimes target children of specific ages and may also focus on those who are younger and less able to report. A police report found an increasing number of online images showing the rape of babies and children too young to disclose the abuse (Townsend, 2008).

Sexual abuse – specific forms and contexts

Grooming

Social workers' confidence was more evident when working with individual familial based cases of sexual abuse than to forms of abuse where grooming, trafficking, internet abuse and other types of exploitative behaviour were identified and where multi-agency responses were required.

(Brady, et al., 2014, p6)

Grooming is an abusive process and refers to actions deliberately aimed at establishing an emotional connection and trust with a child in order to sexually exploit them. In Rotherham (RSCB, 2014, p31) almost 50 per cent of the children sexually exploited had misused alcohol or other substances which was typically part of the grooming process. Grooming may also include threats or bribes which persuade the child that it would be impossible to ask for help. An inquiry into child sexual exploitation involving gangs or groups (OCC, 2013) reported children feeling they had lost all control over their lives. Some children reported the grooming process lasting a long time – months or even two years in one case. They believed they were in a loving relationship. Abusers used threats to ensure compliance including filming sexual abuse and threatening to post images of victims online. Abusers will define abusive behaviour as acceptable, so that the child believes they are enjoying the activity or are responsible for it, even introducing other children, adding to a sense of guilt. Children may mistakenly believe they could have stopped the abuse.

The Sexual Offences Act 2003 included an offence of child grooming with a maximum sentence of ten years' imprisonment. This makes it a crime to befriend a child on the internet or by other means and meet or intend to meet the child with the intention of abusing them. The Serious Crime Act 2015 introduced a new offence of sexual communication with a child for the purposes of sexual gratification where the communication is sexual or if it is intended to elicit from the child a communication which is sexual. Grooming was evident in many cases where TV personality Jimmy Savile sexually abused children (Gray and Watt, 2012).

Social workers should aim to keep the child's world in place – family or placement, school, health services, drug/alcohol counselling, youth clubs/activities and religious/cultural groups. This makes it more difficult for abusers to gain access to the child as there are strong protectors and safe adults around them. Safe accommodation and drop-in centres should be available for children to access in emergencies.

RESEARCH SUMMARY

Caught in a trap provides an insight into the process of grooming as described by 413 children who contacted ChildLine during one year. They were mainly girls being groomed by mainly men. Of the 413 children, 56 per cent said they were being sexually abused and 20 per cent stated that they felt at risk of sexual abuse.

- He makes me feel special because he pays special attention to me and I like that because no-one else does.

- He is there for me when I want to talk to someone about all the bullying at school.

- He is really nice and I really trust him. He wouldn't hurt me. He makes me feel safe.

- The men give me drugs, alcohol and money.

- I am thirteen, he is much older ... I went in his car. I am too scared to tell my mum.

- It's my fault, I agreed to meet him.

- If I tried to stop seeing him I think he would hit me as he says he really loves me.

(Continued)

- They think he is grooming me but we are in love and if he was trying to hurt me he would have tried something but he hasn't.

- I feel so stupid and upset, I never thought I would get in this situation. I feel like hurting myself and ending it all.

(ChildLine, 2012, p8–18)

Forms of abuse based on information and communication technology

They exchanged messages late into the night, Joe carefully tested the boundaries, easing Rachel into mild sexual fantasies, talking about everything from fashion to underwear and swimwear as well as telling all sorts of true life tales from skinny dipping to his first sexual experience ... Sometimes he pushed a touch too hard and stepped back quickly changing the subject, making Rachel laugh or giving her yet another reason to see how lucky she was to have Joe on her side ... This was the worst kind of betrayal. To abuse a vulnerable teenager's innocence...

(Keeble and Hollington, 2012, p142)

The live-streaming of abuse from the developing to the developed world is judged to be an emerging threat. We assess there are four principal factors: the presence of significant poverty in a country, widespread access to well-developed internet infra-structure, access to children and the presence of English-speakers. As access to 4G and broadband becomes increasingly widespread, we anticipate wider availability of live-streamed abuse across an ever-wider range of countries.

(NCA, 2015, p13)

It is an offence to take, permit to be taken, make, possess, distribute or advertise indecent images (photographs or pseudo-photographs) of children and it is a seri-ous arrestable offence to seek out images of child abuse. An indecent image of a child is a visual record of the sexual abuse of a child, through sexual acts by either adults, or other children (or which involves bestiality) or children posed in a sexual way. The Serious Crime Act (2015) introduced an offence of sexual communication with a child if the adult reasonably believes the child to be under 16 years. It is also now an offence for an adult to arrange to meet with someone under 16 having com-municated with them on just one occasion (LSCB, 2015, Part B:7.8.2–4).

Online child sexual abuse is defined as the use of technology to manipulate, coerce or intimidate a child to engage in sexual activity that is abusive and/or degrading. Characterised by an imbalance of power and lack of choice it includes grooming of children for sexual purposes and the production, distribution or possession of inde-cent images of children. It can be preceded by contact abuse and involve serious organised crime (Jutte, et al., 2015, p10). In 2014, the Internet Watch Foundation worked with partner companies to remove 31,266 websites of child sexual abuse images. This was a 137 per cent increase on the previous year (Jutte, et al., 2015, p40). Forty UK police forces reported serious delays in cases while awaiting forensic analysis of online material by hi-tech crime units which deal with retrieval of data from computers, mobile phones and other media devices. Five forces reported a delay of more than a year (BBC, 2015b).

Children can be at risk from strangers online as well as from people they know. They may feel there is no escape as abusers contact them at any time in their home and commonly share images with others. They might target children whose user names have a sexual innuendo or where they see a child has low self-esteem. They might send multiple messages and see which children respond. Sexual exploitation online might include a child taking part in sexual activities via a webcam or smartphone or a child putting sexually explicit images of themselves online. They may be threatened that if they do not comply, the images will be made public. Images may remain online for a long time making recovery and healing very difficult. Online abusive images of children play a key role in motivating and triggering grooming behaviours prior to contact offences.

In one year ChildLine found a 168 per cent increase in counselling sessions relating to online sexual abuse, and the National Crime Agency (NCA) received 3,340 public reports of suspicious online activity, 46 per cent of which involved some form of online child sexual abuse. In addition, NCA and policing have access to digital traces that offer the potential to identify up to 25,000 people with an interest in indecent images of children. These traces are partial or whole bits of data, rather than names and addresses, and require significant resources to identify possible suspects. Some traces will not lead to identifiable individuals (NCA, 2015).

The Marie Collins Foundation (www.mariecollinsfoundation.org.uk) campaigns for a cohesive, multi-disciplinary response to children harmed online – a response that should be based on current, and future, practice wisdom and evidence-based interventions. Childnet International is a website dedicated to advice on how to avoid the potential dangers on interactive services online (www.childnet.com/). Thinkuknow has published guidelines on chatroom safety (www.thinkuknow.co.uk). For an online safety guide for adults and children see: www.barcodediscount.com/articles/online-safety-for-adults-and-kids.htm.

RESEARCH SUMMARY

An NSPCC analysis of 1,000 reported court cases included a snapshot of 100 cases where 4.5 million child abuse images were found. Of 101 convicted offenders, one in three were in positions of trust with the child. More than a quarter were also convicted of other sexual crimes, including grooming, voyeurism and indecent assault, and one in six already

(Continued)

had criminal records for similar offences. Those convicted included doctors, teachers, scout leaders, clergymen, police officers, a magician and a Santa Claus, and two were women (Guardian, 2015). CEOP (Child Exploitation and Online Protection Centre) (2013) reported an estimated 50,000 individuals in the UK downloading and sharing internet abusive images of children in 2012.

Young people who display harmful sexual behaviour

The key message is that children and young people presenting with harmful sexual behaviours are a diverse group with a complex set of motivations, background experiences and varying types of abusive or offending behaviour … Many of the children and young people who require specialist intervention come from very troubled circumstances. As well as being young people who require help to modify and control their behaviour, in order to reduce risk for others, they are also often in need of help to address and move on from their own trauma.

(Hackett, et al., 2013, p244)

Of child sexual abuse in the family, 25 per cent involved a perpetrator under the age of 18 years. This behaviour could in itself be an indicator of childhood experiences of sexual abuse (OCC, 2015, p8). Of contact sexual abuse experienced by children aged 0–17 years, 65 per cent was perpetrated by a young person and 80 per cent of children between 11 and 17 years did not speak about it (Radford, et al., 2011, p9).

Sexual activity will constitute significant harm if the relationship is coercive or involves other forms of abuse and may well be a crime. There is no consent to sexual activity in law under the age of 13 years and between 13 and 16 years sexual activity with a child is also an offence. Between 16 and 18 years young people can legally consent to some types of sexual activity but not where they are in a position of trust, for example they are a mentor or sports leader (Sexual Offences Act 2003). However, children should not be defined as mini-sex offenders as they have a range of needs that include, but are broader than, their harmful sexual behaviour. The separation of youth justice and child welfare policy and services makes an appropriate response difficult for social workers to achieve.

A study of 700 children, referred to UK services for sexually abusive behaviour, found that referrals were mainly for children over 15 years but one-third were aged under 13 years. Of the sample, 97 per cent were male and 38 per cent were learning disabled. A wide range of abuse was perpetrated with just over half the cases involving attempted or actual penetration, and in 75 per cent of cases victims were unrelated to the abuser (Hackett, et al., 2013). As many as 40 per cent of children who sexually harm others are victims themselves of sexual and other forms of harm. They are also likely to be socially isolated (Smith, et al., 2013). Hackett, et al. (2013) suggest that two-thirds had experienced some kind of abuse or trauma and around half of them had experienced sexual abuse. Some children may not realise that the behaviour is wrong and they may also have been exposed to abusive images from a young age.

The abuse should be defined as a pattern of behaviour which may be changed. *There is considerable confusion about what constitutes 'normal' sexual behaviour in children and adolescents, partly because of rapidly changing societal norms ...* Factors which affect the development of abusive behaviour are the age when abuse occurs, its duration, severity, the relationship between the victim and perpetrator and the use of physical force (Vizard, 2006, pp2–4). Power may derive from differences in gender, size, age, material wealth, sexual development, ethnicity, sexuality, disability and levels of sexual knowledge. Adult perpetrators may force children to be abusive or to procure other children. In this circumstance, it is difficult for children to disclose as they may feel guilty about harming other children.

Child sexual exploitation in the context of gangs

Children who harm others are both victims and perpetrators ... when adults treat a young person as just a victim or just an offender, they are not taking into account the complex, cyclical nature of the victim-offender and the factors that influence young people's lives.

(DCSF, 2010b, p7)

Between 2010 and 2011, 16,500 children were at high risk of CSE in gangs (Berelowitz, et al., 2012; 2013). Gangs are defined as street-based, social groups of children and young adults who see themselves, and are seen by others, as affiliates of a discrete, named group who engage in a range of criminal activity and violence, identify or lay claim to territory, have some form of identifying structural feature and are in conflict with similar groups. In gangs control of victims is exerted through: threats of reprisals; violence; terrorising, victimising, corrupting, isolating, filling them with a fear of not being believed if they report what is happening to them; grooming; and coercion.

Berelowitz (2012; 2013) found the majority of victims to be girls although boys comprised a significant minority. The majority of perpetrators were men and 28 per cent were boys. Children may be involved in more than one gang but rarely use the term *gang*; instead they used terms such as *family*, *crews*, *cuz*, or *my boys*. Violence is one way for gang members to gain respect by asserting their power and authority in the street, with much street crime perpetrated against members of other gangs or their relatives.

The high incidence of rape of girls, who are involved with gangs, goes largely unreported. Some gang members groom girls at school using drugs and alcohol, which act as disinhibitors and create dependency. They then coerce them to recruit other girls through social networks. Children identified by the research had been subjected to many types of sexual violence and perpetrators used devious and violent methods to control children. Children struggled to deal with the aftermath of the abuse years after it had ceased. It was found that too many agencies continued to fail children who had experienced contact with multiple social workers making it difficult to build trust. Of 323 gangs believed active in England, only 16 had been associated with CSE and children were still referred to as *putting themselves at risk* rather than *at risk from perpetrators.*

Proactive intervention through problem-profiling is recommended, involving agencies combining intelligence and experience and organising pre-emptive action to flag up and break up the exploitative networks. This approach should become the norm, rather than waiting to be told that a child is being exploited. The problem-profile is led by police and children's services working with other agencies and collates data about children at risk, as well as intelligence from covert policing and information from sexual health clinics, residential and foster homes, youth groups and schools. It should include proactive evidence gathering and mapping of locations of abuse, perpetrators' motivations, and multi-agency intelligence leading to identifying and apprehending perpetrators and monitoring non-convicted suspects (Berelowitz, et al., 2012; 2013; LSCB, 2015, Part B:11.2 and 11.3).

Children were not being heard or protected. The *See Me, Hear Me* Framework (Berelowitz, 2013, p66) sets out a gradual approach towards protecting a vulnerable or exploited child and returning them to a safe life. It includes strategic planning and operational interventions to prevent child sexual exploitation and to deal with it when it occurs. It is child centred, focusing on ensuring that children who are victims of CSE, or at risk of becoming victims, are seen, heard, attended to and understood. It is about making their needs the central and driving force behind all decisions and actions. It is about making the child visible.

Government guidance on this form of child abuse is *Safeguarding children and young people who may be affected by gang activity* (DCSF and Home Office, 2010b). Osman Warnings are letters issued by police if they become aware of a real and immediate threat to somebody's life. When delivered to child victims they should lead to protection procedures (s47, CA 1989; DCSF, 2010b, p25).

Women who sexually abuse

> *A belief persists that being abused by a woman is less damaging than being abused by a man. One has only to talk to the victims to realise what utter nonsense this is.*

> (Keeble and Hollington, 2012, p75)

Women's sexually abusive behaviour is often defined as inappropriate affection rather than sexual crime because women are socially constructed as carers. Children abused by their mothers experience strong feelings of betrayal, and anger is not projected onto non-abusive fathers in the way that it is towards non-abusive mothers (Saradjian, 1997, pp2 and 9). Abuse by women may be less visible than that by men – for instance, it is less obvious when a woman abducts a child.

Female abusers commit all types of sexual offences against children of all ages, groom their victims in the same way as male offenders, use distorted thinking to excuse the abuse and lack empathy for their victims (Ford, 2006, p33). A women might, for instance, claim that she is providing the child with sex education. Bunting (2005) found that there was professional reluctance to accept that women may instigate abuse themselves and that it was often assumed that they are coerced by male partners.

CASE STUDY

Women who abuse

Vanessa George, aged 39 years, sexually abused children in a nursery and swopped indecent images over the internet with another woman. Images of sexual abuse of children and babies were found on her computer. She was given an indefinite prison sentence for seven sexual assaults and for making and distributing indecent images of children but would not identify the children. The judge said that no one had forced these two women to commit these atrocious acts (BBC, 2009a).

In Norfolk, two women and two men were found guilty, following a three-month trial, of a total of 49 offences, including rape, sexual assault and actual bodily harm, carried out against five young children. The judge commented to Marie Black,

Your conduct towards these children can only be described as utterly depraved ... the children were passed around like toys ... The offences included adults conspiring to rape children at so-called sex parties. You used them for your own, and for others', sexual gratification.

(BBC, 2015d, p1; Norfolk Constabulary, 2015)

Children trafficked for sexual exploitation

Under the tight control of a slave driver, victims are unable to tell anyone of their enslavement and the repeated violence and rape that is so often a feature of it. So we must be their voice. Wider society must shout from the roof tops that modern slavery is wrong and it won't be tolerated any longer.

(Cunningham, 2015, p89)

When 15 year old Serena's parents arranged for her to marry a man in the UK, she agreed. She left her home in Gambia, and thought she was heading towards a better life. But as soon as she arrived it became clear things were not as they had seemed. Raped by the man who was supposed to be her husband, she was locked away in a room with no heating, no light and little food. She was then forced into appalling and brutal sex with groups of men and women. Sometimes she would be taken for a drive ... to secluded buildings where she and other young girls would be raped and made to pose for sexually explicit photographs.

(Cunningham, 2015, p6)

Many of them had been raped, some as young as nine or ten years old. They were in so much pain. But we were all too young to really understand what had happened ... The pain was also extreme because all the girls had experienced female genital mutilation.

(Nazer and Lewis, 2004, P100)

The Palermo protocol (ratified in the UK in 2006) provides an international definition of human trafficking:

Trafficking in persons shall mean the recruitment, transportation, transfer, harbouring or receipt of persons, by means of the threat or use of force or other forms of coercion, of abduction, of fraud, of deception, of the abuse of power or of a position of vulnerability or of the giving or receiving of payments or benefits to achieve the consent of a person having control over another person, for the purpose of exploitation. Exploitation shall include, at a minimum, the exploitation of the prostitution of others or other forms of sexual exploitation, forced labour or services, slavery or practices similar to slavery, servitude or the removal of organs.

(UN General Assembly, 2000, p2)

The protocol is clear that **children** are a special case because even if they are agreeable to being moved they cannot consent to exploitation. Smuggling is different from trafficking because migrants usually consent to being smuggled and it involves illegally crossing a border, whereas trafficking can be within one country (UN General Assembly, 2000).

CASE STUDY

Operation Lakeland

Operation Lakeland, a joint operation between police in Slovakia and Kent, included children's services, police and health education and provides an example of the enslavement and sexual exploitation of children by organised crime groups (OCGs). The child victims from Slovakia were trafficked within the UK and kept under the influence of drugs and alcohol. The involvement of Slovak officers assisted the co-operation of the suspects because of the removal of the language/cultural barrier and 22 suspects were arrested, 12 of whom were Slovakian. On the same day, 16 children were taken into protection and were not sent back to their families because of the continued risk of harm. The Centre for Social Justice added that trafficked children are often treated as offenders and pregnant women are sometimes recruited and forced to sell their babies. For trafficked children between the ages of 6 months and 10 years, OCGs can pay between EUR 4,000 and 8,000. In some cases children have been sold for the purpose of exploitation for up to EUR 40,000 (Cunningham, 2015, p16).

The Sexual Offences Act 2003 introduced offences including trafficking into, out of, or within the UK for any form of sexual offence. Intervention in trafficking cases requires joint investigation between social workers and police (s47, CA 1989). End Child Prostitution, Child Pornography and Trafficking (ECPAT) (www.ecpat.org.uk) is a children's rights organisation working against the commercial sexual exploitation of children in the UK and internationally which has produced an online resource, *In Your Hands – Safeguarding Child Victims of Trafficking* (http://course.ecpat.org.uk/).

Pearce, et al. (2009) emphasised the importance of specialist services such as trained interpreters and a dedicated keyworker approach to social work practice with trafficked and sexually exploited children. Local authority accommodation may be a target of traffickers so children may be better protected when placed outside the locality with trained foster carers, supported by a multi-agency child protection team. Launched in 2013, *Say Something if You See Something* is a poster and online awareness campaign that aims to alert hotel staff, taxi drivers, leisure centre staff and takeaways, to recognise the signs of sexual exploitation and be confident to report concerns (The National Working Group for Sexually Exploited Children, www.nwgnetwork.org).

Transnational child sex offenders

Child sex offenders who travel abroad to abuse children usually travel from rich to less developed countries. The use of technology, cheaper air travel, the opening up of borders and visa-free travel all make it more difficult to monitor, prevent and prosecute perpetrators (Bokhari, 2008, p22). Known transnational child sex offenders (TCSOs) continue to be mainly males aged 40 and above. The last three years have seen a diversification in reporting of TCSOs around the world, potentially as a result of more robust procedures to combat child sexual exploitation in parts of South East Asia (NCA, 2015).

Commercial sexual exploitation involves the exchange of cash, clothes or food to a child for sexual contact and occurs in multiple venues, from 'brothels' in red-light districts to coastal areas or hotels. It can occur over a period of time involving grooming. In other cases, the abuser purchases sexual services directly from a third party who has the child entrapped and who then makes the child available to the abuser (Ecpat, 2008).

Since the Sexual Offences Act 2003, British citizens who commit offences against children overseas can be prosecuted in the UK. Despite legal changes there are few prosecutions and British child abusers continue to abuse children overseas (Ecpat, 2011). British child sex offenders travel mainly to Eastern Europe (particularly the Czech Republic and Romania), South East Asia (particularly Thailand, Cambodia, the Philippines and Vietnam), India (Goa), Brazil, Cuba, Spain and Greece, where there is often a lower legal age of consent. ECPAT campaigns for a more co-ordinated police response (Ecpat, 2011) and has devised a Code of Conduct for the protection of children from sexual exploitation in travel and tourism available online (www. thecode.org).

Non-recent abuse

Adult survivors have a right to justice but children may also gain protection through adults coming forward to police and disclosing their history of child abuse. Investigations are conducted by child protection police officers because the abuser may still continue to abuse children and, with sufficient evidence, criminal prosecution may be possible. A referral must also be made to children's services to enable protection of current children. If the abuse relates to alleged abuse within an institution such as a children's residential home or a boarding school or to a network of abuse, then organised abuse procedures are relevant. There is no time restriction on the investigation of non-recent crime and some investigations go back 50 or more years. Police will seek corroborative evidence from potential witnesses, forensic and medical evidence, documentation, information from previous investigations and evidence from scenes of crime. These investigations are thorough and lengthy and may lead to criminal prosecution or inform civil proceedings.

It is very traumatic for an adult to revisit abusive experiences and memories of what happened to them as a child. Social workers should, with the survivor's agreement, inform police at the earliest opportunity and alert their safeguarding manager. The survivor needs to understand that if children are suspected or known to be at risk, then the matter cannot remain confidential because current children must gain pro-tection. The investigation may well extend beyond a single authority boundary and even be international. Responsibility for the investigation is with the police team which covers the area where the alleged abuse is said to have taken place. Social workers will need to assist the survivor in accessing files, a task often allocated to administrative officers, but requiring deep sensitivity to the emotional needs of sur-vivors trying to connect with their past, some of which may be unknown to them. Social workers should provide access to counselling and information about survivors' groups such as National Association for People Abused in Childhood (NAPAC). A num-ber of locally based survivor groups have now been set up such as Forde Park survivors of an approved school in Devon, and East Midlands survivors in Nottingham, both have Facebook pages. Shirley Oaks survivors represent hundreds of survivors from the London Borough Lambeth children's homes (www.shirleyoakssurvivorsassociation.org).

Since 2012, when the Jimmy Savile scandal became exposed, there has been an escala-tion of police investigations into historic abuse of children including those with a focus on the entertainment industry, music schools, religious institutions, care homes and boarding schools. Former inquiries have been re-opened amid allegations of inadequate prior investigation with Operation Pallial, as one example, identifying over 140 cases of abuse of children in North Wales children's homes between 1963 and 1992. A consider-able number of non-recent police investigations are being examined by the Independent Police Complaints Committee (IPCC) following allegations of cover-up and lack of proper investigation of child sexual abuse cases in the past. There have been allegations also of dossiers of evidence presented to government by politicians since the 1980s which have gone missing. A summary and collation of these events is available (BBC, 2015e). Operation Hydrant is co-ordinating police investigations at a national level and the Independent Inquiry into Child Sexual Abuse (www.iicsa.org.uk) was set up in 2014.

RESEARCH SUMMARY

Colton, et al. (2002) interviewed 22 men and two women survivors of institutional abuse and found that:

- *financial compensation was not the motivation leading to disclosure;*

- *some had a strong desire to see the abusers brought to account in order to protect future children, rid themselves of unresolved past trauma;*

- *some had not reported the abuse because they thought they would not be believed;*

- *some had reported the abuse before but no action had resulted;*

- *some felt abuse carried a stigma and they spoke of feeling dirty and of personal shame and guilt;*

- *some feared loss of face with their families and friends and were concerned at being perceived as potential child abusers;*

- *some spoke of the high price they had paid for the abuse, including loss of jobs, relation-ships, mental health problems, self-harm, drug addiction, prison and physical ailments;*

- *some would have preferred an apology even more than a prosecution;*

- *some wanted to access their files to learn more about what had happened to them as children;*

- *support was difficult to access for those in prison;*

- *therapeutic support was seen to be valuable, as were survivors' groups.*

Ritual abuse

The evidence went on for weeks, indescribable, inexplicable, unbearable ... to this day, the official line within which police and social workers are expected to work is that there is no such thing as ritual abuse; they say they are discouraged from pursuing cases ... because it is presumed that juries will instinctively reject them. There is, however, one stunning difference with this account: it could be proved. [Nine people were jailed for crimes against children over 35 years in Plymouth].

(Davies, 1998, p12)

In 1991, the term *ritual abuse* was included within statutory guidance as a subset of organised abuse:

A wide range of abusing activity is covered by this term, from small paedophile or pornographic rings, often but not always organised for profit, with most participants knowing one another, to large networks of individual groups or families ... in which

115

not all participants will be known to each other. Some organised groups may use
bizarre or ritualised behaviour, sometimes associated with particular 'belief' systems.
This can be a powerful mechanism to frighten the abused children into not telling of
their experiences.

(Home Office, et al., 1991: 5.26.2)

Later, (HM Government, 2006, 11.53–57; DCSF, 2010a: 6.10–13) guidance introduced
the concept of child abuse linked to belief in possession or witchcraft and situated
this form of abuse within immigrant communities, and the definition of ritual abuse
was separated from that of organised abuse. However, research confirms that ritual
abuse occurs alongside other forms of organised abuse (Salter, 2014, p13). Salter
(2014) finds no reason to separate out a group that uses religious reasons (i.e. spirit
possession) to abuse children from those that are non-religious – a view consistent
with early statutory guidance (Home Office, et al., 1991: 5.26.2).

In 1994, the Metropolitan Police Ritual Abuse Investigation Team completed
research into 40 cases of ritual child sexual abuse (Mallard, 2008, p327). A former
superintendent of that team stated, that *it would be wrong to dismiss all allega-*
tions of ritual abuse as fantasy. He suggested that in such cases professionals must
listen, retain objectivity and examine each piece of evidence, patiently working
towards a conclusion. *An investigator has to remember that at the heart of an alle-*
gation there may be acts that did take place but they may be rendered distorted or
unbelievable by misinformation (Hames, 2000, p184). This police research was not
made public.

In 1991, in a case where the media was almost entirely sympathetic to parents, nine
children were removed from four families by social workers and police on the main
island of Orkney under suspicion that they were victims of a ritual abuse network.
This followed suggestive evidence given by several children who were members of
another family, known as the 'W' family. The children were returned some weeks later
to their families by a sheriff without the evidence having been tested. A government
inquiry was an analysis of the authorities' response to the allegations and not into
whether abuse had occurred or not. Lord Clyde's inquiry report (Clyde, 1992) presented detail of the 'W' children's original evidence, but questioned the reliability
of it on the basis that, since the children had already been victims of abuse within
their own family, their evidence might have become confused or the result of their
imaginations. However, Nelson, in an analysis of the case, questioned whether this
evidence was childishly imaginative, or instead factual. She commented:

The children described in a matter-of-fact way a series of events where they were
taken from one place in certain cars and trailers by certain people in certain costumes
to another place where they unloaded specific equipment and were joined by named
adults who they claimed sexually abused named children. These lists of people are
very similar to each other. They all named equipment the interviewers do not under-
stand, like the hooker, which appeared to be a kind of shepherd's crook. The children
worry about the accuracy. They grow annoyed when the hooker drawn is too small
or when the car lights are not put in and they make corrections. The only obvious

examples of childish imaginative expression are about emotions as when M, 'drew the sun looking down with a sad face and tears and said that the sun was crying'.

(Nelson, 2008b, p348)

Nelson concluded that this evidence needed police investigation rather than testing by a psychologist or psychiatrist. Despite disturbing comments by some of the children of four other families, also detailed in the Clyde inquiry report, the findings focused mainly on professional practice such as interview techniques and the means of reducing the risk of unfounded action. Nelson, reflecting on the lack of attention by the inquiry to the effective means of investigating organised ritual abuse of children, or indeed to any needs of children relating to suspected sexual abuse, advocates the need for ongoing vigilance in such complex cases. She concludes that *if any of those children on Orkney did need protection, justice or restitution, then they are still waiting for it as adults today* (Nelson, 2008b, p352).

A similar comment was made by Campbell (1997) following the Cleveland inquiry report (Butler Sloss, 1988) stating that it remains unknown whether the 120 children in the case were in need of protection as the focus was again on the professional arrangements for child protection rather than the investigation of child abuse. The failing of both these inquiries is set to be repeated by the Independent Inquiry into Child Sexual Abuse (www.iicsa.org.uk/about-us/terms-of-reference) as rather than the investigation of crimes against children, the main aim is to consider the failings of state and non-state institutions.

CASE STUDY

Operation Kempton in Kidwelly, Wales

Colin Batley was convicted of 11 rapes and numerous other child sexual abuse crimes over 20 years and three women were also convicted of offences against women and children, within and outside the town of Kidwelly. They used occult practices within a secretive group to brainwash victims, including ceremonies where, wearing robes and hoods, they forced children and vulnerable adults to take part in sex acts. Children were procured to take part, suffered extreme threats and were made to wear upside down crosses. One witness described an altar and abusers reading the work of occultist Alistair Crowley. Batley had vicious Rottweilers and told a victim that if she did not follow orders she would be killed by people higher up in the cult. The judge said, *you formed a community, within a community, you were described as evil. That in my view is an entirely accurate statement of your character* (Morris, 2011, p8; Wales Online, 2011).

Sexually exploited children

Sexual exploitation of children and young people under 18 involved exploitative situations, contexts and relationships where young people receive 'something' (e.g. food, accommodation, drugs, alcohol, cigarettes, affection, gifts, money) as a result of them performing, and/or another or others performing on them, sexual activities ... In all cases, those exploiting the child/ young person have power over them by virtue of their age, gender, intellect, physical strength and/or economic or other resources. Violence, coercion and intimidation are common, involvement in exploitative relationships being characterized in the main by the child or young person's limited availability of choice resulting from their social/economic and/or emotional vulnerability.

(DCSF, 2009b)

No matter how children are enslaved, whoever sells or buys them they face similar consequences from this dirty trade. Young children's bodies are simply not ready for sex. They are fragile and tear easily so the children suffer lesions, bleeding, scarring, infections, sterility and sometimes death ... their mental health suffers too as they are introduced to sexual acts which they often cannot understand but which they may feel devalue their bodies and souls. They become confused with their role in life, their sexuality and come to distrust adults who offer them 'love' and then abuse and abandon them.

(Kane, 1998, p5)

If a perpetrator can spot the vulnerable children, why can't professionals?

Why would a 13 year old make it up?

They should have done something to the men not to me.

The social worker didn't understand why I wasn't telling them.

I didn't hide. I told them where I was.

They didn't stop to think why?

They did not look on me as a child. In my head I was older but really truly I wasn't.

The social worker didn't understand the extent or seriousness of what was happening.

(OSCB, 2015, pp13–14)

All the punters go for the young lads – they call us chickens.

(*Guardian*, 2003)

I didn't like any of it to start with, but over time I grew used to it ... they were giving me money and buying me clothes. I regret now what I did but at the time I felt needed and wanted. It seemed better than the children's home.

(D'Arcy and Gosling, 1998, p200)

The Serious Crime Act 2015 amended the Sexual Offences Act 2003 to remove anachronistic references to 'child prostitution' and 'pornography' and changed the language to one of sexual exploitation and abusive images of children. Under-18s are no longer to be prosecuted thus recognising children as victims rather than consenting participants. *Safeguarding children and young people from sexual exploitation. Supplementary guidance* (DCSF, 2009b) is the relevant statutory guidance.

Indicators of child sexual exploitation may include:

- previous and current sexual abuse, neglect, physical abuse and domestic violence;
- family involvement in sexual exploitation, drugs or alcohol misuse;
- children's drug and alcohol misuse;
- eating disorders and self-harm (sometimes extreme, for example genital cutting);
- involvement in theft and petty crime (often organised by an abuser);
- a preoccupation with their mobile phone calls and possession of multiple phones;
- having limited freedom of movement;
- being an unaccompanied child;
- health indicators such as sexually transmitted infections, terminations and pregnancy;
- possession of money and goods not accounted for;
- having an older boyfriend (LSCB, 2015, Part B:6.2.3).

Social workers must not pathologise sexually exploited children. A range of child blaming professional comments showed a lack of understanding about sexually exploited children in Oxford:

- *She is a streetwise girl who is wilful.*
- *She associates herself with adults who have warnings for firearms and drugs.*
- *She is believed to be prostituting herself to pay for drugs.*
- *She deliberately puts herself at risk as she goes off with men who are strangers.*

(OSCB, 2015, p34)

The professionals perceived the children as having consented to the sexual activity; there was a tolerance of underage sexual activity with no recognition of the abuse of power and coercion involved. The offences against the children were not of any less magnitude because they may have been *troublesome* or may have already experienced abuse (OSCB, 2015, pp35 and 37).

> *The fact that scores of professionals from numerous disciplines, and tens of organisations or departments, took a long time to recognize CSE, used language that appeared to blame victims and see them as adults, and had a view that little could be done in the face of 'no cooperation', demonstrates that the failures*

were common to organisational systems. There have been similar cases to those in Oxfordshire, most notably in Rochdale, Derby, Bristol and Rotherham. The same patterns of abuse are seen, the same views of victims and parents, and similar long lead-ins before effective intervention.

(OSCB, 2015, p9)

The focus must be on preventing abuse happening and where children are already involved applying protection procedures, legal safeguards and exit strategies. Targeting abusers may involve prosecution for a range of offences. Police must be robust in seeking evidence to support charges such as grievous bodily harm, unlawful wounding, actual bodily harm, kidnapping, abduction, sexual crimes, false imprisonment as well as drugs offences and benefit or tax fraud. Joint working between children's services, police and the voluntary sector is essential in order to protect sexually exploited children.

Kerrigan Lebloch and King (2006) describe a model of intervention addressing different categories of risk and levels of protective action (LSCB, 2015, Part B:6.3.1) from responding to a child who is at risk of being groomed to immediate action when a child is being sexually exploited. Social workers must work jointly with police. Police and probation services collate information primarily about known and suspected abusers and social workers collate information mainly about the child, family and community networks. It is only when both perspectives are analysed together that children have the best chance of protection and of seeking justice through the conviction of the abusers. Police may provide crime analysts, especially where there are networks of organised sexual crime against children. Social workers must inform the MAPPA of any known or suspected child sex abusers via their representative on the panel. They must also protect identified children from harm and contribute to MAPPA risk strategies.

Child victims must be valued, empowered and informed of their legal rights. These children are already under extreme pressure and need support to develop trust and to talk about what is happening to them. It may be that health or education staff are the only source of professional contact, in which case the protection strategy must preserve this important link and work with those professionals.

CASE STUDY

Becky's story

Becky, age 14 years and in care, was the anonymised subject of a Real Story BBC documentary (BBC, 2006b).

Becky made 40 allegations of sexual abuse by more than 25 men over a two-year period. Although in a children's home, she continued to be the target of child abusers. She told youth workers and professionals at a child protection conference, a counsellor, residential

CASE STUDY *continued*

social workers, hospital Accident and Emergency (A and E) staff, a psychiatrist, behaviour management staff and police about repeated sexual abuse. She was prosecuted for wasting police time even though she spoke of rape and sex work. She said she felt unsafe, even saying that she or her family might be killed, and spoke of being punched in the stomach and given drugs and alcohol. She also said that she had to have sex with men to protect others. She demonstrated many signs of sexual abuse including neglecting and harming herself, attempting suicide, having severe stomach pain, going missing repeatedly and seeking refuge in hospital admissions. Despite the evidence, she was not protected as the child protection conference defined Becky as a nuisance who was placing herself at risk and she was referred for behaviour management and dissuaded from presenting to A and E, her only place of safety.

Although many different agencies were involved in this case, Becky was failed by them all and went unheard. There was:

- no child protection plan or legal safeguards;

- no collation of facts and disclosures indicating abuse – on the contrary a strategy was put in place to manage the disclosures;

- no overview of risk to Becky or other children or plans to keep them safe;

- no ABE (MoJ, 2011) interviews or paediatric assessments;

- no focus on targeting perpetrators;

- no implementation of organised abuse procedures.

The risks of harm to sexually exploited children are high. They experience violence and yet few report to police through fear of retaliation. Children exit this form of abuse when circumstances change, such as when the abusers are convicted, when they have children, access drug treatment programmes or when they have experienced a particularly violent attack or rape. Exiting can be very difficult because of reliance on drugs and lack of self-esteem and they may fear isolation from their peer group.

Parents are frequently defined as neglectful whereas they are also often betrayed, groomed and entrapped by the perpetrators and feel powerless to intervene to stop the abusers' strategies. Social workers need to assess whether or not the parent is protective because a protective parent may be able to assist the investigation. Detailed mapping of shared information about the risk must be undertaken. Protective parents, foster carers and residential staff are well placed to provide information about adult perpetrators by collating vehicle, places or premises details, mobile numbers, names of abusers (including aliases and nicknames) and information about the young person's behaviour. This will inform the investigation and assist in targeting abusers and protecting the child.

ACTIVITY 3.4

How might you respond to a child like Becky? Consider the words you might use as well as your non-verbal behaviour if Becky told you the following:

I've done loads of stuff and if they get a bit pervy I just tell them to back off.

I want a kid, otherwise he'll get my family.

You don't know one thing about my life.

He's my knight in shining armour only he's got a car instead of a horse.

When I'm there I don't feel ugly.

He makes me feel special which is more than anyone else does.

I've got awful stomach pains.

I don't need any help. I can look after myself.

Sleeping with someone for a place to stay isn't prostitution, is it?

I'm disgusting and dirty.

He was really kind to me. I liked the sex.

Why should I tell you? I've told hundreds of times already.

Being on the streets is better than at home.

ACTIVITY 3.5

Consider aspects of professional dangerousness which apply to the professional response to Becky. (The numbers in brackets realte to the different types of professional dangerousness found on page 7).

1. *Becky told over 40 times and was pathologised as inventing accounts. (1 and 14)*

2. *Professionals thought that Becky was responsible for protecting herself and did not define her as a vulnerable child. (2)*

3. *A placement in care was seen to be the entire solution to Becky's situation without a parallel strategy to target the abusers. (3)*

4. *The belief that Becky herself was responsible persisted throughout the case despite new evidence coming to light. (4 and 12)*

5. *Becky was stereotyped as a child who brought the sexual exploitation upon herself and the abusers remained invisible to professionals. (5)*

6. *Becky was not heard and withdrew from the professional network which removed her from sources of help. (6)*

7. *Known facts about Becky and abusers were not collated, so that professional responses were based on guesswork. (7)*

8. *Statutory procedures were not followed leaving Becky exposed to further abuse. (8)*

9. *Becky attended a behaviour management unit where the staff should have recognised that she needed protection. (9)*

10. *Becky's friends would have information about her lifestyle and she also trusted a health worker who should have been identified as a key protector and linked Becky with other help. (10)*

11. *Professionals may have been too frightened to confront the perpetrators. (11)*

Investigating allegations about the sexual exploitation of a child – deciding the threshold for intervention

The following case diagrams are designed to promote a questioning approach as they progress from no ongoing concerns to immediate protective action. You should be informed by the list in the Introductory Chapter. Continue to add your own questions and consider the implications and barriers to safe practice in each case.

Case diagram 3.1

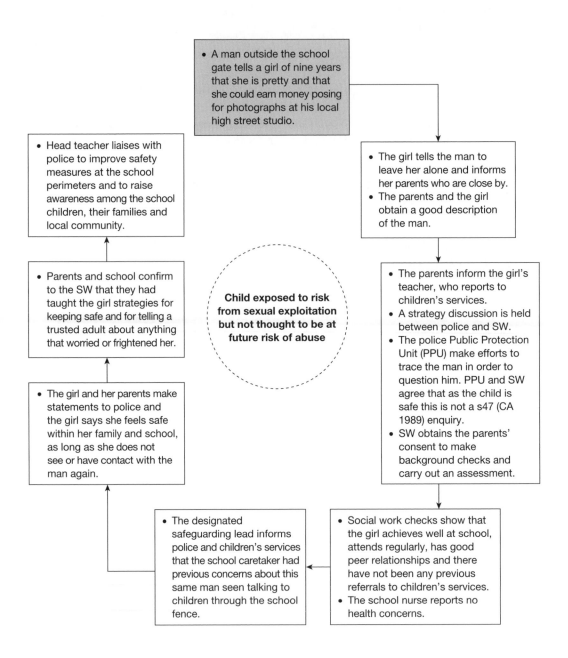

- A man outside the school gate tells a girl of nine years that she is pretty and that she could earn money posing for photographs at his local high street studio.

- The girl tells the man to leave her alone and informs her parents who are close by.
- The parents and the girl obtain a good description of the man.

- The parents inform the girl's teacher, who reports to children's services.
- A strategy discussion is held between police and SW.
- The police Public Protection Unit (PPU) make efforts to trace the man in order to question him. PPU and SW agree that as the child is safe this is not a s47 (CA 1989) enquiry.
- SW obtains the parents' consent to make background checks and carry out an assessment.

Child exposed to risk from sexual exploitation but not thought to be at future risk of abuse

- Head teacher liaises with police to improve safety measures at the school perimeters and to raise awareness among the school children, their families and local community.

- Parents and school confirm to the SW that they had taught the girl strategies for keeping safe and for telling a trusted adult about anything that worried or frightened her.

- The girl and her parents make statements to police and the girl says she feels safe within her family and school, as long as she does not see or have contact with the man again.

- The designated safeguarding lead informs police and children's services that the school caretaker had previous concerns about this same man seen talking to children through the school fence.

- Social work checks show that the girl achieves well at school, attends regularly, has good peer relationships and there have not been any previous referrals to children's services.
- The school nurse reports no health concerns.

Case diagram 3.2

- A boy of 11 years tells a neighbour that his mother's new male partner gives him expensive presents and lets him drink alcohol when his mother is at work.
- The neighbour, who has a child at the same school, shares what she has heard with a teacher.
- The boy has a brother of 13 years.

- Previous referrals to children's services have been made by neighbours about neglect by the mother. They say that the mother binge drinks following the boys' father's suicide.
- The mother works in the evenings in a pub.

- SW identifies some protective relationships within the extended family.

- Checks with police about mother's partner under s47 (CA 1989) procedures reveal no information is available locally or in the town where the boys say he lived previously.
- The school plan to make further referrals should concerns escalate.

Concern about children being sexually exploited

- School attendance and punctuality for both boys has deteriorated since the mother's new partner joined the household.
- Both boys are of average ability but seem distracted and show little interest in their work.

- With the boys' consent the designated safeguarding lead refers both boys to the school anti-bullying programme and invites the SW and the boys' mother to a Team Around the Child (TAC) meeting at the school.
- The SW in consultation with the school and a manager decides to make checks with police about the mother's partner without the mother's consent because sharing this information may place the children at further risk.

- The 13 year old tells a school nurse that he thinks he might be gay and is being bullied. He wants to go to a local gay youth club.
- He says that his mother's partner tells him he is an attractive boy who could easily find a boyfriend.
- He says that his mother's partner is 15 years younger than she is.

- With the boy's knowledge, the school nurse informs the designated safeguarding lead of her concerns that the older boy is being bullied about his sexuality.
- She has also noted that both boys now have expensive computer games and iPhones.

Case diagram 3.3

- A boy of 15 years tells the school nurse that he wishes to resume contact with a man he calls 'uncle' who sexually abused him in the past.
- The abuser was convicted of sexually abusing a number of boys after giving them cigarettes, alcohol and somewhere to stay.
- The boy has missed the attention from his 'uncle', believes that his 'uncle' has changed and is truly sorry for what happened.
- The nurse reports the boy's account to children's services with the boy's consent.

- Children's services contact the boy's mother who states that after the abuser was imprisoned, the boy was no longer the subject of child protection procedures.
- She did not believe the initial allegation because he was a friend of the family and she visited him in prison several times.
- Consent from the mother to further checks was not sought as the SW decided this might place the boy at further risk.

- CAMHS have remained involved with the young person and family since the sexual assault and will continue to support the child and assess both parents' capacity to protect the boy from future harm.
- The SW begins the process of making a claim under the Criminal Injuries Compensation Scheme in relation to the past sexual abuse of the boy.

- The school nurse tells the SW he is concerned about the boy's weight gain. In the last year he has become overweight and now has difficulty taking part in school sports activities.

Suspicion of actual or likely significant harm to a sexually exploited child, s47 (CA 1989) enquiry

- The MAPPA risk strategy states there should not be any contact between the abuser and the boy.
- The Public Protection Unit will monitor the abuser's activities.

- The SW checks with the school and learns that the boy has an Education Health and Care Plan (EHCP) and receives extra tuition. He enjoys and excels at drama.
- He has spoken with his tutor about looking forward to going round to see his 'uncle' with his mates to play music and watch movies.

- The father, although separated from the mother, lives close by and tells the SW and police that he is very worried for his son's safety since the abuser returned to the community.

- SW makes enquiries and holds a strategy discussion with police.
- The abuser is monitored and should he have any contact with the boy there will be a joint investigation and child protection conference.

- The MAPPA panel inform children's services of the abuser's release from prison and recommend s47 (CA 1989) enquiries.
- The abuser started a treatment programme in prison which continued in the community provided by the probation service. The abuser is remorseful but still fantasises about sex with children. He is assessed by MAPPA as being at low risk of re-offending.

Case diagram 3.4

- A girl of 12 years with cerebral palsy tells her mother during a weekend visit home, that a member of staff from the care home where she lives has upset her.
- She says he touched her breasts under her pyjamas when he took her on a camping trip and filmed her with his mobile phone.
- The girl lives in a small residential care home 100 miles from the family home, with eight other disabled children.

- The girl is too traumatised to return to the home. The SW identifies an alternative placement.
- The SW begins to support the girl's application for criminal injuries compensation and the organised abuse investigation continues.

- The mother reports what she has heard to the child's SW in the local disabled children's team who makes a referral to the police CAIT.
- The staff member concerned is suspended by the director of the home, pending investigation.
- The police visit the mother to take a statement.

- Other authorities with placements in the home are informed of the allegation. A strategy meeting is organised by the authority where the home is located and all relevant authorities are invited.
- Child protection planning takes place at a local level for every child who attends the residential home.
- Given police and SW knowledge of prior allegations within the children's home, and the production of images of the child, organised abuse procedures (DCSF, 2010a) are implemented.
- Consideration is given to pursuing criminal proceedings against the staff member.

S47 (CA 1989) investigation of a sexually exploited child

- During an interview with the police and SW, the mother states she believes her daughter's allegation.
- The mother is herself a survivor of sexual abuse from a teacher.
- The daughter was also physically abused while in nursery school and her mother understands safety issues.
- The mother has three younger children and the SW arranges a family support worker so the girl can remain at home during the investigation.

- A residential worker tells the police that the two staff previously dismissed were still visiting the home and were friends of the alleged abuser. He also said that the alleged abuser was not qualified and only got the job through fake references.

- A paediatric examination takes place, with the girl's consent, which confirms some minor physical trauma to her vaginal area which the paediatrician said was not inconsistent with the girl's account.

- A strategy discussion is held between police and children's services and the Local Authority Designated Officer (LADO), and a joint investigation is agreed.
- Police and SW contact colleagues in the area where the children's residential home is located and a strategy meeting is convened.
- There have been two other child abuse investigations at the home in the past two years about two staff members who were dismissed for gross misconduct.
- The girl is interviewed according to ABE guidance (MoJ, 2011) with her own and parental consent, by a police officer, SW and an intermediary who understands the girl's communication needs. She discloses that the staff member, who she named, also *gives kisses on the lips and puts his finger inside her bottom.*

Case diagram 3.5

- At the strategy meeting it is decided that should the child run away from the new placement, an application for secure accommodation will be considered.
- In line with local child sexual exploitation protocols, and in order to assist prosecution, all multi-agency information is to be collated to inform the police investigation and child protection planning.
- An application for criminal injuries compensation is prepared by the SW.

- A girl of 14 years is found naked in bed with a man of 52 years following a raid on a massage parlour and is placed in police protection.
- Four other young people are discovered at the scene.
- Police use their powers of protection to remove her and the other young people and inform children's services immediately.
- A strategy discussion takes place between police and children's services and a joint investigation is agreed under s47 (CA 1989).

- Children's services records state the girl is currently missing, has been reported missing many times and began to run away from home and foster care from the age of 13 years.
- Police have located her in various parts of the country including coastal resorts.

- The SW obtains an Interim Care Order (s31, CA 1989) with directions for a paediatric assessment including drug screening and a visually recorded interview.
- A placement in residential care, a long distance outside of the authority, is identified.
- A strategy meeting is to be convened as soon as possible.
- The outreach worker visits the girl in her new placement.
- Appointments are made for the girl with the sexual health clinic.
- Organised abuse procedures will be implemented by police in relation to all the children removed from the massage parlour.

Immediate action to protect a child from sexual exploitation

- Further social work checks show that the girl has been missing from school for over a year. Previously, she was achieving well and is described by her school as sociable and popular with other children.
- The girl's mother has severe mental health problems and a history of alcohol misuse, and cannot protect her daughter.
- The girl's father is in the army and away from home for long periods.
- The SW, in consultation with a manager, decides not to seek consent from the parents or the child for making checks as this would not be in the child's best interests.

- The SW interviews the girl at the police station who says she will continue being a sex worker and that it is her choice. She also says she can look after herself.

- A worker in an outreach service has engaged with the child and reports to the SW that the girl smokes crack cocaine and has engaged in unsafe sex.

- The SW telephones the parents to inform them that their daughter has been found, that she is to be interviewed and an Interim Care Order (s31, CA 1989) is to be applied for.

- The foster carer tells the SW that she cannot manage the girl's behaviour or stop her running away and that older men persistently call at the house and wait outside in cars.
- There have also been several threatening and abusive phone calls from men to the girl.
- The foster carer keeps a record of the men's names, car registration numbers and mobile phone numbers to pass to police.

C H A P T E R   S U M M A R Y

This chapter reflects concern at the considerable reduction in the numbers of sexually abused children gaining protective intervention and how this contrasts with the findings of Operation Hydrant and the Children's Commissioner for England as to current prevalence. The scale of sexual abuse and its relationship to power, at every level, requires social workers to be courageous in how they understand and respond to ensure that children are protected. Many forms of child sexual abuse, including within the context of organised abuse, have been presented as well as strategies used by child sex abusers, including women and children, to target vulnerable children. The case diagrams provide an opportunity to consider child protection procedures when children are sexually exploited.

Survivor accounts:

Cooper, T (2007) *Trust no-one*. London: Orion.
Cooper's account of her childhood in Kendall House children's home where she was forcibly drugged and sexually abused and her struggle for justice for herself and other survivors of this home.

Montague, R (2014) *A humour of love – A memoire*. London: Quartet Books.
Montague writes about sexual abuse by his father, a member of parliament.

Rhodes, J (2014) *Instrumental*. London: Canongate.
Rhodes, an internationally renowned pianist, writes about the impact of sexual abuse.

St Aubyn, E (2012–15) The *Patrick Melrose* novels.
St Aubyn writes a series of fictional accounts based on his experience of the impact of sexual abuse by his father.

www.mosac.org.uk
Support for non-abusive parents and carers.

www.ceop.police.uk
The Child Exploitation and Online Protection Centre (CEOP), part of the National Crime Agency, provides a dedicated 24-hour online facility for reporting instances of online child sexual abuse.

www.spotlightonabuse.wordpress.com
An archive of press coverage of non-recent abuse.

https://shatterboysuk.wordpress.com
Male survivors of child abuse inspiring change through shared experience.

Chapter 4
Neglect

Introduction

Neglect is when parents ignore you ... when parents leave you and you get hurt, if you are bullied at school and you have no one to turn to, neglect is scary.

Young people might think it's their fault that they're being neglected so they go along with it.

Most young people can't tell anyone that they're neglected.

(Hicks and Stein, 2010, pp 7, 12 and 16)

The unwanted and unsung heroes and heroines of British society, who suffered at the hands of 'care' and 'don't care' with thousands of other 'unwanted' children. That these children grew up to make something of their lives from the chronic neglect that was the 'care system' is a tribute to their courage and fortitude ...

(Frampton, 2004, p290)

As we entered the hall I clocked the kitchen to my left. Stacks of dirty plates, mouldy food, an overflowing, stinking bin – actually make that overflowing stinking flat. I couldn't see the kitchen worktop. I didn't want to know about the fridge. Dirty nappies and cat faeces covered the sticky floor. I was standing there speechless when a young woman appeared in the hallway. She was holding a child. He was also covered in little scabs, they were on his arms as well as his face. My head spinning I said, Show me the child's bedroom ...

(Keeble and Hollington, 2010, p47)

I considered the options. Would it be right to split the children from their struggling but loving mother who would be able to cope with the right help? Or had the line been crossed? Was this a case of serious neglect which meant the family must be split, possibly forever?

(Keeble and Hollington, 2010, p49)

This chapter focuses on protection of children from neglect. It begins by looking at definitions and moves on to consider the knowledge required to make professional judgements. The complexities of this form of abuse will be examined to support an informed approach to individual children's circumstances. Research into children's views and survivor perspectives provides a basis for sound decision making. The chapter concludes with case examples of neglect involving children left at home alone, which will take the reader through an investigative process, escalated through five levels of social work intervention to support in-depth analysis.

Definition of neglect

The persistent failure to meet a child's basic physical and/or psychological needs likely to result in the serious impairment of the child's health or development. Neglect may occur during pregnancy as a result of maternal substance misuse. Once a child is born, neglect may involve a parent or carer failing to:

- *provide adequate food, clothing and shelter (including exclusion from home or abandonment);*
- *protect a child from physical and emotional harm or danger;*
- *ensure adequate supervision (including the use of inadequate care givers);*
- *ensure access to appropriate medical care or treatment.*

It may also include neglect of, or unresponsiveness to, a child's basic emotional needs.

(DfE, 2015, p93)

Learning about neglect

ACTIVITY **4.1**

Think about what persistent, basic and serious mean in the context of the definition of neglect in Working Together to Safeguard Children (DfE, 2015, p93).

COMMENT

None of the 6 children who died from extreme deprivational neglect (mostly starvation) had ever been the subject of a child protection plan so the severity and dangerous nature of their life threatening neglect had not been recognised ... the family's contact with any agency was almost non-existent by the time of the child's death or serious harm ... the family's isolation added to the invisibility of the child.

(Brandon, et al., 2013, p10)

This guidance specifies persistent as an essential component of neglect, yet one incident of neglect could be fatal, for example when a child falls from an open window. Brandon, et al., (2013, p82), in an overview of serious case reviews, concluded that the statutory definition failed to emphasise that neglect can be not only harmful but fatal. Neglect is defined often as a factor in the case, rather than associated with fatality, though the impact of neglect can lead to suicide. The same applies to cases of sudden unexpected death in infancy where neglect was a concern and accident cases where there were forewarning signs such as lack of parental supervision. It seems that cases may have more difficulty getting through the 'front door' of children's services unless the level of neglect is extreme. In the case of Family Z (HSCB, 2012) (which involved chronic neglect of ten children between the ages of 10 months and 16 years, over a seven-year period), when strategy meetings were called, it was mainly in response to an incident or injury to one of the children. Only two meetings were prompted by concerns about neglect.

The House of Commons inquiry into the child protection system in England (HC 137:1, 2012–13, p20) expressed concern that information about neglect was not being systematically collected by local authorities other than for those children who were subject to a child protection plan. An Action for Children report (2013) discovered that a high percentage of professionals felt powerless to intervene in cases of suspected child neglect and the main barriers to intervention were the lack of available services and resources.

Gorin's research into children's views of neglect (2004) found that children mainly spoke to friends, siblings and extended family or their pets and did not know how to contact professionals for help. They found some professionals hard to talk to and wanted information given in a way they could understand; often they were confused about what was happening. Some were very worried about their parents' safety and spoke of witnessing violence or experiencing violence themselves.

The fact that neglect is not only harmful but can also be fatal should be part of a practitioner's mindset, as it would be with other types of harm. Harm from neglect can be minimised, downgraded or allowed to drift.

(Brandon, et al., 2013, p82).

There is little support for neglected young people in the transition to adulthood.

(p75)

Brandon, et al. (2013) studied 645 serious case reviews carried out between 2005 and 2011, where the child had been subject of a child protection plan. Neglect was a category of abuse in 101 cases and a child protection plan was in place at the time of death, but for 42 cases the plan had been discontinued and it was clear that these children needed the plan for longer and had fallen through the child protection net although their cases were serious. The lack of recognition by practitioners of the severity and impact of neglect was of recurring concern. The review noted that large families lead to individual children not always being seen as individuals. There was also a failure to involve men who were protective influences and who could contribute to the children's wellbeing.

Loss, death of a significant adult and rejection were a common feature of some children's lives. They were often left to their own devices and experienced no emotional warmth. As they grew up they experienced an unpredictable or frightening family life, characterised by inconsistent bouts of parental mental ill health, alcohol or drug misuse, violence towards them and their siblings and between adults, and for some, sexual abuse. Some had experienced multiple types of harm, multiple losses, separation and

(Continued)

feelings of abandonment and there was little evidence of professionals taking into account the children's early histories. Children asked to be accommodated but were generally refused by children's services and referred on to other agencies for support.

The research highlighted six main themes:

Malnutrition: *Extreme deprivation by withholding food or water from the child where the child died or was close to death.*

In some cases, withholding food was a way of asserting powerful adult authority whereas others were on inappropriate restricted diets as a result of faith or lifestyle choices. A small number of older children were malnourished in the context of virtual imprisonment. For some children the mother's eating disorder had an impact on their ability to feed their children. None of the six children in the sample who had died of extreme deprivational neglect, such as starvation, had ever been the subject of a child protection plan so the dangerousness of their situation had not been recognised. The children and their families were isolated making it difficult for professionals to observe what was happening and a sudden change in parental behaviour, such as increased hostility or non-co-operation, could signal life-threatening harm to a child in this situation.

Some neglected children were isolated through being absent from school and some in a context of being home educated. A decision to home educate is a parental right (s7(b) Education Act 1996) and for many families a positive choice. However, for the neglected child, this means the school is unavailable as a protective factor. There is no mandatory framework to monitor, assess or inspect the quality of the home education provision and no formal route for the child to express their views about it. The local authority is not required to keep a list of home educated children and has no right to impose home visits on the family.

Medical neglect: *The child may have been born with complex health needs or disabilities or may have developed a serious illness.*

The children died or nearly died as a result of parents' non-compliance with medical advice or failure to administer medications. All the children in the sample who were medically neglected required long-term, often complicated care and some parents would not accept the child's diagnosis or were unable to understand the condition. Professionals sometimes did not realise that a parent's situation had changed, such as with the birth of a baby or arrival of a new partner, and that the child was no longer receiving appropriate treatment. This suggested the importance of recognising tipping points in the family's ability to provide good quality care. In these cases, the rule of optimism operated and a lack of challenge to parental behaviour led to cases not being referred to children's services.

Parental learning disabilities were rarely highlighted but, analysis of these reviews has shown that there are often indications that parents had learning problems which were not assessed or addressed. The rigorous demands of these children's highly complex health care needs present serious challenges to parents with a learning disability (p53). For some parents this aspect of neglect was indicative of a struggle to respond to professional requirements such as appointments or to understand transport arrangements.

Physical abuse combined with neglect: *Physical assault both fatal and resulting in very serious injury in a context of chronic neglect where assumptions masked this danger to the child's life.*

A mindset of this is only neglect led to a dilution of very real risks from physical harm. The report stressed that neglect does not preclude physical abuse. The serious case reviews identified physical abuse in one-third of the children who had a child protection plan for neglect. A quarter of the children who had died of neglect had died as a result of physical assault. In these cases professionals had not taken account of family histories of violence or injuries to siblings. There was also parental hostility towards professionals leading to fear, paralysis and uncertainty. Some assessments were incomplete even in the context of section 47 (CA 1989) investigations and services withdrawn. Missed appointments, family hostility and non-co-operation should trigger greater not less professional vigilance.

Suicide of a young person: *In the context of a long-term history of neglect or extreme isolation having a catastrophic effect on a child's mental well-being.*

A history of neglect ran through almost all the cases of young suicide in serious case reviews. Most of the children had been well known to agencies over a number of years but for some, particularly those who were constantly on the move, their problems were largely unrecognised. These children found it hard to trust and were viewed by professionals as disengaged. *There was concern about children in care who felt compelled to return home who remained unsafe.*

SUDI (Sudden unexpected death in infancy): *Unexplained infant deaths within a context of neglectful care and a hazardous home environment, which was not anticipated by professionals or carers within 24 hours prior to the child's death. (This differs from SIDS (sudden infant death syndrome) where the cause of a child's death is not understood following investigation.)*

A history of child neglect in the family did not lead to professional reassessment when a new baby was born, particularly in the context of large families. Even when a child protection plan was in place, professionals were falsely reassured by parents about the baby's safety and did not assess a known risk such as a parent misusing substances and sleeping with the baby. Known risk factors such as co-sleeping, parental smoking, low birth weight, babies sleeping on their fronts and premature birth were not always considered in these families.

Accidents with some elements of forewarning: *Accidents, both fatal and resulting in serious harm, occurring within a context of chronic long-term neglect, lack of supervision and an unsafe environment, 'an accident waiting to happen'.*

(Continued)

While the precise circumstances of accidents were often unpredictable, the reviews conveyed the sense that the risk of accidental harm from some source was high, due to either the precarious living conditions and/or the inadequate level of supervision. Environmental factors were relevant, such as families in high-rise, temporary accommodation where children were playing unsupervised.

Many serious case reviews referred to a lack of urgency in professional response to neglect cases, thresholds for services were deemed not to be met, assessments were delayed and poorly completed. Years could pass with the children's safety remaining compromised. [Professionals often] tacitly accepted domestic conditions ... which were hazardous to the child *(p58). High staff turnover and vacancy rates led to unallocated cases and overwhelming workloads, drift and confused responses. Professionals seemed to interpret children's behaviour as happy or playful when they were in fact living in hazardous environments and showed poor development (Brandon, et al., 2013, Pemberton, 2013).*

Prior to a strategy meeting, and as part of a section 47 (CA 1989) investigation, information is sought from other agencies. A teacher may have noticed other indicators of neglect such as the child's lunch box containing little food, or a child not being dressed appropriately for the weather, or having little concentration in class. The housing department may have information about environmental health issues such as complaints from neighbours about rubbish or infestations. Probation or police may know about family members with criminal histories relevant to the care of the child or of domestic violence or substance misuse in the home. Health professionals may have the early history of the child, even pre-birth, which has been shown to be particularly relevant to the assessment of neglect (Reder, et al., 1993). As well as professionals close to the world of the child, it is often neighbours, relatives and friends who have a wealth of information and if they report neglect their voices should be heard. Allegations may be malicious, but checks must be made on their authenticity. In a section 47 (CA 1989) investigation it is not necessary to obtain parental permission for making these checks although it is good practice to do so if this does not place the child at further risk of harm.

The case may be stepped down if there are few concerns, or a section 47 (CA 1989) investigation will lead to decisions regarding formal interviews of the child and family, paediatric assessments, a child protection conference or other protective action such as a legal order to remove the child to safety.

If police are pursuing a criminal investigation, it will be important for them to obtain forensic evidence such as photographs, medical evidence of any impact of the neglect, items of clothing or bedding, mobile phone messages and e-mails. They may also need to interview witnesses such as siblings or neighbours to see if they corroborate the child's statement or other evidential findings. Social workers can assist police by being aware of these possibilities and making sure that they preserve such evidence and do not contaminate what may become a crime scene. Police may want to interview the parent under caution as a suspect. Any social work interview of the parent must be agreed with police to make sure that there is no interference with the criminal investigation. It is essential to obtain the view of the child who would usually be interviewed on their own.

The child's view may not be the same as their best interests. A carer may have told them what to say to keep professionals at a distance and the child's view may not reflect the degree of risk as, for instance, they may be trying to protect a vulnerable parent. Children repeatedly neglected may define their situation as normal and on interview present as confident and content with their lives. It is important to remember that children often retract initial allegations about abuse and a child who has complained at school about being hungry or cold at home might state the very next day that everything is fine. Social workers must be vigilant that the rule of optimism, which is the overwhelming desire to think that the child is unharmed, does not prevent them being open to the possibility that the child is suffering significant harm. In the case of Paul, who died in 1993 aged 14 months, despite gaining reports of the children's extremely neglectful home conditions, social workers defined them as a *dirty but happy*, loving family with their problems mainly stemming from housing conditions (Bridge Child Care Consultancy Service, 1995).

ACTIVITY 4.2

Do you think the following are signs of neglect:

- *obesity;*
- *not having a child vaccinated;*
- *lack of age-appropriate toys;*
- *poor attendance at school or nursery;*
- *global developmental delay;*
- *frequent out-of-hours GP consultations;*
- *frequent hospital admissions;*
- *poor concentration or learning;*
- *speech delay;*
- *poor self-care;*
- *involuntary urinating/ soiling;*
- *non-attendance for medical appointments?*

(Continued)

COMMENT

More children are overweight in more unequal countries (Wilkinson and Pickett, 2009). Obesity may be the result of neglect if a carer continually feeds a child inappropriate foods and takes no notice of medical advice. The child may be defined as at considerable risk of significant harm because of the medical and psychological risks. But there are other reasons for obesity such as medical conditions or depression. A child may choose to look obese in order to change their body image and appear unattractive to a child sex abuser or in response to emotional harm.

Parents have a right to refuse immunisations for their children. This is a clear matter for parental choice and in itself is not a child protection concern. Severe dental decay may indicate neglectful parenting but it may be the parent has been misinformed about a certain food and drink which causes dental decay. If a parent did not seek medical advice and refused to provide the child with treatment, this would be evidence of neglect. Frequent hospital admissions could indicate a parent who is very anxious and seeking support about their child's health. Perhaps they had a previous child who died or was seriously ill and a plan to support them could be put into place.

Neglect – the evidence

- In 2014, 20,970 children were the subject of a child protection plan under the category of neglect. Neglect comprised the largest category (DfE, 2014b).

- In Radford, et al.'s (2011, p43) study, neglect was the most prevalent type of abuse. This equates to five per cent for those under 11 years, 13 per cent for those of 11–17 years and 16 per cent of those 18 years and over who said they were neglected during their childhood.

- Police recorded 9,516 cruelty and neglect offences against children under 16 years in the UK in 2013–14 (Jutte, et al., 2015, p30).

- Neglect is a serious factor in the majority of serious case reviews (60 per cent) and for children of all ages, not only younger children (Brandon, et al., 2012a).

- A quarter of the children who had died of neglect had died as a result of physical assault (Brandon, et al., 2013, p10).

- 1,016 children called ChildLine about neglect issues between 2014 and 2015 (NSPCC, 2015).

- 70 per cent of children who had run away had not been reported as missing (Rees, 2011).

- On average each young offender institution provides only 12 hours of education for children per week (CRAE, 2014, p96).

- 2.6 million children in the UK are living with parental alcohol misuse (Turning Point, 2011).

- A history of neglect ran through almost all the cases of young suicide in serious case reviews (Brandon, et al., 2013, p70).

- There are between 250,000 and 350,000 children of parents who misuse drugs in the UK (ACMD, 2011).

- More than 43,000 homeless households with dependent children were living in temporary accommodation at the end of June 2013 (Shelter, 2013).

- Of a poll of 2,000 parents, a quarter said children were more likely to be neglected during school holidays; 15 per cent had cared for a child they thought was being neglected (Action for Children: https://yougov.co.uk/news/2011/08/09/neglect-summer-holidays/).

- Ofsted (2014a) found that social workers had high thresholds for intervention and gave too many chances to parents to demonstrate their good care of the child often in the face of substantial evidence to the contrary.

CASE STUDY

Daniel Pelka – 'invisible' to professional networks

The serious case review described Daniel as *invisible* because

much of the detail which emerged from witness statements and the criminal trial about the level of abuse which Daniel suffered was completely unknown to the professionals who were in contact with the family ... his poor language skills and isolated situation meant that there was often a lack of a child focus to interventions by professionals ... At times he was treated as inhuman, and the level of helplessness he must have felt in such a terrifying environment would have been overwhelming.

(CSCB, 2013, pp6 and 34)

When [Daniel's stepfather] was too much drinking, my brother had a cold bath and I asked [stepfather] to stop it ... I got my brother from the bath and I pulled the plug out and I hugged him ... I was downstairs, I heard him screaming. I came upstairs and asked [stepfather] to stop it, and he stopped it ... [stepfather] didn't bother to look after him properly. He didn't even give him food or clean him. He didn't let him go to the toilet. ... I had to make food for him. He pooed and weed in his bed and I have to clean him up. [Daniel's mother] would ask how many pieces of toast I wanted. I would say two and go upstairs really quietly and give it to [Daniel]. He was not allowed to come downstairs.

(Dimmer, 2013)

On the night Daniel died his sister described that she... *tried to wake him up but I couldn't. Then I tried to listen for his heartbeat but I could not hear anything.* These statements from Daniel's sister were presented at the trial. She tried to protect Daniel and at the same time was expected to cover up the abuse by explaining his injuries as accidental to the school.

(Continued)

On 3 March 2012, Daniel, aged 4 years and 8 months, died of a head injury which was almost certainly the result of a direct blow to his head. The forensic pathologist concluded that there had been longstanding neglect as Daniel was grossly malnourished and dehydrated with over 40 injuries and bruising all over his body. For a period of at least six months prior to his death Daniel had been starved, assaulted, neglected and weighed just 10 kg. Both his mother and her partner were convicted of murder. Daniel had an older sibling aged 7 years and a younger sibling aged 1 year. The apparent good care of the other children by Daniel's mother may have given professionals a false sense of reassurance that she was not harming Daniel.

There was no record of any conversation with Daniel about his home life or his relationship with his family. Daniel was subjected to torture including putting him in cold baths, holding his head under water until he passed out and force-feeding him salt. He was made to do military-style endurance punishments such as sit-ups, standing in corners, squatting and running on the spot. Denied food, he was kept locked in a filthy room from which the door handle had been removed from the inside. This room had no furniture, smelt of urine, had a soiled mattress and was cold. Daniel was the scapegoat of the family.

As Daniel's mother had not worked for a year in England the family were not entitled to benefits including for housing or free school meals. This fact was not taken into account in any assessment where its impact on Daniel and his siblings should have been considered. He knew little spoken English and school staff relied on his gesticulations and on his sister or his mother to interpret for him. He was noted by school staff to engage in ritualistic behaviours such as cutting paper into small pieces for long periods, to be isolated, to have poor attendance and to look in bins for food.

His mother told teachers that Daniel had health problems and was a secret eater with an excessive appetite and when seen, just three weeks before his death by a paediatrician, a health cause was thought likely. Explanations went unquestioned and a key professional error in the case was an unwillingness to define the mother as abusive.

Police had records of 27 incidents of domestic abuse, with three different partners, including evidence of serious misuse of alcohol and violence towards the mother. *What is clear was that these children lived in a climate of arguing, fighting and drunkenness* (CSCB, 2013, p30). Police conducted *safe and well* checks but showed little understanding of the children's situation or of investigating the risks to the children in situations of parental conflict. The children had also experienced frequent house changes and contact with different professionals.

Daniel had a history of physical injuries for which the mother provided various explanations which were too readily accepted by the social worker. The paediatrician was concerned at delay in bringing Daniel to the hospital. High workloads for social workers and understaffing were a factor in poor decision making, but the possibility of child abuse was not fully explored. The serious case review referred to the *rule of optimism ... in these conditions workers focus on adult strengths, rationalise evidence to the contrary and interpret data in the light of this optimistic view* (CSCB, 2013, p43). The review also stated that social work assessments showed a level of naivety and lack of analysis, and did not take into account the cumulative effect of a series of incidents and pieces of information (CSCB, 2013, p47–48; Morris, 2013).

Neglect of disabled children

About seven per cent (0.9 million) of children under 16 years are disabled, meaning they have a long-standing illness or impairment which causes substantial difficulty with day-to-day activities. Parental isolation, as well as stigma, discrimination and financial pressures, contribute to the break-up of one-fifth of families (Contact a Family, 2011). All disabled children are likely to experience housing difficulties, especially overcrowding and inaccessible kitchens, toilets and bathrooms. The *great majority of families of disabled children reported that their homes were unsuitable* (Beresford and Rhodes, 2012, p2). Four out of ten disabled children were living in poverty – a total of 320,000 children. Of these more than one-third lived in extreme poverty. Half of disabled children living with a disabled adult lived in poverty. Many families did not access their full benefit entitlement (The Children's Society, 2011). Carers' rights have been strengthened within the Children and Families Act 2014. Local authorities have a duty to provide assessments to carers of disabled children if it appears that the parent/carer has needs, or the parent/carer requests an assessment.

Disabled children are nearly four times more likely to be neglected than non-disabled children. Children with special educational needs (SEN) are 17.9 per cent of the school-age population and are children with a learning difficulty or a disability who require specific educational provision. Children with SEN, long-standing illness or disability are more likely to experience multiple forms of abuse (Radford, et al., 2011).

Out of a sample of 47 serious case reviews, five per cent concerned disabled children with issues mainly relating to neglect and delayed medical treatment (Brandon, et al., 2008, p39). Disabled children still enter care because of their impairment, suggesting a failure to gain support before this becomes necessary. Mencap (2013) reported eight out of ten families had reached breaking point because of a lack of short breaks which were reduced by local authority cuts despite this being a requirement (CRAE, 2014, p16). Children rarely have an opportunity to socialise with other children who are not disabled (Aiden, et al., 2014).

Disabled children are neglected through a lack of resources and support services, particularly for black and minority ethnic disabled children and their families. Little evidence has been found of the children's wishes and feelings being ascertained. Communication difficulties may make it difficult for a disabled child to tell others about abuse or present evidence in court. *These factors taken together increase their vulnerability and make them targets for abusers since the risk of disclosure is low and the risk of a successful prosecution even lower* (Utting, 2005, p83). Disabled children should not be separated from their parents on the basis of their disability, yet they continue to be over-represented in care systems (UN, 2006). Children with learning disabilities, dyslexia and Attention Deficit Hyperactive Disorder (ADHD) are also significantly over-represented in young offender institutions and their needs are not identified (Murray and Osborne, 2009, p30).

A number of barriers can get in the way of protection for disabled children. *Children are left in situations where there is a high level of neglect … because a professional feels the parent, carer or service is doing their best* (Brandon, et al., 2013, p76). Sympathy with the family may lead to collusion and signs of abuse may be attributed to impairment rather than to neglect. Social workers unfamiliar with a child's needs may over-rely on the main carer for information (Stalker, et al., 2010), therefore specialist advice may be necessary (Murray and Osborne, 2009).

The following indicators of neglect are particularly relevant to disabled children:

- denial of access to food;
- neglect of basic health and hygiene needs such as hair washing;
- failure to provide means of communication;
- keeping a child apart from the family, locked in a room, confined to a buggy, bed or cot;
- misuse of medication;
- not keeping health appointments;
- ill-fitting equipment such as splints;
- abusive behaviour modification through deprivation of food, liquid, clothing;
- not acknowledging a child's impairment or having unrealistic expectations;
- treatment without pain relief;
- invasive procedures without consent (see Wonnacott, et al., 2013).

Systems designed to protect all children may fail disabled children because of a division between specialist disability and children's teams (Murray and Osborne, 2009). Disabled children are seldom involved in child protection conferences and are less likely to be defined as credible witnesses by police with insufficient use of intermediaries (Stalker, et al., 2010). Considerable benefits were found in facilitating communication in court when intermediaries were used (Plotnikoff and Woolfson, 2008). A study of three serious case reviews described a lack of reporting of concerns and poor knowledge and experience of staff working with disabled children (DfES, 2006b).

In 12 local authorities, Ofsted (2012b) reported that disabled children too often had unidentified child protection needs, but when child protection concerns were identified they generally gained protection. When concerns were less clear children experienced delays in protective intervention. The report found that advocacy was rarely considered or used. Deaf children's needs are specifically not well served by dis-ability teams (Young, et al., 2009). Franklin and Knight (2012) recommend advocacy to assist disabled children's participation.

Neglect of children at different ages

ACTIVITY 4.3

Social workers sometimes think that children are more vulnerable to abuse at particular ages. At what age do you think children are more likely to experience neglect?

COMMENT

Neglect featured evenly across the age groups in a study of serious case reviews, but was much more common for children of 11–15 years (Brandon, et al., 2013, p39). Evidence of serious neglect also applies to older children. Hicks and Stein (2013) ask for a re-examination of current definitions of neglect in the light of age-related distinctions and perspectives, and a fuller understanding of the particular needs of adolescents who are experiencing neglect. More knowledge is needed about neglectful parenting and effective intervention to protect older children.

In the UK an estimated 1 in 50 children are forced to leave home before the age of 16 years. These children are unlikely to receive services and are more aptly described as throwaways. Once on the street they are at great risk of neglect and serious harm. One in seven is hurt or harmed and one in nine sexually assaulted. About 70 per cent of children who run away overnight were not reported as missing (Rees, 2011). Children over age 16 years are not protected by some legislation in the same way as younger children. It has been suggested that the Children and Young Persons Act 2008 needs amending to ensure that older children living at home would have the same protection as younger children. The Housing Act 2004 should also be amended to ensure 16–17 year olds at risk of homelessness can never be evicted and be defined as intentionally homeless. Children over 16 should also be included in the remit for CAMHS provision as a right (Pona, et al., 2015).

Neglect – specific forms and contexts

Faltering growth

Although guidance (DfE, 2015) does not specify faltering growth in children, this condition may very well be caused by neglect. Faltering growth is defined as when weight, height and head circumference of the child are significantly below age-related norms or the rate of increase is of concern. Unless there is reason for immediate protection of the child, child protection procedures will usually only begin when a paediatrician has decided that the cause is non-organic (i.e. when a child's growth and development are not what would be expected in relation to normal mile-stones and this lack of development is not due to genetic or physical causes).

Some faltering growth may be caused through under-stimulation as well as poor feeding. Percentile or growth charts are an essential tool in monitoring the development of children and for assessing changes when the children are in different environments. Health professionals should present percentile charts at child protection meetings where a health analysis is needed about the child's height, weight and head circumference over time.

Social and economic inequality and neglect

Poor children are more likely to eat unhealthy foods; live in substandard, insecure and unsafe housing; have fewer places to play; be worried about household finances and their parents' health and mental health; try to hide their poverty from others; and do less well at school. Poverty impacts on the child's right to be safe, to be educated and to be healthy.

(CRAE, 2014, p58)

Social and economic inequalities are matters of life and death for children. Countries that spend more on social protection have lower child mortality rates. The messages are stark and crucial. Poverty kills children ... Equity saves lives.

(Wolfe, et al., 2014, p24)

RESEARCH SUMMARY

In a survey about poverty 2,000 children responded. Of children who defined themselves as not well off:

- *76 per cent said they worried about how much money there was in the family;*

- *53 per cent said they do not have enough space and their home was too cold;*

- *26 per cent said damp or mould was a problem;*

- *55 per cent said they felt embarrassed and 14 per cent had experienced bullying (Pople, et al., 2013).*

When families do not have enough to live on, children have a right to financial support from the government in order to enjoy a standard of living which will meet their basic needs, in particular with regard to food, clothing and housing (UN, 1989, Articles 26 and 27). There are currently 3 million children living in poverty in the UK (The Children's Society, 2014).

Sixty per cent of poor families were cutting back on food, 17 per cent of children went without new clothes and one-third of children living in poverty in England were not entitled to free school meals (Whitham, 2012). The number of children living in families with multiple vulnerabilities is set to increase dramatically owing to changes in the benefit system and cuts in public services (Reed, 2012; CRAE, 2014). Increased parental employment does not automatically move children out of poverty but moves them from low income workless households to low income working households (CRAE, 2014). Since 2010, there have been wide-ranging benefit cuts severely affecting disabled children (OCC, 2013). Babies from poorer families are more likely to be born with low birth weight and to die than children from richer families. Child outcomes are related to income inequality in rich countries such as the UK. These include higher infant mortality, lower birth weight, overweight children, lower educational achievement, poor peer relations, more bullying and more teenage births (Wolfe, et al., 2014; Wilkinson and Pickett, 2009).

Neglect is often located within disadvantaged communities, yet these families are more visible to the authorities and therefore more likely to be assessed for services than children of wealthier families. The eradication of poverty would ease stress on poor families but neglect is to do with modes of thought and behaviour rather than experiences of poverty (McSherry, 2004). Therefore, ending poverty would not lead to ending child neglect.

Separation: Child migrants

I was told I was going on a picnic.

I was told I would ride on horseback to school and pick fruit from the trees.

We can't give them back their childhoods but allowing them at least to be able to say who their parents were, perhaps meet cousins, hear stories, understand the very few vague memories they may have is huge.

(Rhodes, 2015)

The very first UK child migrants were sent in 1618 to Virginia in the United States and the last in 1970 to Australia (Bean and Melville, 1989). It is estimated that child migration programmes were responsible for the removal of over 130,000 children from the UK to Canada, New Zealand, Zimbabwe (formerly Rhodesia) and Australia although government statistics are woefully lacking in accuracy. Children were sent by specialist agencies and well-known charities to populate the empire with 'good, white British stock'. Many of the children lived in large institutions and were used as cheap labour suffering abuse, cruelty and neglect. As early as 1882, Dr Barnardo was sending to Australia, New Zealand and Canada *young people of good physique, trained to make use of their hands, of tested moral character, of an age where they were easily adaptable with few home or family ties to bind them to the mother country* (Williams, 1943, p118).

Margaret Humphreys, a social worker from Nottingham, established the Child Migrant's Trust (www.childmigrantstrust.com/) and has struggled to obtain justice for the survivors of this wide-scale trafficking programme. Her book *Empty Cradles*

(Humphreys, 1996) was the subject of the film *Oranges and Sunshine* (2010). Many child migrants had no idea who their birth families were or the reason why they were sent to the colonies and their parents were not told what had happened to their children. A child migrant survivor stated that they were deported to a prolific, predatory group of child sex offenders with a long history of abusing young, vulnerable boys.

Baby-trafficking from Ireland is described in the book *Banished Babies. The children involved in Ireland's transatlantic adoptions were frequently referred to as 'orphans' and the institutions they came from as ' orphanages' yet almost without exception they were the children of unmarried mothers, 'illegitimate' children in the stigmatizing language of the day … the practice continued for 20 years … It was organized by nuns with full official sanction* (Milotte, 1997, p15). The film *Philomena* (2013) presented the story of a woman who searched for 50 years for her forcibly adopted son who was sold by the Catholic Church from Ireland to North America (Sixsmith, 2010). The story of child migrants is a current survivor campaign. The children were exploited for political and economic reasons and the practice went unchallenged for decades.

Children in the midst of parental divorce and separation

When parents are separating, children's needs and wishes can become lost within the parental conflict. In 2014, 90,000 children were involved in new cases in the Family Courts (Bowcott, 2015). Of the 118,140 couples divorcing in England and Wales in 2012, 48 per cent had at least one child under 16 years. Children rarely have a voice in what happens after their parents separate. Children may experience the same emotions as a parent at these times, such as loss, grief, guilt and a sense of abandonment. Although the vast majority of separating parents do not wish to harm their children, many do as they become preoccupied with their difficulties.

Changes in legislation are intended to reduce delays and public costs. The Children and Families Act 2014 made the presumption that both parents will continue to be involved in their child's life where consistent with the child's welfare. Also, parents applying for divorce, judicial separation or an end to a civil partnership are now required to attend mediation before going to court, but there is no right for children to take part. One young person reported, *In my case, I had to wait 4 years before my voice was heard and I was considered to be too young to know my own mind or listened to individually and simply just lumped together with my younger sister* (Bowcott, 2015).

Children aged over 10 have direct access to judges in family cases to make their views and feelings known (Hughes, 2014). However, children now have less access to legal representation in their own right because of changes in the legal aid system. Legal aid is only allowed in cases which involve domestic violence or child abuse (CRAE, 2014).

The National Youth Advisory Service (NYAS) offers independent advocacy to children in situations of parental conflict if a child feels unsafe, unheard or unfairly treated and in need of advice (www.nyas.net). However, a majority of local authorities have reduced by half their spending on youth advocacy services (CRAE, 2014).

Brothers and sisters separated in the care system

I'm too young to go by myself.

They are too far away.

I do not know where they are.

There is no one to go with me.

It costs too much to go to see them.

(A National Voice, 2006, p4)

The level of sibling separation in care is a national scandal ... as without family net-works, children in care are likely to have poorer life outcomes and contribute less to society. This could be avoided with better planning and multi-agency collaboration between government, local authorities, fostering agencies, social services and chari-ties like ourselves.

(www.siblingstogether.co.uk)

During 2014, 71 per cent of looked after children with a sibling in the care sys-tem were separated from a brother or sister, and for those in residential homes the figure was considerably higher at 95 per cent (Morgan, 2014). In the absence of parents, siblings provide a continuity of care strengthening family bonds and stability which promotes their welfare. *Siblings Together* estimates that there are approximately 40,000 children in care who are separated from brothers and sisters who are also in care, and a further 4,000 children entering care who are separated from siblings each year.

Sometimes there is a reason for sibling separation because it might be in the child's best interests, for instance when a relationship is abusive, when there are timescale pressures or a lack of expertise inhibiting proper assessment, and some-times there is a shortage of foster carers or homes willing to take sibling groups (CSJ, 2015).

Institutional and organisational neglect

In 2015, the charity Article 39 estimated the number of children in England living in institutional settings to be 80,000 (www.article39.org.uk/). This includes children in independent boarding schools, residential care settings, hospitals, mental health wards, custody and immigration detention. Based on data provided by local councils, research concluded that there were 3.34 confirmed cases of abuse by staff for every 100 children in residential care in England in 2011/12. There were 15.41 abuse allega-tions per 100 children during this same period (Biehal, et al., 2014).

Neglect may also be a form of secondary abuse. This is abuse caused by the sys-tems designed to protect children. Key examples of such neglect are children abused within institutions or while in care. Frampton provides an account of his childhood in care in the 1960s, which he describes as *the social dustbin* and as chronic neglect. *I unconsciously but stubbornly followed my instincts, side stepping danger, drawing back from cliff edges, unsafe situations and unsafe people* (Frampton, 2004, p235).

Most children in care will have lived in more than one placement. In 2013–14, 7,500 children in care experienced three or more placement moves, 5,000 experienced five or more moves and 1,500 experienced ten or more moves (Ofsted, 2014b, p24). Also, more than a third of children were placed outside their home locality and one-sixth lived more than 20 miles away (CRAE, 2014, p40; Biehal, et al., 2014, p70; Ofsted, 2015). The care system may not always provide the high standard of care required; however, this factor must never deter professionals from being prepared to remove children from harmful situations.

In 1991, Frank Beck received five life sentences for sexual and physical assaults against children between 1973 and 1986 in children's homes in Leicestershire. His regime involved so-called regression therapy, which included the humiliation of children and promotion of aggression which resulted in restraint.

> *The kids were in their early teens – the older kids had drinks in bottles with dummies. It was an attempt to dig down to the supposed roots of children's problems by returning them to a state of infancy. Younger children might be dressed in nappies. Social workers might cut up the food on their plates as if feeding infants. Children would be given toys designed for younger children ... children were provoked into violent temper tantrums, physically restrained ... and sometimes choked around the neck with a towel ... children were dressed and undressed by staff, kept in pyjamas for days.*

> (D'Arcy and Gosling, 1998, pp8 and 28)

The abusive regime illustrates *the way in which theoretical labels and concepts were used to confer credibility and intellectual respectability on abusive practices* (Stanley, et al., 1999, p20).

Children in custody

The child custody population at the end of July 2015 was 1,003, which includes 37 girls. Willow (2014, p8) describes a large reduction in the number of detained children although the UK remains one of the main incarcerators of children in Europe. Despite the reduction, Ofsted's (2015) assessment of children in care shows that those from black and minority ethnic communities are more likely to be locked up. They represented 41 per cent of the 453 children in care, or held in secure units or prisons on 31 March 2014. Girls comprise four per cent of the detained child population and in 2013 the government announced it would stop sending them to prison. Of all child prisoners, 96 per cent are between the ages of 15 and 17 years. Between 2012 and 2013, less than a quarter were imprisoned for crimes of violence, just five per cent for sexual offences and 13 children for the offence of murder (Willow, 2014, p42).

The young age of children entering the adult court system has led to concern that children lack understanding of adult court processes, that they share transport, custody suites and waiting rooms with adult defendants and are subjected to professionals who lack training in work with children (CRAE, 2014, p93). Of specific concern is the transportation of children from court to prisons in security vans for long journeys, often late at night and without adequate food, drink or toilet facilities. Willow reports the use of gel bags given to children who needed the toilet during the journey (2014, p205) and the continued use of handcuffs on children being taken to hospital or funerals.

The age of criminal responsibility is the age at which children can be legally prosecuted for a crime. In England this is ten years. It is believed that *children aged 10 are able to differentiate between bad behaviour and serious wrongdoing and it is right they should be held accountable for their actions* (HM Government, 2014, p55). However, the UNCRC (UN, 1989) has consistently recommended that this age should be raised and replaced by a welfare approach. Willow comments that an analysis of the forms completed when a child enters the criminal justice system showed that more than a third of girls have been abused and many experienced bereavement or witnessed family violence (Willow, 2014, p10).

The UNCRC (UN, 1989) states that children can be deprived of their liberty as a last resort but do not then lose other human rights such as food, education, health care, religious observance and family contact. They should be placed close to their families unless this is not in their best interests, yet in March 2013 most children in custody were placed on average 45.6 miles from their home. It is unacceptable that children can be deprived of family visits as a punishment for poor behaviour (CRAE, 2014, p95). There is much concern about chronic societal neglect of children in custody.

An inspection of a Staffordshire prison, where 119 children were detained, stated that *cells were filthy, gloomy, covered in graffiti and contained offensive material, heavily scaled toilets, damaged furniture and smashed observation panels. Many of the cells holding children on their first night were in an uninhabitable state and there were 44 cells with double occupancy* (HMIP, 2014, p33). Other inspection reports described beds close to toilets and that boys sometimes had less than 15 minutes daily exercise outside (Willow, 2014). In 2013, an inspection of Feltham young offender institution described wide-scale physical decay and squalor as well as violence. It found a third of children had reported victimisation by staff and 300 violent acts perpetrated by children against other children within a six-month period (HMIP, 2013) Children referred to being hungry with long periods between meals. A British Medical Association report (2014) noted that children's mental health needs were unmet in custody and systems for accessing medical care were limited (OCC, 2011).

Youth homelessness

That was my biggest worry … her sleep and rest. She never got to bed at the time she needed to be in bed. Even if I could get her into bed she couldn't fall asleep because it was the time people were making such a big noise in the B&B.

The toilet was through the communal area which was shared by us and the other family.

The kids wouldn't want to use the toilet. They'd sit there and hold it in saying they don't want to go.

It was such a small room as soon as you got a couple of toys out you were tripping over them. The kitchen area wasn't guarded off and Poppy had an accident. I didn't know where the nearest hospital was.

You have 12sqm and have to spend all your time in this space. It was horrible – especially at weekends. We didn't want to open the door because the house was full of strangers.

There was no space to play at all. They had a garden but there was rubbish and debris everywhere.

(Shelter, 2013, p5)

There is a lack of local government strategies for homeless young people. Changes in the benefit system have led to an increase in homelessness and family displacement. At the end of June 2013, more than 11,100 homeless households in temporary accommodation were placed in another local authority's area leading to severe disruption to the lives of children (BBC, 2015f).

Secure and adequate housing is a right under the UNCRC (UN, 1989, Article 27). Homeless children are more likely to have mental health problems and be absent from school (CRAE, 2014). Local authorities are legally required to find accommodation for homeless families with children, 16 and 17 year olds who are not living with their families and care leavers. However, at the end of June 2015, 100,000 children in England were living in temporary accommodation with more than 2,500 in bed and breakfast, and 830 had been there for over six weeks (BBC, 2015f). This negatively affects children's health, education and family life. Families are living in crowded bedrooms, often with no cooking facilities, and are forced to share bathrooms with strangers. Families report that their children have nowhere to do homework and have witnessed disturbing incidents, including threats of violence, sexual offences and drug misuse (Shelter, 2013).

CRAE have produced a factsheet, *Children's Human Rights and Housing,* available at: www.crae.org.uk/publications-resources/childrens-human-rights-and-housing/

RESEARCH SUMMARY

In 2011, a survey of 7,349 children aged 14–16 years, found prevalence rates of 8.9 per cent had run away overnight on one occasion and 6.2 per cent had run away overnight in the last 12 months. This equated to an estimated prevalence rate of 74,000 children in England who run away overnight each year at least once. In terms of incidence, 36 per cent ran away once, 33 per cent more than once and 22 per cent on more than three occasions leaving an estimate of 100,000 incidents of running away each year. Included in the survey were 90 children who lived in care and ran away far more often.

The survey reported that more than 18,000, aged 14 to 15 years, who run away overnight each year were either hurt or harmed while away. A third of the children had run away before the age of 13 years. On the only or most recent occasion, 11 per cent of the children said they had been hurt while away from home. 18 per cent said they stayed with someone they did not know and nine per cent said they had begged. There were strong connections between family change, poverty and running away. The children were more likely than other children to be depressed, have poor school attendance, misuse alcohol and drugs and be in trouble with police (Rees, 2011).

Research into 216 homeless children in four European countries; UK, Portugal, Netherlands and the Czech Republic found that prior to becoming homeless nearly half had run away on more than one occasion and many were not reported missing. They said that what might have made a difference was if their parents had been supported. Especially in the UK and the Netherlands, children said they had been brought up by a single parent and this was the result of the death of a parent or separation, which left one of the parents (in most cases, the mother) with responsibility for raising the children. In many families, the arrival of a new partner or step-parent created new tensions precipitating the child leaving the family home.

Overall, 85 per cent reported stress prior to leaving their last permanent home, and in the UK 12 per cent reported having attempted suicide and 20 per cent reported self-harming. However, after leaving home both suicide attempts and self-harm fell to five per cent. There was a marked decrease in most of their mental health problems but trouble sleeping was the one experience that appeared to remain the same or increase after leaving home (Smith, et al., 2015; CSEYHP, 2010).

Children who go missing

There is a scandal going on in England involving children missing from care – and until recent cases of child sexual exploitation in Rochdale and other places put the spotlight on this issue – it was going on pretty much unnoticed. Going missing is a key indicator that a child might be in great danger. About 10,000 children go missing from care every year.

(APPG, 2012)

In a period of 5 years children went missing from council care in south-west England more than 350 times. A child of 6 years was missing 4 days and a teenager 529 days. Many children, mostly teenagers, went missing on multiple occasions.

(BBC, 2015g)

Sixty per cent of trafficked children in care go missing, a third within a week of arrival, and most are never found. They are frightened to report what is happening and are subject to multiple forms of exploitation (CSJ, 2013, p24).

Children from care who had run away were interviewed and gave accounts of a punitive response from residential workers with little evidence of sympathy or a desire to know what caused them to go missing.

They look at you as if you are a piece of shit on the bottom of their shoe.

They put you in a room and shut the doors to stop you getting out and they restrain you.

They hid my shoes, like I went out in socks and she put ketchup in my shoes.

They should say 'why did you run away? Is there a problem?'

(Taylor, et al., 2012, pp7–12)

Martin Allen went missing in 1979. His family continue to appeal for information about him and believe him to have been abducted as part of a child sex abuse network (Gill, 1984). Better known cases include Madeleine McCann, who went missing in 2003 in Portugal, and Ben Needham, who went missing in 1991 on the Greek Island of Kos. Although some missing children gain news coverage, most remain unknown and there are no statistics for the numbers who are not found. Ofsted reported that children went missing from foster care 13,305 times between 1 April 2013 and 31 March 2014, an increase of 36 per cent on the previous year. Almost 530 incidents were linked to sexual exploitation and 113 were missing longer than one week. It was the first time Ofsted had asked foster carers to record reasons for the disappearance of foster children (Hill, 2015b). *Turning one's gaze away from children apparently settled in long-term foster care is not acceptable* (Biehal, et al., 2014). An All Party Parliamentary Group (2012) reported into children who go missing from care and the findings led to the *Statutory guidance on children who run away or go missing from home or care* (DfE, 2014e). Part of this guidance is the Runaway and Missing From Home and Care Protocol (RMFCH) which includes the requirement for an independent person to interview the child within 72 hours of the child's return, and guidance about risk assessment. The charity Missing People (www.missingpeople.org.uk) offers advice and support.

A serious case review (OSCB, 2015, p17) reported that in the context of a network sexually exploiting children in Oxford, even police did not see children going missing as the result of organised abuse and accepted the children's explanations of being with friends. The six girl victims were reported missing between one and 193 times mainly while in the care system (p38).

Abducted children

Article 35 (UN, 1989) states that children have a right to protection from being abducted or sold. A study of over 500 UK cases showed that 17 per cent were taken by parents, 2 per cent by other family members, 35 per cent by someone known but unrelated and 42 per cent by strangers. Most victims are girls under the age of 12 years and are abducted in the absence of their carers. In 95 per cent of attempted abductions by strangers it was not possible to see a clear motive and in the majority of cases children went willingly with the abductor after being offered a ride in a car or being engaged in conversation (Newiss and Traynor, 2013). It has been estimated that at least one child out of 600 will experience an actual abduction by a stranger (Gallagher, et al., 2008). Child abduction warning notices need to be extended to children over 16 years to enable police to protect children of this age group targeted by perpetrators for sexual exploitation or other crime (Pona, et al., 2015).

Child Rescue Alert (www.childrescuealert.org.uk) is a system available throughout the UK which works by interrupting media channels regularly with news flashes that a child has been abducted, alerting the public to the incident immediately – asking them for vigilance and to call 999 with crucial information.

Unaccompanied asylum seeking children (UASC)

They helped me a lot. She was the first person I met in the social services. She came and picked me up [from the immigration office] and she took me to the foster carer and I used to receive calls all of the time – sometimes every day. And after that she used to come and meet me … At the time I couldn't speak English so they used to bring a translator for me. So they came just to ask me how I'm doing and make sure I'm ok. They helped me.

(OCC, 2014, p53)

Thousands of children are among the refugees fleeing Syria, Iraq, Somalia, Albania and Afghanistan. Hundreds of children of all ages have died during lengthy sea crossings in unsafe boats and dinghies, in the backs of trucks, on overcrowded trains and during the marches of hundreds of miles in an attempt to reach safety and stability. *So the boat – they are for three people, or five people. The agent, they put in about 20 people. And when they are moving there are some strong waves because of the weather. Some people they lose their lives* (OCC, 2014, p50).

In 2014, 1,861 children claimed asylum in the UK, seeking safety from countries where the state has caused them harm or has been unable to protect them (Refugee Council, 2015). An UASC is a child under the age of 18 years who is not living with their parent, relative or guardian in the UK and needs the care and protection of welfare services in the country of asylum while their claim is being examined and settled. In 2012, around a quarter of unaccompanied children claiming asylum in the UK were successful in obtaining refugee status while the remainder had their claims refused outright or were granted limited leave to remain until age 17½ (OCC, 2014, p9). Davies and Kerrigan Lebloch emphasise the importance of social workers using their authority to promote the rights of young refugees (2011).

When unaccompanied children arrive in the UK, following journeys spanning many months and often having stopped off in many different countries, they are unwell, severely traumatised, hungry and exhausted. An OCC (2012) report concerning the interview process on arrival of UASC in Dover found that they were met with a response of detention and interrogation. The Independent Chief Inspector of Borders and Immigration (Vine, 2013) found that decisions were not always based on the best interests of the child and there was no attempt to trace the child's family in the majority of cases. Although the UK government made a commitment to end the detention of children for immigration purpose, they continue to be detained in short-term holding facilities. The Prison's Inspectorate reported that, for children kept in detention, there were no dedicated child friendly interview rooms, sometimes no telephone was available and children were held for between 8 and 30 hours (HMIP, 2011). Of 136 unaccompanied children held at English ports between April and July 2013, 65 were held over 12 hours (Gower, 2014). Children have said that interviews were stressful and adversarial, and sometimes their accounts were met with disbelief from the interviewing officer (OCC, 2012, p12).

UK immigration officers are required to accept a local authority age assessment, but many children are defined wrongly as adults and then made destitute, detained or accommodated as adults. The Refugee Council (2014) secured the release from detention of 36 children wrongly defined as adults, some as young as 15 years, and raised serious concerns about the trauma to children (Refugee Council, 2014). However, numbers may be higher as there is no proper statistical analysis of unaccompanied children who were not defined as children by the Home Office and not referred to local authorities (Vine, 2013). There is no statutory guidance on age assessments and it is not an exact science but a matter of professional judgement. Physical appearance and demeanour do not determine age. Social workers should obtain information about the young person's life history and development. Some children provide inconsistent accounts because many societies calculate age differently from the UK and also because children may have been coached to state certain facts on arrival. *The first time you come they don't know you, you don't know them. 90% of people might not want to say the truth because for me I didn't know who they are or where I am* (OCC, 2014, p52).

Home Office statistics do not state clearly the numbers of dependent and unaccompanied children being deported/returned each year. The Minister for Security and Immigration in response to a parliamentary question showed that 3750 UASCs were returned to Afghanistan, Albania, Iran, Iraq, Libya and Syria between 2007–15, (Secretary of State for Home Department, 2016). A film, *Hamedullah: The road home,* follows the journey of a young person deported to Afghanistan from the UK. He is put on a chartered flight and visually records what happens when he lands and finds his family home destroyed in the war (Clayton, 2011). Between 2009 and 2015, over 600 young people over 18 years who had settled in the UK as UASC have been returned to Afghanistan as just one country defined as a safe place for return. Since 2013, 228 Afghan children have asked the Red Cross to help trace their families but only eight have been successful. Hakim, an UASC, spent six years in the UK after age 13. At 19 years he was returned to Afghanistan, where he was unable to find his family and lived in a derelict warehouse. *When I returned it was the worst situation of my life … I don't want to be kidnapped again. I don't want to be killed … here the security situation is getting worse day by day* (McClenaghan, 2015). Of returned children, many were born or spent most of their lives in the UK. They experience lost friendships and school disruption with no guarantee of protection in their own country. They may be punished with imprisonment, torture or murder.

There are an estimated 120,000 undocumented children in the UK who do not have leave to enter or remain in the UK (CRAE, 2014). The Legal Aid, Sentencing and Punishment of Offenders Act 2013 has meant that the vast majority of children, including those in care, can no longer access legal aid for immigration claims, *a lot of times in lessons I would be crying and asking 'Sir, can I take time off?' or maybe lie to my teachers and say I needed to go home where really I had to go get in contact with these immigration people* (Pinter, 2015, p10). Such children remain vulnerable as their status is unresolved, they must fend for themselves and become targets for exploitation and trafficking. Many local authorities have now closed their specialist asylum teams, which are much needed given the complex nature of the knowledge base and ever changing legislative context.

Families with no recourse to public funds

A House of Commons Education Committee expressed serious concern about the correlation between government policies on immigration and the incidence of destitution among asylum seeking and migrant children stating that, *it would be out-rageous if destitution were to be used as a weapon against children because of their immigration status* (HC 137:2, 2012–13, p42).

Asylum seeking families receive 70 per cent of income support benefits. They are not allowed to do paid work and are denied any legal means of providing for their families. Many are displaced to deprived parts of the UK where social infrastructures are poor. Asylum seeking children require educational, psychological and social support, yet these services have been drastically cut back (Hardwick and Hardwick, 2015, p285).

Social workers need to critically examine individual cases where parents have no recourse to public funds and assess the impact on children of this policy. While children have a right to protection from harm they also have a right to family life and must not be separated from their families unless there is evidence of child abuse and they are not being protected. Social workers may find themselves under pressure to remove children when parents are under threat of removal because they have been refused the right to remain in the country. Some parents are denied public funds because of their employment status and this also applies to women fleeing violence who may be denied a refuge place. In 2013, a parliamentary inquiry into asylum seeking children concluded that authorities were failing to meet the welfare needs of children and families who were being left destitute, living in poor accommodation and moving frequently with many school changes (Teather, et al., 2013).

The Refugee Council website (www.refugeecouncil.org.uk) provides lists of destitution support services as well as other resources for those with no recourse to public funds.

Children in the armed forces

Child Soldiers International [hold a vision of a world] where all children (boys and girls below the age of 18) can grow up under conditions that allow them to realise their full potential and enjoy their fundamental human rights. We believe that to achieve this, children must be protected from any form of military recruitment by armed forces or groups and involvement in armed conflict, as well as from other human rights abuses that occur in these environments.

(www.child-soldiers.org/about_us.php)

The statement below from *Working Together to Safeguard Children* (2010) about UK child soldiers has been omitted from *Working Together to Safeguard Children* (DfE, 2015), which focuses solely on the children of service families.

Looking after under-18s in the armed forces comes under the Ministry of Defence's (MoD) comprehensive welfare arrangements, which apply to all members of the armed forces. Commanding Officers are well aware of the particular welfare needs of younger recruits and trainees and, as stated above, are fully committed to co-operating with statutory and other agencies in safeguarding and promoting the welfare of under-18s. Local authority children's social care already has a responsi-bility to monitor the wellbeing of care leavers, and those joining the armed forces should have unrestricted access to local authority social care workers.

(DCSF, 2010, 2.177)

Children under 18 years may be in the armed forces as recruits or trainees, and may be stationed overseas or in the UK. More than one in ten new army recruits are boy soldiers of just 16 years, according to the MoD, and more than one in four of all new army recruits are under 18 years and therefore too young to be sent into com-bat, although this policy may be overruled if there is military need and by reason of the nature and urgency of the situation. There are more than 1,700 children in the armed forces. Many children begin the enlistment process at 15 years. The organisa-tion Child Soldiers International has concerns that targeting children for recruitment places them at risk of harm as they are more likely than adults to be bullied, to develop mental health problems, to be injured in training and to be killed once they reach the age where they can be in active service (Owen, 2014a). In 2015, the cam-paign ForcesWatch (www.ForcesWatch.net), which scrutinises the ethics of the armed forces youth recruitment practices, reported that the MoD had attempted to access personal information from the National Pupil Database in a bid to increase school age recruits. Through the creation of a mobile App it was aiming to promote army recruitment by matching a career profile to a career opportunity. The Department for Education refused to co-operate with this request.

When four army trainees died in 2006 in the barracks at Deepcut, Surrey, there were no serious case reviews on the two under the age of 18 years (Blake, 2006). Child recruits have a right to the same protection as other children in institutional settings, including a right to family contact, access to advocacy, the opportunity to raise child protection concerns with external agencies and external inspectors. If the recruits are care leavers they have a right to contact their social worker.

The four UK Children's Commissioners stated to Child Soldiers International (www.child-soldiers.org) that the recruiting of children breached the UNCRC.

The UK is the only state in Europe to recruit 16 year olds into the armed forces. We support the growing global consensus that the minimum age for entry into the armed forces in the UK should be raised, to 18, as children should not be involved in hostilities, either directly or indirectly, and to protect their mental health, education and long-term life chances, especially those in our most disadvantaged communities.

(Hellen, 2015)

Children trafficked for domestic labour

Trafficked children have been deprived of almost every right: the right to identity, to health, to education, to be safe, to be free – and are unlikely to be aware that they even have rights. When identified they need to be supported through child protection services. This support is often compromised by their uncertain immigration status.

(CRAE, 2014 p88)

As the weeks passed I became more and more depressed. I was a stranger to the children. I was completely isolated and alone. I stayed in the house and worked from early morning to late at night – unloved and uncared for. I was trapped in the middle of this strange city that I had been told was dark and dangerous. All I did was work, work, work. The only thing I looked forward to was sleeping in my cold room.

(Nazer and Lewis, 2004, p263)

Mende Nazer was a child slave in London trafficked from Sudan.

Trafficking involves the exploitation of children through force, coercion, threat and the use of deception and human rights abuses such as debt bondage, deprivation of liberty and lack of control over one's labour. Exploitation includes children being used for sex and sex work, domestic servitude, sweatshop and restaurant work, drug dealing and credit card fraud, begging or pickpocketing, benefit fraud, drug mules or decoys for drug traffickers, forced marriage, trade in human organs and in some cases ritual killings (LSCB, 2015, Part B:8). About 25 per cent of all UK trafficking victims are children who may be trafficked to the UK, within the UK or in transit through the UK to another country (such as Italy, Canada, the USA and Ireland) for financial gain. Some enter the UK as unaccompanied children or as students or visitors and may be brought in by adults claiming to be their carers as individuals or part of organised gangs. Once in care, children may be removed and abducted by the traffickers and go missing from protective systems.

Even when a child understands what has happened, they may still appear to submit willingly to what they believe to be the will of their parents. Children may be recruited to escape poverty, warfare, discrimination and/or a lack of education, with the parents not realising the risks to the child, but also parents may sell children for profit. Even before they travel, children can be subjected to abuse and exploitation to establish the trafficker's control over the child. The child's identity documents may be confiscated, the child may be locked up and isolated, and some are told that they must repay the debt of the air fare, accommodation and food and must work to pay this off. Belief systems are sometimes used to frighten children into thinking that if they tell anyone about the traffickers, they and their families will die.

The UK has set up a National Referral Mechanism to identify victims of trafficking (DfE, 2014d). In 2014, the Home Office launched a public awareness campaign (mod-ernslavery.co.uk). In 2015, the Modern Slavery Act consolidated previous legislation and introduced new offences for slavery, servitude, forced labour and human traf-ficking. The law made provision for child advocates and pilot schemes are in place. However, it failed to include a non-prosecution principle for trafficked children.

A comprehensive range of indicators are available on the London Safeguarding Children Board website (LSCB, 2015, Part B:8) and government guidance is available from *Safeguarding children who may have been trafficked* (DfE, 2011c). If traffick-ing is suspected, the police CAIT must be informed and a section 47 (CA 1989) joint investigation implemented. The child must be given a safe place to stay and be pro-vided with support and legal advice. Social workers must work with police to identify and prosecute traffickers and to locate safe relatives including in the country of origin. Children in care must be protected and monitored for signs of meeting traffickers such as through phone calls, sometimes by placing them in foster care outside the locality.

Victoria Climbié was taken by Kouao from her family in the Ivory Coast via France to London under a false name and passport. She stood to attention and was deferen-tial in the presence of Kouao (described as a master–servant relationship). Although Laming (2003) did not examine the possibility of Victoria having been trafficked in the inquiry, Garrett (2006) considered transnational migration as a core aspect of the tragedy of Victoria's death.

CASE STUDY

Hien, a victim of trafficking

Hien was 10 when he arrived in Britain in 2008, having been taken from his village aged 5 years. He spent five years travelling with someone who claimed to be his uncle and was forced for three years to cook and clean at a London house. Forced to drink alcohol, he was severely abused and told he had to stay to pay off family debts. He ran away and slept rough but later worked on cannabis farms in Manchester and Scotland. He had no idea what the plants were. He was unpaid, locked in and isolated, had to use pesticides which made him ill. Eventually he was prosecuted and sent to a young offender institution but was released after a crown prosecutor identified him as a victim. Hien remains worried that traffickers might come to his house and find him. It is estimated that about 3,000 children trafficked from Vietnam are in the UK being exploited by criminal gangs on can-nabis farms (Kelly and McNamara, 2015).

A child left at home alone

Being left alone in the house was scary. I never let on to my parents how scary, as I didn't want to disappoint them. But I was pretty terrified. I would lie in bed, wide awake, listening to the strange noises of the night, analysing every squeak and rustle, until I heard the welcome crunch of their car tyres on the driveway. (Sarah, 8 years)

(Hamilton, 2007)

A mother and aunt were convicted because they left a boy of 8 years alone until 1.00 am. He had left the house and they did not report him missing for six hours. The judge said: *I have heard a heart-rending account by the child where he describes being left alone but feels secure as he is with his teddy bears* (Parker, 2015).

There is no law stating at what age a child can be left at home alone. The Children and Young Persons Act 1933 applies to anyone over the age of 16 who has responsibility for a child under that age and wilfully neglects or exposes the child in a manner likely to cause unnecessary suffering or injury to health. For police to prosecute a parent, the situation has to be severe. Police statistics, for the last three months of 2014 in England and Wales, stated that 105 parents had been charged for leaving children alone. These included 30 cases of no further action, 24 parents who accepted a caution and 19 parents who were charged. The Crown Prosecution decision to charge is based on a range of criteria including age, the period of time and the potential dangers of the environment where they were left (Turner, 2015). Children of all ages are at risk from being left alone.

Social workers often make judgements about less clear situations of harm when deciding whether the child is in need of protection and if immediate action is indicated. Social workers must visit the home and make an assessment of living conditions – this will mean looking in the kitchen, bedroom and other rooms and outdoor space. Children in locked rooms is the most significant single factor in many cases where a child has died from abuse. Checks should be made for when handles have been removed from the inside of doors preventing the child leaving the room and where bolts are on the outside (Reder, et al., 1993).

It is usually police who first become aware of a child left alone, make an assessment of risk, intervene to protect and refer to children's services. Keeble provides an example from his practice of a police constable who found a baby tied to a cot who had been left alone for some time. The officer removed the baby and police powers of protection were in place. The baby was already the subject of a child protection plan.

'The problem was the social worker disagreed as to what we should do next.'

'I've interviewed the mother and she says that her daughter had got into the habit of climbing out of her cot and had almost fallen. The mother was just trying to make her secure by fastening her to the bars of the cot. The ties weren't taut.'

'And the excrement?' I asked.

'The child's nappy had simply been left too loose. There's no reason for us to remove the child'.

For some reason the social worker had 'decided to put a positive spin on the mother's interview when to me it was obvious the baby was in real danger'.

(Keeble and Hollington, 2010, p211)

CASE STUDY

Home alone

Being left alone may not reach a threshold of the crime of cruelty or civil standard of significant harm. For instance, one father said he went into a chemist's shop for just five minutes and left his child in the car and was later arrested. He won his case on appeal (Turner, 2015). At the other end of the spectrum it may be one sign among a cluster of very serious indicators of harm as in the following case.

Tiffany Wright, aged 3 years, died of starvation having been left alone in a room above a pub where her mother worked. Her leg and arm bones were marked with growth arrest lines meaning she had experienced long periods without food. She was likely to have been dead three days before emergency services were called. Insect larvae were found on her naked body which lay on a urine-soaked bed with no covers. In 2008, her mother, Sabrina, pleaded guilty to manslaughter and her partner to child cruelty and neglect. They both received prison sentences.

For DCI Powell the symbol of how badly Tiffany was failed were the lilac flakes he had found in her bedroom, evidence he finally came to understand. Without toys or food, the three-year-old had resorted to licking or eating the paper from her wall spending hours picking it off in pieces, an entire arc cleared by her bed head as she foraged, tiny scraps were found stuck to her locked wrists. All the while she would have heard the drinkers down below, stamping and singing … Sabrina spent that Christmas working round the clock, while Tiffany and her brother were locked upstairs.

(Levy and Scott-Clark, 2010, p36)

A disabled child is more likely to be dependent on others for their care and so left alone they may be at an increased risk of harm. A child with certain learning or physical disabilities may not understand levels of risk and how to protect themselves or be unable to escape dangerous situations. However, it may be that a disabled child has safeguards in place for their needs and feels entirely confident about being at home alone and social workers must take advice from specialists and others who know the child well.

For all children, the parent's or carer's attitude to the social worker is of significance. *I just popped out for five minutes to get medicine for the sick baby,* will evoke a different professional response from an avoidant reaction such as, *why don't you go across the road and see Mrs X who hits her kids.* Compliant parents who are remorseful may certainly be genuine but they may also be trying to conceal an abusive situation. It is important to collate information and analyse whether their responses are consistent with the child's explanation and witness accounts. Parents may need support to keep their child safe and then a risk assessment will be needed, in consultation with specialists such as psychologists, to consider their capacity for change.

Every time police attend a child left at home alone they send a referral to inform children's services because even an isolated incident may constitute significant harm. A parent's actions may be deliberate or unintentional. The impact on the child may be equally harmful, but a carer who is anxious and says the train from work was delayed will evoke a different professional response from one who seems uncaring and is absent because of a chaotic drug-related lifestyle. In the first case it would be important to check the details of the account and consider what precautions were taken to allow for such an eventuality. The parent may be struggling themselves through illness or have language or communication difficulties. The social worker needs to assess parental support needs but also be prepared to acknowledge that the child may nevertheless be neglected intentionally or unintentionally.

Social workers may be told by carers that it is normal in their culture for siblings to care for children of a young age or to be deemed mature enough to be left alone. Their view may or may not accurately reflect a specific culture and even within a community, practice may differ between families. Professional sensitivity is needed to assist the family to understand the risks posed by life in the UK for a child unsupervised and isolated.

ACTIVITY 4.4

Think about the following parental responses during an interview about neglect and how you might respond to adults who:

- are compliant: *You are quite right – she wasn't old enough to be left alone – things haven't been right in this house for some time.*

- see themselves as experts: *We are professionals, we can judge when he can take care of himself. It's just been a difficult time for us. We don't need your help but thank you.*

- are angry: *We don't want you snooping round our house coming in when we're not here. Who do you think you are? I have rights you know.*

- are avoidant: *No you can't come in. We are busy feeding the kids. We'll come to your office tomorrow when they're in school.*

COMMENT

Morrison provides a seven-point scale model of evaluating parental responses to professional intervention to enable social workers to assess risk to children (1998, pp140–1). For instance, a parent might respond in one of the following ways.

(Continued)

I accept my child has been placed at risk by leaving her at home on her own.

At this stage the child will need a protection plan in place because there is insufficient evidence of change.

I know I neglected her. She is too young to be left on her own but she had driven me mad not taking her bottle.

The parent admits that they are in some way responsible for the neglect but they locate the problem in the child's behaviour. Such an admission does not indicate that they accept responsibility that abuse might recur.

I feel bad about leaving her on her own. She's too young really.

The parent feels uncomfortable about the neglect. Yet caution must be taken as this could indicate false compliance as a result of the agency intervention.

We can't go on working these long hours and caring for my elderly Mum. The kids are suffering being left alone so much.

The parent does realise the need for change and may well do as the professionals ask but they may have little idea of how to achieve the changes needed.

I know I can manage to improve things. I'm going to start sharing child care with my neighbour so the children aren't left alone any more.

The parent has a plan for change, shows motivation and can be assisted to make changes.

Even though I do not want my child to have a child protection plan, I recognise it will help me get support in how to manage my kids better and not to leave them.

The parent realises they have to make decisions and accept professional support. This is a basis for working in partnership with the parent.

I have organised a child minder for when I can't get back in time.

The parent is determined to change and the social worker needs to respond positively so that the momentum is not lost. It is the time to identify goals and how these may be achieved.

ACTIVITY 4.5

What are important questions to ask about safeguards in the home when investigating the case of a child left at home alone?

You might consider some of the following.

- *Does the child know how to use a telephone? Do they have credit on their mobile or can they contact a neighbour in an emergency?*

- *Is there an alarm? Can the child exit the home easily in an emergency?*

- *Are basic safety precautions installed in the house such as stair gates, cooker guards, fireguards, socket covers and smoke alarms? Are medical and toxic substances stored safely?*

- *Is the child of sufficient age and understanding to know what might constitute an emergency such as the sound of a smoke alarm?*

- *Is there an unreasonable expectation for the child to cook food? Is there food in the house that the child can access?*

- *Is there light? Has the gas/electricity/water been cut off?*

- *What is the general level of hygiene? Are the children's beds clean and dry?*

- *Are harmful substances out of the child's reach such as alcohol or drugs? Are they exposed to risk from the paraphernalia of drug misuse such as syringes?*

- *Are the children protected from online abuse?*

- *Do pets pose a risk to the child? Are pets well cared for?*

- *Does the child open the door to strangers?*

- *Are there adults who pose a risk to the child who can gain access?*

- *Is the child at risk of harm from their own behaviour? Are they likely to hurt themselves, run into the road or cause a fire?*

Investigating allegations about a child left at home alone unsupervised – deciding the threshold for intervention

The following case diagrams are designed to promote a questioning approach as they progress from no ongoing concerns to immediate protective action. You should be informed by the list in the Introductory Chapter. Continue to add your own questions and consider the implications and barriers to safe practice in each case.

Case diagram 4.1

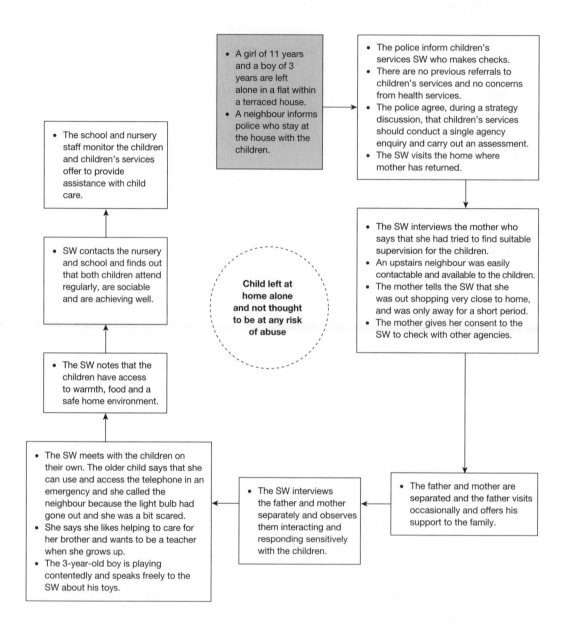

- A girl of 11 years and a boy of 3 years are left alone in a flat within a terraced house.
- A neighbour informs police who stay at the house with the children.

- The police inform children's services SW who makes checks.
- There are no previous referrals to children's services and no concerns from health services.
- The police agree, during a strategy discussion, that children's services should conduct a single agency enquiry and carry out an assessment.
- The SW visits the home where mother has returned.

- The SW interviews the mother who says that she had tried to find suitable supervision for the children.
- An upstairs neighbour was easily contactable and available to the children.
- The mother tells the SW that she was out shopping very close to home, and was only away for a short period.
- The mother gives her consent to the SW to check with other agencies.

- The school and nursery staff monitor the children and children's services offer to provide assistance with child care.

- SW contacts the nursery and school and finds out that both children attend regularly, are sociable and are achieving well.

Child left at home alone and not thought to be at any risk of abuse

- The SW notes that the children have access to warmth, food and a safe home environment.

- The SW meets with the children on their own. The older child says that she can use and access the telephone in an emergency and she called the neighbour because the light bulb had gone out and she was a bit scared.
- She says she likes helping to care for her brother and wants to be a teacher when she grows up.
- The 3-year-old boy is playing contentedly and speaks freely to the SW about his toys.

- The SW interviews the father and mother separately and observes them interacting and responding sensitively with the children.

- The father and mother are separated and the father visits occasionally and offers his support to the family.

Case diagram 4.2

- Children's services implement s17, (CA 1989)
- Following advice from the RSPCA, police arranged for the dog to be returned to the family and the mother is told that should there be any further incidents child protection procedures will be initiated.
- The girl is offered a school counselling service to support any further reporting. She tells the SW that her mother has told her that she will not leave her alone again until she is much older.

- A girl of 11 years is left at home alone with a boy of 5 years, in a flat on a large housing estate.
- The girl calls the GP surgery when the boy is bitten by the family dog.
- The GP calls an ambulance and makes a referral to children's services.

- Checks within children's services by the SW show that there are no previous referrals and the schools have no concerns.
- The hospital doctor tells the SW that the children are well cared for.
- The hospital SW interviews the children. The girl says that she doesn't like being left alone to care for her brother, she wants to be out with her friends playing instead and no neighbours were around for her to contact.
- The SW contacts police (CAIT) who have no record of the family. A single agency approach by children's services is agreed.

- The SW makes a home visit and finds there is plenty of food; the home is warm and a child-centred environment.
- The mother says that the dog has never been known to bite a child before.
- The mother is very upset by the incident and acknowledges that she should not have left the children alone.
- The girl tells the mother in front of the SW that she does not want to be left in charge of her brother and wants her dog back.

Concern about a child left at home alone

- Police contact the Royal Society for the Prevention of Cruelty to Animals (RSPCA) to arrange collection of the dog which is not a breed covered under the Dangerous Dogs Act 1991.

- Children's services decide that the children should return home and that they will conduct an assessment (s17 CA 1989).
- The dog bite is not serious and the hospital discharges the boy with medication.

- The mother provides the father's details and when the SW contacts him he explains that he has the children for holidays as he lives with a new partner, some distance away.

- The hospital SW interviews the mother who, when called, arrived at the hospital immediately.
- The mother explains that she had gone shopping for half a day and thought the children would be fine because the girl can use and access the telephone.

Case diagram 4.3

A boy of 12 years and a girl of 2 years are left at home alone in a small block of private flats.
- The boy calls police from a friend's mobile phone because his mother has not come home and he is anxious that his father might turn up.
- Police refer to children's services and remain with the children until the SW arrives.

- The SW interviews the boy at his home and he tells the SW he finds caring for his sister a chore and he is cross with his mother for leaving him in charge.
- The boy also says that his father uses drugs, sometimes visits unannounced and that there is no one he can call on for help.
- The boy has asthma and uses an inhaler daily.
- The home environment is safe and child centred. However, after looking in the fridge and cupboards the SW finds there is little food available.

The SW reports back to police and it is agreed that, should there be a further incident, there will be a joint investigation and child protection conference.

- SW checks show that there have been previous referrals to children's services for concerns about neglect and that the school is concerned because the boy often arrives late.
- The health visitor reports that the girl has delayed speech development and the mother often misses appointments.
- The SW holds a strategy discussion with police. Checks show the police have no previous information about either parent and an initial single agency investigation is agreed (s47 CA 1989).

- The school offer the boy one-to-one support from the school counsellor.
- An application is made for a nursery place for the 2 year old.

Suspicion of actual or likely significant harm to a child left at home alone, s47 (CA 1989) enquiry

- The GP sees the mother about her depression and arranges to see the boy about his asthma.
- The SW implements child in need (s17, CA 1989) protocols and explores any risks posed by the father's contact.
- The SW interviews the father who agrees to a parenting assessment.
- The SW visits the children the following day, sees them on their own and observes the 2-year-old playing.
- The SW assesses the mother as protective but as needing support.
- The mother asks the children's grandmother to stay for a while to help out.

- The SW contacts the father by phone to assess the risk to the children of him visiting and to reassure the children that they are safe.
- The father explains that he will not visit without informing the mother and children in advance.

- The mother returns to the home and tells the SW she doesn't know what the fuss is about as her son is very responsible.
- She says that she had to go out to collect her medication as she gets very depressed. She also had to see a friend who owes her money.
- When asked about the father's visits, the mother says that he is away at the moment and always lets her know when he is coming round.

Case diagram 4.4

- A girl of 13 years with a moderate learning disability and a boy of 3 years who has epilepsy are left at home alone.
- The boy requires regular medication.
- They live in a street property.
- The girl runs into the street to call an adult passer-by because the boy is having a seizure. The adult immediately calls an ambulance and the police arrive.

- Police report to children's services that there is little food in the home and no heating on a cold day.
- The children do not have access to a telephone and the girl is vulnerable because she cannot use the public telephone.

- A strategy meeting is arranged for the next day to plan the investigation and to consider the need for a paediatric assessment and a child protection conference.
- The boy is to remain in hospital overnight for monitoring.
- The girl returns home to the care of both parents with support from the Disabled Children's Team.
- The mother begins attending a support group for parents of disabled children while the SW arranges for a family support worker to be with the 3 year old.

- The SW makes checks and learns that there have been two previous referrals to children's services because the children were left alone.
- School staff report that the girl is often left waiting for her mother to collect her and does not always have sufficient food in her lunch box.
- The health visitor reports that the boy is reaching his developmental milestones and the mother takes him for regular hospital check-ups.
- Children's services ask the hospital SW to interview the children.
- The girl tells the SW that there is no neighbour available and that her mother had gone to church.
- A strategy discussion takes place with police and a joint investigation is agreed.

S47 (CA 1989) investigation of a child left at home alone

- The police decide it is not in the children's interests to pursue a prosecution.
- The police and SWs decide that the family need support services and that the boy needs to be provided with a nursery place as a matter of urgency.

- The parents are separated and the father visits at weekends. The children tell the SW that they enjoy his visits.
- Checks by the SW show that the father is not known to police.

- The SW checks with the Disabled Children's Team who report concerns about neglect issues and who have known the family for some time.
- The allocated SW agrees to support the father in addressing the basic need for food and warmth in the home.

- The father is contacted by the Disabled Children's Team SW who meets him at the family address where he agrees to stay during the investigation.
- The home is cold as there is no electricity and there is little food in the fridge or cupboards.
- The father says that he has had concerns about the impact on the children of the mother's religious commitments although he sees the church community as supportive.

- The mother tells the interviewers that she had to attend an important church service on the instructions of the pastor.
- The mother is worried about the little boy and shows both children affection to which they respond.

- The mother responds to a note left by police and attends the hospital. Police and the SW interview the mother at the hospital.

Case diagram 4.5

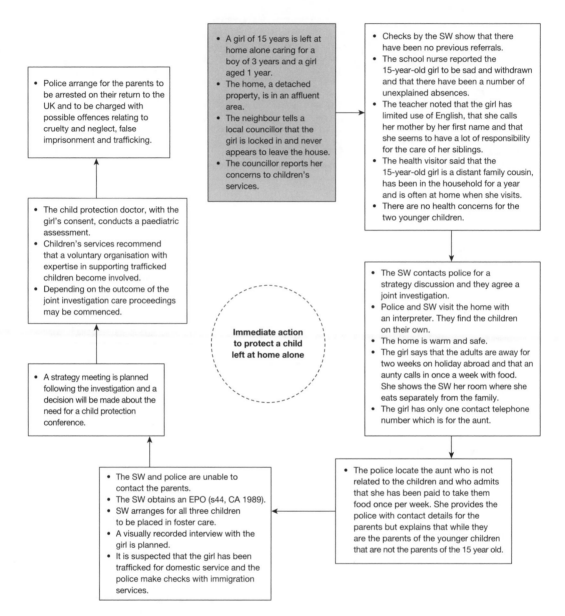

- Police arrange for the parents to be arrested on their return to the UK and to be charged with possible offences relating to cruelty and neglect, false imprisonment and trafficking.

- A girl of 15 years is left at home alone caring for a boy of 3 years and a girl aged 1 year.
- The home, a detached property, is in an affluent area.
- The neighbour tells a local councillor that the girl is locked in and never appears to leave the house.
- The councillor reports her concerns to children's services.

- Checks by the SW show that there have been no previous referrals.
- The school nurse reported the 15-year-old girl to be sad and withdrawn and that there have been a number of unexplained absences.
- The teacher noted that the girl has limited use of English, that she calls her mother by her first name and that she seems to have a lot of responsibility for the care of her siblings.
- The health visitor said that the 15-year-old girl is a distant family cousin, has been in the household for a year and is often at home when she visits.
- There are no health concerns for the two younger children.

- The child protection doctor, with the girl's consent, conducts a paediatric assessment.
- Children's services recommend that a voluntary organisation with expertise in supporting trafficked children become involved.
- Depending on the outcome of the joint investigation care proceedings may be commenced.

Immediate action to protect a child left at home alone

- The SW contacts police for a strategy discussion and they agree a joint investigation.
- Police and SW visit the home with an interpreter. They find the children on their own.
- The home is warm and safe.
- The girl says that the adults are away for two weeks on holiday abroad and that an aunty calls in once a week with food. She shows the SW her room where she eats separately from the family.
- The girl has only one contact telephone number which is for the aunt.

- A strategy meeting is planned following the investigation and a decision will be made about the need for a child protection conference.

- The SW and police are unable to contact the parents.
- The SW obtains an EPO (s44, CA 1989).
- SW arranges for all three children to be placed in foster care.
- A visually recorded interview with the girl is planned.
- It is suspected that the girl has been trafficked for domestic service and the police make checks with immigration services.

- The police locate the aunt who is not related to the children and who admits that she has been paid to take them food once per week. She provides the police with contact details for the parents but explains that while they are the parents of the younger children that are not the parents of the 15 year old.

C H A P T E R   S U M M A R Y

The main difficulty for social workers is deciding at what stage the neglect of a child has escalated to the point where a protective multi-agency response is indicated. This decision is reached only through effective joint working, debating the thresholds of intervention and reaching agreement about when a section 47 (CA 1989) should be implemented. Social workers may exhibit helplessness in the face of chronic neglect and this reflects the child's experience. This aspect of professional dangerousness is covered in the Introduction and is further developed in this chapter. Neglect within the family and in wider societal contexts is included to extend social workers' awareness of structural influences on child and family life. The case diagrams provide an opportunity for deep analysis of intervention when a child is left at home alone.

FURTHER READING

Crawley, H (2012) *Working with children and young people subject to immigration control*, 2nd edition. London: Immigration Law Practitioners' Association.
A guide to good practice with unaccompanied asylum seeking children.

Daniels, H (2104) *Hackney child*. London: Simon and Schuster.
An account of a childhood in care – a child abused by those who should have protected her.

WEBSITES

www.howardleague.org
The Howard League raises awareness about child deaths in prison and chronic neglect of children within custodial settings.

https//modernslavery.co.uk
Home Office and NSPCC awareness campaign on modern slavery including child trafficking.

Chapter 5
Physical abuse

A C H I E V I N G   A   S O C I A L   W O R K   D E G R E E

This chapter will help you to develop the following capabilities, to the appropriate level, from the PCF.

- **Professionalism**
  Represent and be accountable to the profession.
- **Values and ethics**
  Apply social work ethical principles and values to guide professional practice.
- **Diversity**
  Recognise diversity and apply anti-oppressive principles in practice.
- **Knowledge**
  Apply knowledge of social sciences, law and social work practice theory.
- **Critical reflection and analysis**
  Apply critical reflection and analysis to inform and provide a rationale for professional decision making.
- **Intervention and skills**
  Use judgement and authority to intervene with individuals, families and communities to promote independence, provide support and prevent harm, neglect and abuse.
- **Contexts and organisations**
  Engage with, inform and adapt to changing practice contexts and operate effectively within own organisational frameworks and within multi-agency and inter-professional settings.
- **Professional leadership**
  Take responsibility for the professional learning and development of others through supervision, mentoring, assessing, research, teaching, leadership and management.

It will also introduce you to the following academic standards as set out in the social work subject benchmark statements:

5.1.2 The service delivery context
5.1.4 Social work theory
5.5 Problem-solving skills
5.6 Communication skills
5.7 Skills in working with others
7.3 Knowledge and understanding

(www.qaa.ac.uk/en/Publications/Documents/Subject-benchmark-statement-Social-work.pdf)

Introduction

We do not know how long the attack lasted, but at least fifty blows were rained upon her, interspersed with repeated demands that she spelled her name Sukina ... when she was too weak to stand she tried to crawl out of the room to the stairs, asking her father to stop hitting her... Sukina's mother tried to intervene and was herself assaulted, causing injuries to her face.

The attack on Sukina continued until she was barely conscious, at which point she was taken by her parents to the bathroom and placed in a bath of warm water in an attempt to revive her ... As she slipped into unconsciousness Sukina told her father she was sorry. Although an ambulance was called, Sukina was already dead on arrival at the hospital.

(Bridge Child Care Consultancy, 1991, p7)

Sukina Hammond, aged 5 years, was murdered by her father in 1988 in Bristol.

Sita told me to take my jumper and vest off, she pulled a knife and she did little marks. I was bleeding. They stood round me in a circle, hitting me and laughing ... my aunt said that my mum and me have got witchcraft ... she laughs when she hits me. She says if I tell anybody she hit me, she will take a knife and stab me.

(BBC, 2005)

This chapter focuses on the protection of children from physical abuse. It begins by looking at definitions and moves on to consider the knowledge required to make professional judgements. The complexities of this form of abuse will be examined to support an informed approach to individual children's circumstances. Research into children's views and survivor perspectives provides a basis for sound decision making. The chapter concludes with case examples of physical harm to children involving physical punishment, which will take the reader through an investigative process, escalated through five levels of social work intervention to support in-depth analysis.

Definition of physical abuse

Physical abuse may involve hitting, shaking, throwing, poisoning, burning or scalding, drowning, suffocating or otherwise causing physical harm to a child. Physical harm may also be caused when a parent or carer fabricates the symptoms of, or deliberately induces, illness in a child.

(DfE, 2015, p93)

The Domestic Violence Crime and Victims (Amendment) Act 2012 extended the offence of causing or allowing the death of a child or vulnerable adult to cover causing or allowing serious physical harm.

Learning about physical abuse to children

Sometimes injuries remain medically unexplained and doubt exists about the origin of unusual markings or conditions. For example, some of Victoria Climbié's injuries were described by paediatricians as looking like belt buckle marks and yet no evidence ever explained the causes of these markings. Despite the uncertainty, these should have been thoroughly investigated as they were in fact indicative of future harm she suffered. Some forms of punishment are unusual, such as making a child kneel or stand in fixed positions for hours or pulling out a child's hair. Cooper, in her account of being a child in care, describes having her mouth washed out with soap for saying bad words. I choked and retched but she kept ramming it back into my mouth (Cooper, 2007, p8). Stobart (2006) studied cases of children in particular faith communities who had experienced chilli pepper rubbed into their genitalia and eyes, being hit, beaten and burnt when considered possessed by spirits.

Physical abuse – the evidence

- In 2014, there were 4,760 children who were the subject of a child protection plan under the category of physical abuse (DfE, 2014b).

- Research showed that in the UK 1.3 per cent of under 11s, 6.9 per cent of 11–17s and 8.4 per cent of 18–24s had experienced some form of physical violence by their parents or guardians during childhood, while 0.8 per cent, 3.7 per cent and 5.4 per cent respectively of each age group had experienced severe physical violence (Radford, et al., 2011).

- In 2014–15,10,155 children contacted ChildLine about physical abuse (NSPCC, 2015).

- A study of domestic violence found that child victims will not necessarily grow up to be violent or become adult victims themselves and that there is no conclusive evidence of a cycle of violence (Mullender and Morley, 1994).

- In a study of 139 serious case reviews in England in 2009–11, 63 per cent of cases included domestic violence as a risk factor (Brandon, et al., 2012a).

- There were 67 child homicides across the UK in 2013–14 according to police statistics. The number of children who die where abuse or neglect is suspected is much higher (Jutte, et al., 2015, p15).

- A survey showed that 86 per cent of adults would be happy to shop in a smack-free shop (Child Rights International Network, 2007; Saunders and Goddard, 2010).

- A safety survey of 2,420 children, aged 9–16 years, found that 55 per cent reported being physically assaulted and 80 per cent had experienced harassment which they found frightening. The reports were not exclusive to deprived areas and most took place in streets and parks (Deakin, 2006).

- The Metropolitan Police said there had been 60 crimes linked to faith in London in 2015 in a nine-month period (BBC News, 2015h).

- Between 2005 and 2015, 183 children have been killed in London, 68 per cent by stabbing and 18 per cent were shot (www.citizensreportuk.org/reports/teenage-murder-london.html).

- Children aged 11, 13 and 15 years experience more conflict in more unequal societies, more fighting, bullying and finding peers unkind and unhelpful (Wilkinson and Pickett, 2009).

CASE STUDY

A lack of focus on children B, C and D

Three children made numbers of disclosures about severe and recurring physical and emotional abuse and neglect by their adoptive parents, mainly perpetrated by the adoptive mother (M). Following charges of child cruelty, M and father (F) were convicted. The serious case review questioned the quality of the adoption assessment and approval and the introduction process carried out with haste (CESCB, 2011, p17). The review also considered that many professionals struggled to maintain a child focus when faced with M and F's aggressive behaviour, their *disguised compliance* and that their approach was affected by perceptions and assumptions made regarding the parents' social class, professional status and *high academic qualifications and the attitude of M and F toward them* (p21).

During a six-month period, Child B had made eight disclosures and Child C one disclosure. Section 47 (CA 1989) enquiries began in response to only three of these. The chronology below lists the nine disclosures, the response to these and the outcomes at each stage for the children. There were also observations by school staff of M showing a lack of warmth towards the children, of the children being frightened of her, of insufficient food in their lunch boxes and of the children looking thin. The GP had made a referral to the CAMHS but other agencies were not aware of this and M did not attend after the first appointment. The health visitor noted two injuries which might have been accidental and also realised that M and F had chosen to change the children's first names.

The serious case review criticised the lack of referral to children's services by health and education services and stated that the CAMHS were adult focused and had not seen the children. Professionals *misread the signals* about Child B, defining his running away as teenage rebellion against parental discipline. M and F appeared concerned for his wellbeing, making efforts to find him when he went missing, but each event was dealt with in isolation from the children's experiences and statements over time. The children did not feel confident to confide in professionals as they felt unprotected and unsafe, *the children's perception must have been that disclosing what was happening to them would make no difference. The risk was if they talked and they were not removed, M and F would know and might result in the abuse being taken into unknown and even more dangerous territory* (p19). For these children, the role of friends and responsible members of the public was very important in reporting concerns to professionals but, *in this case professionals did not give sufficient weight to the information they provided* (p19).

The review stated the importance *of the maintenance of up-to-date chronologies in building up a picture of events and concerns over time to inform assessments and decisions* (p20). A chronology would have informed protective action. Without a context of formal child protection protocols the disclosures were not properly evaluated, the risk to all children was not considered at an early stage, information was not effectively collated and too much emphasis was given to paediatric findings which needed to be considered in the context of other information. Particular criticism was made of a decision to accommodate the children (s20, CA, 1989) which did not guarantee their safety and enabled the parents to take the children home leaving them exposed to further abuse (CESCB, 2011).

A chronology

The chronology below is adapted from the original *Bridge Chronology* (Fitzgerald, 1999) used in many serious case reviews which enables multi-agency collation of information prior to analysis of facts and is based on the Serious Case Review regarding the B, C and D children (CESCB, 2011).

Date	Allegation	Intervention	Outcome
1.03.2009	B alleged to residential care staff abuse by both parents. Red mark above eye said to be caused by F.	Emergency duty team (EDT) took B home. F denied allegation but said M hit child. Referral to adoption team instead of investigation team for follow up.	No medical assessment. No s47 investigation. Police not informed. B retracted allegation.
17.03.09	B had two red marks under his eye and told residential care unit (RCU) that F had hit him and that both parents frequently punched him.	Police and EDT responded. B placed in foster care. Paediatric assessment inconclusive about marks under eye.	B returned home at M's request prior to ABE interview. M said she would protect B from F. B did not want to go home and was very distressed. No account taken of child's allegations and father's comment about abuse by M.
30.03.09	B went to the RCU and alleged assault by F and said he did not wish to go home.	EDT arranged collection of B by M and F without interviewing the child. Police saw M but not B and believed her account that B was going into care which was untrue.	B was returned home. No s47 took place.
3.06.09	Teacher, whose son was a friend of B, said B would not self-refer as he said he was not previously believed.	Teacher made referral to children's services.	No s47 investigation or s17 assessment.

(Continued)

CASE STUDY *continued*

Date	Allegation	Intervention	Outcome
6.06.09	B approached a stranger for help and was brought to hospital with injuries caused through jumping out of window at home. He said he did this to escape abuse.	Admitted to hospital for observation but EDT decided he should return home after telephone calls with M and B. When M came to hospital she was intimidating to ward staff.	No face-to-face interview with B by EDT. Police not informed of disclosure. M's behaviour on the ward did not escalate concerns. No s47 investigation.
07.06.09		B accommodated for two weeks at parents' request because he was continually running away and had behaviour problems at school.	Returned home 26 June. No s47 investigation.
29.06.09	B was found by police sleeping rough. A man told police that B was running away because he was being hit by his parents and bullied at school.	Police spoke to B but he would not confirm the allegation.	B was returned home. No s47 investigation.
02.07.09	Friend of B called police to report B being scared to go home because of being hit.	B told police he did not want to return home but EDT decided M and F could collect him.	No interview of B by EDT and no follow up of allegations.
22.07.09	C tells friend that M had assaulted her and showed the bruises. She did not want this reported.	Teacher referred to children's services. C refused to be medically examined. S47 investigation was begun.	Investigation deemed inconclusive as C would not make a statement or be examined. Police not informed.
8.09.09	B made allegations at hospital about physical and verbal abuse by M and F and had bruising to his arm.	B admitted to hospital and would not return home. Social worker believed no evidence to support prior allegations and thought problems were school based.	Paediatrician disagreed and would not discharge B who was then accommodated when M discovered B didn't want to see her. No s47 investigation.
23.09.09	B disclosed to Independent Reviewing Officer (IRO)	S47 carried out. B gave account in an ABE interview of abuse over	ICO obtained but no guardian ad litem allocated because of staff shortages.

Date	Allegation	Intervention	Outcome
	the serious physical and emotional abuse by M and F.	nine years. Strategy meeting decision to apply for ICO to enable ABE interviews with Children C and D. Police concerned of risk to children if M and F informed of this so they interviewed C and D at school but C and D did not corroborate B's account.	
02.10.09			M and F arrested on suspicion of abusing all children.
05.10.09	Because C and D had not made disclosures, local authority made decision to return C and D home.	There was no discussion by the local authority with the IRO or police. The court revoked the ICOs at the local authority's request.	C and D were returned home and later said they were abused that same day.
10.11.09	Foster carer for B informed police that C and D wished to disclose abuse.	Police interviewed C and D without parental consent and they corroborated B's account in ABE interviews. M and F arrested same day.	Later C and D were the subject of police powers of protection and later ICOs were obtained.

Disabled children and physical abuse

She like asked me if it had happened and I said yeah. I think if she hadn't asked me I probably wouldn't have told her.

(Taylor, et al., 2015, p16)

Taylor, et al. (2015, pp13–37) collated accounts from ten disabled adults who had experienced all forms of abuse in childhood. Some had made multiple disclosures to a range of trusted adults but only two resulted in protective action. Six of the ten participants disclosed as children and three led to police investigations. One disclosure made at age 18 years led to a conviction for a sexual offence.

Disclosures did not always gain a sensitive response leaving the children feeling disempowered and disbelieved.

I tried to tell people quite a lot of times, like when I was nine and I was sectioned because I tried to kind of take my life kind of thing cos I couldn't handle it anymore ... and even then nobody asked me why did I do it.

The social workers should have thought why I was always so angry, why I was always behaving badly to the foster parents.

The children were largely invisible to protective services. They could be in close contact with services yet the abuse went undetected.

It was wrong but I kept quiet. I didn't know how to tell anyone. I didn't know how to break the silence. I didn't know how to tell my Mum that he had been touching me.

I remember the social worker saying to me 'Oh that's good that you get on with your mum's boyfriend, some kids don't.' And I felt like I would have been betraying everyone if I'd said 'well actually sometimes he's not very nice'.

They (social workers) didn't look at me when I was talking and try to pay attention to what I had to say. They would be looking at their papers.

Abusers exploited the children's isolation, low credibility, fear and self-blame. The lack of advocacy and interpreting services for deaf children was a key factor in non-detection of abuse.

I wish, wish, wish that we had an interpreter then. My wee sister would be fine. She would have had a happier childhood. Now she is dead, aged 41. I wanted to protect her. I failed her.

I was the quiet one ... I'm the only deaf person in my immediate family. I couldn't use the phone to speak ... If you are deaf you can't phone ChildLine.

Participants described isolated childhoods with few friends or family and a lack of formal professional support.

If I told them what happened to me, they would be upset. I couldn't do that to them. I didn't want the family to break down.

I knew from very early on that I had to put on a front because I thought I would be the one taken away.

I had ... two sisters; my worry was that he would start to pick on them, that's why I kept it up until I was 14.

They would attack me if they knew I tried to tell someone was hurting me ... I would be helpless and stuck.

The research identified the need to define the children as credible court witnesses to enable them to achieve justice.

> *They never took him to court. Never. No charge or court. Nothing. The police said I had to forget about it. There was nothing more they could do about it. He was free to walk. I was so upset.*

Disabled children are nearly four times more likely to be physically abused than non-disabled children (Jones, et al., 2012). The presence of multiple disabilities appears to increase the risk of abuse. Abuse is under-reported because of the relatively powerless position of disabled children. The lack of specialist communication services is a key factor in non-disclosure and non-detection.

ACTIVITY 5.2

Why do you think disabled children are particularly vulnerable to physical abuse?

COMMENT

- *Disabled children are more isolated socially – particularly in institutional care away from their locality, making it difficult to be noticed by protective adults.*

- *At all ages they are more dependent on others for personal care, allowing abusers' close contact which goes unquestioned.*

- *A child may be unheard when trying to disclose abuse because of communication difficulties or inability to access support.*

- *Abusers target disabled children thinking that the indicators of physical abuse will be misinterpreted as signs of disability and the abuse will remain hidden.*

- *Disabled children may experience specific forms of physical abuse such as force-feeding, excessive physical restraint or rough handling.*

The physical abuse of children at different ages

ACTIVITY 5.3

Social workers sometimes think that children are more vulnerable to abuse at particular ages. At what age do you think children are more likely to experience physical abuse?

All children are at risk of physical harm even though babies are more vulnerable. Children under the age of 1 year are three times more likely than other children to be subject of a child protection plan for physical abuse. In England and Wales, babies are eight times more likely to be killed than other children. In 2007, of babies under age 1 year, 19,000 lived with a parent who has used Class A drugs, 39,000 lived in households affected by domestic violence, 93,500 lived with a parent who misused alcohol and 144,000 lived with a parent with a mental health problem (Cuthbert, et al., 2011, p5).

In a study of serious case reviews Ofsted (2011b) noted that 24 per cent of the sample were over the age of 14 years. There is a risk that older children are defined as more able to cope and are less likely to receive a child protection response, often falling in a gap between children and adult services. There is more likely to be a professional focus on older children as having behavioural problems rather than looking for the causes of the behaviour and considering whether they are victims of harm (HC 137:1, 2012–13, p32).

Physical abuse – specific forms and contexts

Physical abuse of children within violent families

Serious case reviews of child deaths from abuse highlight a history of violence including parental conflict and violent, criminal histories, such as sexual crime, as significant. Each year around 2.1 million people experience some form of domestic abuse in England and Wales which includes 1.4 million women and 700,000 men. In 2013–14, police recorded 887,000 domestic abuse incidents and seven women a month were killed by a current or former partner. The rate for women murdered in a context of domestic violence has been consistently around the 100 per year mark for the past decade (ONS, 2015). In the absence of engaging with male perpetrators, social workers commonly focus on mothers' failure to protect children and also expect them to manage the man's violence.

Perpetrator programmes are co-ordinated and run by Respect (www.respectphoneline.org.uk/), which also delivers counselling for male victims of violence. Stanley, et al. (2010) argue for perpetrator programmes to feed into parenting assessments. This applies to investigations of domestic violence perpetrated towards both men and women. It is indicative of societal attitudes to male victims of domestic abuse that a major retail store, Superdrug, sold an inflatable punch-bag which encouraged hitting men into which a photograph of a man could be inserted where the face should be. The punch bag had an arrow pointing to the head stating *hit him here* and an arrow pointing to the groin stating *kick him here*. Following a complaint from The ManKind Initiative (http://new.mankind.org.uk/) the item was withdrawn.

Reder and Duncan found that *a clear history of violent, criminal or other antisocial behaviour from at least one of the caretakers* was evident in a significant number of their sample of serious case reviews (1999, p63). Key risk factors are the young age of the child, health problems in the child, young mothers, drug misuse and men's criminal histories. About a third of children living in violent households try to intervene to stop it, thereby risking harm to themselves.

> *I tried to help. I tried to guard my Mum so he couldn't hurt her. I didn't talk about it with anyone. I used to run downstairs to see mum was OK.*

> *I make myself be awake so that I can jump up when it happens and get between them.*

> *I didn't really try to stop the fight. I was too frightened. I used to think 'He'll just beat me up too'.*

> (Mullender, et al., 2003a, pp21–3)

There is a high correlation between parental violence and violence to children. Some 130,000 children live in homes where there is domestic abuse (Safelives, 2015) and 62 per cent of children living with domestic abuse are directly harmed by the perpetrator of the abuse, in addition to the harm caused by witnessing the abuse of others (Caada, 2014). There were 1,669 children living in refuges on one day in 2014 (Women's Aid, 2014). Stanley, et al. (2010) argue for a long-term approach rather than stop/start repeated assessments with cases being opened and closed with little continuity.

The risk of violence increases during pregnancy and child birth as does the risk of miscarriage, stillbirth, pre-term and low birth weight babies. This may be the direct result of violence but also of poor maternal health, substance misuse and non-engagement with services (Peckover, 2009). Knowledge of family violence will indicate the need for a pre-birth child protection conference to ensure a protection plan is in place for the child from the moment of birth. Sharpen, of Against Violence and Abuse (www.avaproject.org.uk/), expressed concern about the numbers of children killed on contact visits, *often a woman will leave for the sake of protecting her children, and then she is put in the impossible position where the courts are saying,* 'but the children must have contact with this man who is too dangerous to live with'. *What kind of message is that giving her?* Contact often may be supervised by an unqualified worker without the expertise required to ensure the child's safety (HC 137:1, 2012–13, p29). Professionally staffed contact supervision should be accessible on a voluntary basis not just through a court order or children's services involvement. Handover times between parents can be especially problematic for children (Stanley, et al., 2010). Adding to risk of harm to a child is the fact that few refuges accept boys over 12 years, which places protective mothers in untenable situations.

Wood, et al. (2011) interviewed 44 boys and 38 girls between the ages of 13 and 18 years who were not in mainstream education and found:

- *over 50 per cent of the girls said they had been in a sexually violent relationship;*

- *50 per cent had experienced physical violence;*

- *25 per cent of boys said they had been in relationships with physically aggressive partners.*

The study followed previous research (Barter, et al., 2009) of 1,400 girls aged 13–17 years who were not considered to be from vulnerable backgrounds which found:

- *a third had been sexually abused and a quarter experienced violence from boyfriends;*

- *the violence levels with girls were high – they had been punched, had bruised eyes or broken teeth, had been pushed downstairs or dragged by the hair;*

- *25 per cent of boys had experienced some form of domestic violence but not at this level;*

- *young women had opted to stay with violent partners rather than be a single mother.*

Many of the children in this study had come to view violence as a normal aspect of intimate relationships. Violence for some was present in their families, peer groups and in their intimate partner relationships, as recipients, instigators or both. For several, violence had become so ingrained in their childhoods that to acknowledge the emotional or physical impact of violence, including intimate forms, was viewed as an indication of weakness. This severely restricted their ability to seek help. However, the research also showed that many young women had a range of positive protection and survival strategies which they used in response to violence.

Homes where animals are abused or used to intimidate

To make matters worse he [Tiffany Wright's father] bought a succession of large dogs, a great dane, a staffie, a Rottweiler ... dog excrement had been trampled all over the flat.

(Levy and Scott-Clark, 2010, p35)

She [the police officer] described the 6ft 4in man as 'sadistic – fascinated with pain' ... Barker spent a lot of time alone with Peter [Connolly, aged 17 months], which is when much of the abuse took place. He kept a Rottweiler dog, Kaiser, and it was suggested in court that some of Peter's injuries might have been inflicted by the animal. Connelly's home was described as disgusting. When police searched it, they found dog mess and human faeces on the floor and rat holes burrowed into the walls. The bodies of dead chicks, mice and a dismembered rabbit were strewn around.

(BBC, 2009b)

Violence in a household may extend to cruelty towards animals as part of a continuum of abuse within a family. Animal abuse is defined as intentional harm of animals, including wilful neglect, inflicting injury, pain or distress, or malicious killing. There is increasing evidence of links between abuse of children, vulnerable adults and animals (LSCB, 2015, Part B, p32). A review of the literature (Hackett and Uprichard, 2007) identified that professionals should be aware of the role and meaning of pets in family life, which is often positive, but also assess the risks and seek specialist advice when needed. The risk assessment needs to take account of the nature of the animal concerned and the specific meaning and motivation behind any cruel act. The Royal Society for the Prevention of Cruelty to Animals (www.rspca.org.uk) can always be consulted to assist risk assessment.

Shaking injuries

One of the most dangerous forms of violence towards children is shaking. When a baby is shaken the blood vessels may bleed as the brain impacts repeatedly against the skull. For those babies who survive, between 50 and 80 per cent may suffer paralysis or a long-term learning impairment such as cerebral palsy, visual problems, epilepsy, learning and behavioural problems. Abusive head trauma, involving injury to the brain or bleeding within the structures around the brain, is the leading cause of death among children who have been abused and may arise from shaking or impact injuries. Children younger than 2 years are most affected, with an estimated prevalence of 1 per 3,000 babies younger than six months. Boys appear to have more head injuries than girls, from any cause. Children who have brain injuries may also have other physical injuries. Children may also suffer spinal injuries as a result of abuse such as neck, chest and lower back injuries (NSPCC, 2013a). Many parents who shook babies said it was because of incessant crying, and post-natal depression can be a factor (Shepherd and Sampson, 2000, pp721–35). A DVD for parents, *Coping with crying*, has led to increased safety in babies from this type of injury (Owen, 2014b).

Bites and oral injuries

The labial frenulum is the fold of tissue inside the mouth that joins the upper or lower lip to the gums and injury to it is indicative of physical abuse. However, this injury can be caused accidentally and needs assessment in the context of the developmental stage of the child, a full examination and the parental explanation. When present in an abused child, it is frequently associated with multiple injuries and serious harm.

A bite mark may be human or animal, child or adult size. Any human bite could be abusive and should be fully assessed by a forensic dentist who can have an important role in child protection. If involved early enough, they can take photographs and casts of the bite, and possibly retrieve DNA, which can help identify the perpetrator. Dogs and other carnivores (such as ferrets or rats) tend to leave characteristic bites involving tearing of the skin causing deep puncture wounds. These are also much narrower bites than human ones (NSPCC, 2012a).

Burns and scalds

Burns include scalds from hot liquids, contact burns from hot objects or flames, chemical and electrical burns. Between 10 and 14 per cent of burns are caused through abuse. Burns due to neglect outnumber intentional burns (NSPCC, 2102c). Medical opinion about burns is often definitive and essential to investigating social workers. A child who runs into a cigarette may not have a deep circular burn, which would be left if a burn had been purposefully inflicted. Sometimes burns may indicate a shape, such as from an iron, hair tongs or electric fire, and patterns may be matched against the objects described by the child or family. A child may pick up an iron and be burnt but this will leave a different mark from an iron held close to the skin. Intentional contact burns are frequently multiple and may involve areas of the body other than the hands.

Children will naturally move away quickly from contact with hot liquids and splash marks will occur, but if a child has been dipped or held in hot water or other liquid there may be a clear demarcation line of a burn which would be more indicative of a non-accidental injury. However, an adult may throw a hot drink over a child in anger and this would leave splash marks. Intentional immersion scalds may not affect less exposed parts of the skin such as behind the knees (NSPCC, 2012c). Rope and friction burns can be caused deliberately, such as when a child is restrained during sexual or physical abuse. The presence of old scars from burns may indicate a lack of treatment for previous injuries. A child protection paediatrician must always be consulted and will advise who is the appropriate medical specialist to respond in each case.

A police officer interviewed children who had been burnt on their eyes and genitals through the application of hot chillies:

> One child stated,
>
> 'He went to the kitchen. When he came back he had some green chillies. He rubbed them into me' …
>
> Where did he rub them?
>
> 'Between my legs inside'
>
> This was torture a long lasting and agonising burn – they must have felt like they were on fire.
>
> (Keeble and Hollington, 2011, p134)

Endurance punishment

Endurance punishments are the use of a stress position to punish a child. *Whenever Sefu or Tanesha were naughty their father would not only make them stand in the corner, he'd force them to hold a hardback Bible straight above their heads or to hold their arms straight out in front of them* (Keeble and Hollington, 2011, p125). Another practice is referred to as *Pick a Penny* where the child places one finger on a penny on the floor and at the same time holds the other arm high in the air, balancing on one foot for a long time.

Bruising

Bruises are the most common injury in children who have been physically harmed. Some bruises are more likely in children learning to walk, who bump into objects and fall over, usually on parts of the body that protrude like knees and elbows. Bruising in a non-mobile child is very unusual and, even on older children, it must be seen in the context of any existing concerns about harm. Professional perceptions of parents' rough handling of a child need to be questioned in the context of known domestic violence, physical aggression or mental health problems. Dating bruises is very difficult and medical assessment is essential. If a child has a disability such as epilepsy and has frequent falls, advice must be sought to clarify whether patterns of bruising are consistent with the disability or not. A child may bruise easily due to various medical conditions and this can be proved by medical tests thus eliminating suspicion.

Bruising must be considered in relation to the parent's capacity to supervise responding to the child's developmental needs. Patterns of bruising may be particularly indicative of abuse.

- There may be bruising to the softer parts of the body such as the face, abdomen, buttocks, arms, ears and hands.

- The head, ears and neck are the commonest sites of bruising linked to child abuse.

- As a result of defending themselves abused children may have bruising on the forearm, upper arm, back of the leg, hands or feet.

- Clusters of bruises on the upper arm, outside the thigh or on the body are indicative of abuse.

- Symmetrical bruising may be indicative of gripping or holding a child down.

- Bruises which have petechiae (dots of blood under the skin) around them are more commonly caused by abuse than by an accident.

- Two simultaneous bruised eyes are rarely accidental.

- Bruising on the inner thighs and buttocks may be indicative of sexual abuse, as may bruising in and around the mouth, which in babies may also indicate force-feeding.

- Abusive bruises may carry an imprint of the hand, fingertips, knuckles or an implement.

- Non-accidental head injury or fractures can occur without bruising.

- Severe bruising to the scalp, with swelling around the eyes and no fracture, may occur if the child has had their hair pulled violently (NSPCC, 2012d).

Fractures and dislocations

Accidental fractures are common in children and about 66 per cent of boys and 40 per cent of girls will sustain a fracture by their fifteenth birthday. Some 85 per cent of accidental fractures are seen in children over 5 years but they can also be indicative of abuse. Fractures occur in a significant proportion of physically abused children and 80 per cent of these are seen in children under 18 months (NSPCC, 2012b). Non-mobile children rarely sustain fractures. Social workers need to understand child development and to know that a baby aged 3 months does not roll over and that an infant of 6 months rarely walks or may not be crawling. Not all young children with fractures display pain or discomfort which can make it difficult to detect when a fracture has happened. There are many types of fractures, some more indicative of abuse than others (NSPCC, 2012b).

RESEARCH SUMMARY

In an analysis of 17 serious case reviews involving 28 children from 17 families and including 19 children who died, the most common injuries were brain damage, skull fractures, rib fractures, other fractures and poisoning. Ten died before the age of 10 weeks. In every case it was the youngest child or only child in the family who died. Half had previously been treated for suspicious injuries. We conclude that a great many serious injuries with discrepant explanations, cases both fatal and non-fatal, are preventable. *Most had been assessed as children in need and not in need of protection despite parental histories of substance misuse, mental illness and domestic violence (Dale, et al., 2002, p35).*

Poisoning

The most commonly used substances in poisoning children are salt, paracetamol and prescription drugs. When investigated, parents often say that they had not realised the toxicity of the substance and had not considered that the child might be harmed. In 2014, Child BT died from an overdose of methodone, which was found in his feeding cup. The parents were convicted of manslaughter (BSCB, 2015).

RESEARCH SUMMARY

In one study, 100 mothers were interviewed and all defined salt as a serious poison and had a concept of a safe dosage of paracetamol, but a third did not realise paracetamol could be lethal. The conclusion was that it is highly unlikely that a mother could administer a harmful dose of salt or paracetamol in the belief that their actions would have no ill effect (Smith and Meadows, 2000, p16). Poisoning is more likely to be non-accidental if:

- *a substance is repeatedly administered or ingested in large amounts;*
- *there are other features of abuse;*
- *the child is aged outside 2–4 years;*
- *a history of self-poisoning is implausible;*
- *there is a previous history of unusual presentations to hospital (Meadows, 1997).*

Forced ingestion including of non-food substances

This form of abuse is when a child is forced to eat or drink, including inedible, non-food substances. For example, child sex abusers may force a child to drink alcohol or take muscle-relaxant drugs. In her book *Trust No One*, Cooper described her child-hood in care where she was forced to take a range of anti-psychotic and sedative drugs (Cooper, 2007). The Laffoy Commission on child abuse in Ireland highlighted the exploitation of children in care for use in drug trials. Numbers of children were vaccinated in trials for rubella, whooping cough, polio and diphtheria (Ring, 2003). Krugman, et al., (2007) described cases of young children who have been suffocated through being forced to swallow baby wipes.

CASE STUDY

Baby Diamond

A mother was convicted for 'causing or allowing' the death of a 10-month-old baby 'Diamond' through force-feeding her to boost her weight. In 2010, Diamond died of pneumonia having been found with excessive amounts of food in her lungs. Similar concerns relating to an older sister had been raised in 2009. The serious case review found that social workers made cultural assumptions about African feeding practices and interpreted the mother's behaviour as motivated by her concern for the child. The review stated that, *it is likely that the mother's professional status encouraged the rule of optimism ... an accompanying confidence in her ability to cope with a child with feeding difficulties and to learn from the experience with her elder child* (WFSCB, 2011, p10). Knowledge of the family was not collated across health and other agencies and there was insufficient involvement of the older siblings in the investigation. There was lack of risk assessment or forensic approach to the case. This approach was said to be influenced by a national policy of assessment leading to *a tendency for child protection enquiries to be subsumed as part of an assessment without adequate investigation and risk assessment taking place* (WFSCB, 2011, p11).

Fabricated or induced illness

Children present a rosy picture to the external world whilst they were being subjected to extensive physical and emotional abuse at home.

(DCFS, 2008, p11)

Fabricated or induced illness is a condition whereby a child is harmed through the deliberate action of their parent which is attributed by the parent to another cause. In 93 per cent of cases it is by the mother (Lazenblatt and Taylor, 2011). Illness induction can cause death, disability and physical illness and lead to emotional problems. Children affected are commonly confused about what is happening to them and find it very difficult to speak about it. Professionals must provide children with the opportunity to express their views but be fully aware of not increasing the risk to them prior to protective measures being in place. An existing diagnosed illness in a child does not exclude the possibility of induced illnesses but may provide the parent with opportunities for inducing symptoms (LSCB, 2015, Part B:2.1.1–3). It is possible that a parent might invent a symptom in order to protect the child from other forms of abuse. The action may be a strategy to get the child into hospital for a few days and away from an abuse network.

Safeguarding children in whom illness is fabricated or induced (DCSF, 2008) is the relevant guidance and supplement to *Working Together to Safeguard Children* (DfE, 2015) A training resource, *Incredibly Caring*, supports the guidance (DCSF, 2009a), as does *Fabricated or Induced Illness by Carers*, published by the Royal College of Paediatricians and Child Health (2009).

This category of physical harm may include:

- deliberately inducing symptoms in children by administering medication or other substances, by obstructing the child's airways or by interfering with the child's body to cause physical signs;

- interfering with treatments by overdosing, not administering medication or interfering with medical equipment such as infusion lines;

- claiming the child has symptoms which are unverifiable unless observed directly, such as pain, frequency of passing urine, vomiting or fits – these claims lead to unnecessary investigations and treatments which may cause secondary physical problems;

- exaggerating symptoms, causing professionals to undertake investigations and treatments which may be invasive, are unnecessary and therefore harmful;

- obtaining specialist treatments or equipment for children who do not need them;

- alleging psychological illness in a child;

- interfering with medical documentation (DCSF, 2008, 2.6).

This form of abuse is most commonly identified in younger children and it may take a considerable amount of time to identify what is actually taking place. Older children may collude in the sick role with the parent (Lazenblatt and Taylor, 2011 p2). Parents and carers in these cases may have histories of childhood abuse and considerable medical, obstetric or psychiatric histories. There may be experience of miscarriages, stillbirths or other losses in parents' lives which have often taken place within a short timespan (DCSF, 2008, 2.31). Sometimes the adult knowledge of medical conditions indicates a background in medicine. Child protection conferences must only be held after reaching the point of discussing professional concerns openly with the parent/s, i.e. when it has been agreed that to do so will not place the child at increased risk of significant harm. This may be some time after the commencement of enquiries under section 47 (CA 1989) and a series of strategy discussions/meetings which allows time for the medical professionals to undertake continuing evaluation and police to progress any criminal investigation. Legal action may be needed prior to any conference.

A strategy meeting must consider specific issues when responding to this form of abuse. The child may require constant medical observation and a dedicated medical clinician to co-ordinate treatment. Medical records of the family must be collated to assess the risk and the accuracy of carer accounts. Professional records must be exceptionally confidential in such cases. The strategy meeting will need to include decisions about the nature and timing of any police investigations, including analysis of samples and covert surveillance (this will be police led and co-ordinated). The use of covert video surveillance must only be used if there is no alternative way of obtaining information which will explain the child's signs and symptoms and if the strategy meeting considers that its use is justified based on the medical information (DCSF, 2008, 6.36).

Use of tasars (electrical discharge weapons)

A tasar is an electro-shock, non-lethal weapon used by police. It delivers an electric current to cause incapacitation. The UN Committee against Torture (2013) recommended that the UK ban the use of tasars on children. The UK government responded that it could not implement the recommendation as the prime responsibility of law enforcement agencies is to protect the public (HM Government, 2014 p56). The use of tasars on children is increasing. In 2013, 15 police forces used tasars on 230 children. In 7.5 per cent of cases the tasar was used on drive stun mode which causes pain but not incapacity (CRAE, 2014, p30).

Children in custody and use of restraint

No child shall be subjected to torture or other inhuman or degrading treatment or punishment. No child should be deprived of his or her liberty unlawfully or arbitrarily. The arrest, detention or imprisonment of a child shall be in conformity with the law and shall be used only as a measure of last resort and for the shortest possible period of time.

(UN, 1989, Article 37)

Since 1990, there have been 33 deaths of boys in prison (Willow, 2014, p68).

The death of children fills us all with a particular horror. First that the children must have been intolerably unhappy and second that responsible adults have failed ... to keep children safe from harm. In many cases outside prison, child suicides come as a surprise but as far as young offender institutions are concerned this manifestly cannot be the case as every child prisoner is known to be at risk of suicide.

(CRAE, 2002, p64)

Carlile (2006) said that many practices in child custody would be regarded as child abuse in any other setting and clarified that restraint should not be used primarily to secure compliance. It should only be used to prevent escape from custody, to stop a child hurting themselves, others or damaging property or inciting another trainee to do certain defined acts.

The Howard League stated that the UK government is breaching at least ten articles of the UNCRC (UN, 1989):

> *The profligate use of prison for children, the infliction of pain and injury to control children behind closed doors, child deaths in custody, lack of physical exercise and the use of segregation blocks that resemble modern day dungeons are all ways in which the treatment of children in custody amounts to child abuse and in some cases may be criminal.*

> (2007, p1)

Children appearing in court are not generally named. Yet the law does not prevent naming in public before a child is charged. Courts may also remove reporting restrictions in specific cases. There is much concern that publicly named children become at increased risk of verbal and physical attack or exploitation and the exposure places their families at risk (CRAE, 2014, p28).

Genital integrity – female and male genital mutilation

> *States parties to take all effective and appropriate measures with a view to abolishing traditional practices prejudicial to the health of children.*

> (UN, 1989: Article 24.3)

In a documentary, *The day I will never forget*, Fouzia, aged 5 years, recites a poem to her mother saying she will forgive her only if she promises to spare her sister the practice of FGM:

> *In the morning I was dragged and pinned on the ground. I cried until I had no voice. The only thing I said was 'Mum, where are you?' and the only answer I got was 'Quiet, quiet, girl'. The pain I had experienced was one I will never forget for the rest of my life and I would not wish it to happen to my friend or anyone else. That night I had a sleepless night. I could see an old lady with many blades doing it again and again and again. I screamed. My loving parent, is this what I really deserve?*

> (Longinotto, 2002)

Adult survivors have also written about their experience of FGM (Nazer and Lewis, 2004; Walker, 1993; Dirie, 1998).

Both female genital mutilation (FGM) and non-therapeutic male genital mutilation (MGM) are irreversible procedures performed without the child's consent. Sometimes these practices are said to be justified for cultural or religious reasons but these reasons must never stand in the way of the protection of children from harm (HM Government, 2011). Genital Autonomy (www.genitalautonomy.org.uk) is an advocacy and children's rights charity campaigning to seek an end to non-therapeutic genital surgery on all children.

Female genital mutilation

It is estimated that 127,000 women aged 15 to 60 years who have migrated to England and Wales are living with the consequences of female genital mutilation (FGM). Also, approximately 10,000 girls under 15 years who have migrated to England and Wales are likely to have undergone FGM (Home Office, 2014). Statistics from general practice and mental health trusts found over 1,000 reported cases in England in just two months (Health and Social Care Information, 2015). Police reported that 50 girls were taken from the UK to Somalia by their mothers or grandmothers for FGM between ages 11 and 17 years leading to an investigation (BBC, 2015i).

FGM has been illegal since 1985 in the UK. The Female Genital Mutilation Act 2003 made it illegal to take a child abroad for the procedure with a penalty of 14 years imprisonment. The Serious Crime Act 2015 (s73) extended the legislation to include a new offence of failing to protect a child from the risk of FGM, granting lifelong anonymity to victims and making the Act apply to habitual as well as permanent UK residents. An FGM Protection Order was introduced to place a mandatory duty on those in regulated professions (such as teachers, social workers and health workers) to report any suspicion of FGM appearing to have been carried out on girls under 18 years (Home Office, 2015c). FGM Protection Orders may include:

- confiscating passports or travel documents to prevent girls being taken abroad;
- forbidding anyone from aiding another person to commit or attempt to commit an FGM offence such as bringing a 'cutter' to the UK for the purpose of committing FGM.

An emergency order can be made so that protection is immediately in place. In 2015, police obtained the first order preventing two girls from being taken abroad (BBC, 2015i). Breach of an FGM Protection Order is an imprisonable criminal offence.

Prosecution for this crime can be difficult as very young, and traumatised children, may not remember details about exactly what happened (BBC, 2010c). The lack of implementation of child protection protocols was a concern of a House of Commons Education Committee, *we were appalled to discover that despite 148 referrals of FGM in the past four years, police and social services do not place girls at risk on the child protection register. This must change* (HC 107, 2013–14, p24). FGM in the UK is a form of physical child abuse and is addressed in child protection guidance as a supplement to *Working Together to Safeguard Children* (DfE, 2015; HM Government, 2011). A section 47 (CA 1989) child protection investigation must take place. Specialist advisors should be invited to inform a strategy meeting.

FGM comprises all procedures that involve partial or total removal of the female external genitalia and/or injury to the female genital organs for cultural or any other non-therapeutic reasons (WHO, 1995, 3). The procedure is mainly carried out by older women with no anaesthetic using knives and razor blades, for example. The practice is surrounded in secrecy and girls are often completely unprepared for what happens. FGM is carried out at any age but the age is becoming younger (HC137:1, 2012–13, p 47). In some countries prevalence rates can be as high as 98 per cent (Egypt, Ethiopia, Somalia and Sudan) and as a result of migration the practice has spread to the UK (NSPCC, 2013b).

There are wide-ranging reasons given for performing FGM including preserving virginity, cleansing, upholding family honour and complying with religious beliefs. FGM results in some children's deaths and the harmful long-term emotional, psychological and physical consequences are well documented (Momoh, 2005; NSPCC, 2013b). A child in school may be noticed to have a sudden change of demeanour and behaviour following the trauma, take a long time to urinate, have difficulty walking or standing, be reluctant to attend medical appointments, take time off school following urine and menstrual infections or be absent from physical activities. Children may be identified as at risk of harm if they are from a community or family known to practise FGM, if the procedures have been performed on siblings or if there is a sudden threat to take the children abroad for no clear reason. There is little research about children's perceptions of FGM (Dustin and Davies, 2006).

There is guidance on the London Safeguarding Children Board website (www.londonscb.gov.uk/fgm) including information on Project Azure, a police initiative (LSCB, 2015, Part B:24). Information is also on the Forward website, which is a campaigning group against the practice of FGM (www.forwarduk.org.uk). A statement opposing FGM with relevant contact details has been provided for girls to carry with them especially if they go abroad (Home Office, 2012). *No Laughter Here* (Williams-Garcia, 2004) is a children's story on this topic.

Male genital mutilation

Male genital mutilation (MGM) is not against the law in the UK and is not defined as child abuse. The campaign group 15 Square (www.15 square.org.uk) considers MGM to be abusive because it involves irreversibly removing the foreskin, usually for cultural or religious reasons. The child does not and cannot consent and it infringes a child's right to bodily integrity. Usually carried out on the eighth day after birth, there is no legal requirement for the person undertaking MGM to be medically trained or to have proven expertise. It is common for religious leaders to conduct this practice.

An essential difference between FGM and MGM is that sometimes male circumcision, unlike FGM, may be medically required. However, there is no medical basis for non-therapeutic MGM as a routine practice. MGM can constitute harm when the child acquires an infection as a result of neglect, sustains physical or cosmetic damage, is emotionally, physically or sexually harmed from the way the procedure is carried out, or emotionally harmed from not having been consulted. The procedure is sometimes conducted incompetently or facilities are inadequate or unhygienic. Some babies have died from bleeding and other complications and some are injured (Greenshields, 2009). Freedom of information (FOI) requests to Great Ormond Street Hospital in London found that on average over a five-year period, following complications and bleeding, staff repaired two male circumcisions a week, Manchester Royal Children's hospital treated around three cases a month and in 2009 a Birmingham hospital treated 105 boys (Fogg, 2012). The *London Child Protection Procedures* (LSCB, 2015, Part B:25) provide guidance on MGM and advice as to when to report the procedure to children's services.

Ritual child abuse linked to accusations of 'possession' and 'witchcraft'

Child abuse is never acceptable wherever it occurs and whatever form it takes. Abuse linked to belief, including belief in witchcraft or possession, is a horrific crime which is condemned by people of all cultures, communities and faiths.

(DfE, 2012b, p2)

The power of these beliefs and the power of those religious leaders who espouse them cannot be overestimated. The congregations in these churches hang on the pastor's every word. If they say a child is possessed – for them that is the word of God.

(BBC, 2005)

He believed Khyra [Ishaq] was possessed by a 'jinn', a type of evil spirit that features prominently in Islamic scripture.

(Taylor, 2010)

The traffickers or witch-doctors take your hair and cut your arms, legs, heads and genitals and collect the blood. They say if you speak out I can kill you ... the witch-doctor told me that one day he would need my head.

(Rogers, 2011)

A House of Commons Education Committee drew attention to this form of ritual abuse citing reports that in a period of four years over 400 African children had been abducted and trafficked into the UK, some for the purpose of blood rituals (HC 137:1, 2012–13, p46). The term *spirit possession* is defined as the belief that an evil force has entered a child and is controlling them. Sometimes the term *witchcraft* is used indicating a belief that a child is able to use an evil force to control others. Other language connected to such abuse includes *kindoki, ndoki, djinns, obeah* and *muti murders*. The beliefs are genuinely held by families and religious leaders who make attempts to exorcise evil spirits from the child – sometimes referred to as *deliverance*. It is thought that a large number of cases remain undetected and some children are taken abroad for the procedure (Stickler, 2005). Between January and October 2015, the Metropolitan Police *Project Violet* saw 60 cases involving ritualistic or faith-based beliefs including homicides (BBC, 2015h). A National Action Plan states, *we are clear that this is not about challenging people's beliefs, but where these beliefs lead to abuse that should not be tolerated* (DfE, 2012b, p2).

Disabled children are particularly vulnerable to this form of abuse including those with epilepsy, Down's syndrome, autism, learning disability or mental health problems.

Also vulnerable are children who are left-handed or whose parents have been branded as witches (AFRUCA, 2009). It is important to recognise other indicators which include:

- unexplained marks, burns, bruises, red or sore eyes and complaints about painful genitalia (from rubbing in chilli pepper, salt or ginger) or incision marks;
- a child becoming withdrawn, confused and isolated;
- a lack of bonding with the carer;
- a child accused of being evil;
- poor school attendance;
- limited freedom of movement;
- a malnourished child;
- carers who do not take a child for medical treatment;
- a child with faeces smeared on their clothes;
- carers who have financial obligations to religious leaders (LSCB, 2015, Part B, p26).

Eno's Story is a children's story about the issue of witchcraft accusations (Olofintuade, 2010).

CASE STUDY

Child victims of faith beliefs

Victoria Climbié died from hypothermia and malnourishment following multiple, severe inflicted injuries in 2000 just one week after being taken by her aunt to two pastors who concluded that her incontinence was the result of possession by evil spirits and advised that the problem could be solved by prayer (Laming, 2003). A childminder and hospital staff witnessed Victoria's aunt calling her *a wicked girl* and *little Satan*.

In 2001, the torso of Adam, a 5-year-old boy, was found in the Thames. Hoskins (2012) the expert advisor to the police investigation provides an analysis of this case including a cultural context. *Adam* had been made to eat poisonous substances prior to his death and his body had been drained of blood, indicative of a ritual killing. Police traced Adam's origin to Nigeria. In 2011, a woman provided police with the boy's name and said he had been killed by a group (Crawford, 2013; Goodwin, 2001).

Kristy Bamu, aged 15 years, was drowned in a bath during a supposed exorcism. Kristy's sister and her partner were convicted of murder. They had believed that Kristy had bought *Kindoki* into the home. He was starved, denied sleep, tortured and suffered 101 injuries prior to being drowned. The judge said that *the belief in witchcraft, however genuine, cannot excuse an assault on another person let alone the killing of another person* (BBC, 2012).

Tunde, an Angolan child aged 8 years, was placed in foster care following severe injuries inflicted as an exorcism by three adult family members including Sita Kisanga, imprisoned for the crime of cruelty.

> *Tunde had been beaten with a belt buckle and stabbed with a stiletto shoe, was sliced with a kitchen knife and had chilli pepper rubbed in her eyes. She was also starved for days at a time. She was stuffed naked into a sack and told that she would be thrown into the river. Tunde had scar tissue three centimetres long from one cut to her face. Whip scars and stab marks covered her back and legs. There were at least twenty marks made by a knife. She was extremely malnourished ... Sita believed in Kindoki (possession) and the torture was to 'cleanse' Tunde's spirit ... This is not a cultural issue ... it's child cruelty whatever religious or cultural excuse the abuser gives.*

(Keeble and Hollington, 2010, p116–17)

RESEARCH SUMMARY

Stobart (2006) identified 38 cases of ritual child abuse linked to belief in spirit possession in families from Africa, South Asia and Europe, referred by police, social workers and teachers. Perpetrators were usually the carers but not the natural parents and abuse took place mainly where the child lived, although five were abused in places of worship. Carers often had numbers of partners and siblings were sometimes involved in the violence. Abuse was mainly physical but some cases were classified as sexual abuse. The children were powerless and thought that if they told they would not be believed. They were moved regularly between schools and unmonitored. The children were scapegoated mainly because of perceived difference including disability, rebelliousness and being a high achiever. The abuse was seen by carers as forcing the evil spirit out of the child.

Twenty-four of the children reported being beaten, kicked or punched.

Ten children were scalded or burnt with an implement

Four children were stabbed to create a way out for the evil.

Three children were semi-strangled.

Ten children were made to fast for up to three days.

Isolation was enforced to prevent the evil spreading to other people. Some children were only to be touched by a stick and others were forbidden to eat with the family or were confined to separate rooms.

Some were made to sleep in the bath, forced to have cold baths, tied up, or had salt, ginger or chilli pepper applied to their eyes and genitals.

In 11 cases there were concerns about the mental health of the carer.

Physical 'punishment'

Corporal punishment of children is a violation of their rights to respect for their human dignity and physical integrity. Its widespread legality breaches their right to equal protection under the law.

(Global Initiative to End All Corporal Punishment of Children, 2015)

The Committee remains concerned that corporal punishment still is not fully outlawed in the home and certain educational and alternative care facilities. It is also concerned about the existing legal defence of 'reasonable punishment'. The State Party should take practical steps to end corporal punishment in all settings including the home and should repeal all existing legal defences. It should encourage non-violent forms of discipline as alternatives to corporal punishment and should conduct public information campaigns to raise awareness of its harmful effects.

(UN Human Rights Committee, 2015, p9)

There is growing progress towards universal prohibition of this most common form of violence against children: 46 states have prohibited all corporal punishment of children, including in the family home. The experience of these countries shows convincingly that legal reform along with promoting positive discipline strategies reduces reliance on physical punishment and the need for intervention in family life including prosecutions.

(www.endcorporalpunishment.org)

The debate about physical discipline commonly centres on whether or not parents and carers should smack children. Parental attitudes towards physical punishment are changing. A study involving focus groups with 70 parents found that although most had used physical punishment they did not find it acceptable or effective. A significant number of parents said they would be happy for it to be banned (Prince, et al., 2014). However, the practice remains extensive. In 2011, 2,160 parents of children under 11 years were interviewed about their childhood experiences. Of these parents, 41.6 per cent said they had physically punished their child in the past year (Radford, et al., 2011). Also a report on madrassas (supplementary schools for Muslim children operating outside the mainstream system) found that children in some settings experienced being smacked, hit with a belt and threatened with a stick (Cherti and Bradley, 2011).

Lyon (2000, p48) found that physical punishment is more likely to escalate when used frequently, is a response to parental stress, and that there are unrealistic expectations of a child's behaviour or the parents lack knowledge of alternative ways to respond to their children.

RESEARCH SUMMARY

An international study, involving 32 countries, looking at evidence for the effects of spanking on mental health and crime informed by longitudinal research, found:

- *about 90 per cent of toddlers in North America are spanked and high rates of toddler spanking exist in most other countries as well;*

- *spanking tends to decline with age;*

- *spanking is inversely associated with social class, positively related to number of children in the home, more likely to be used in single-parent than two-parent families;*

- *people who spank tend to support other types of violence such as in resolving disputes;*

- *frequent and infrequent spanking is associated with behaviour problems and impacts negatively on cognitive development;*

- *the consequences of spanking do not vary by level of nurturance by mothers;*

- *the detrimental impact on the child is the same whether spanking is delivered in an impulsive or in a calculated way;*

- *there is no evidence that spanking is ever an effective disciplinary strategy;*

- *spanking is related to risky sexual behaviour because a weakened bond with parents decreases the parental boundary setting so children may have lower self-control, lack self-esteem and may be more accepting of violence in relationships; therefore, they are more likely to be impulsive and seek immediate gratification or to seek acceptance from a partner through sex;*

- *data collected demonstrated the consistency of the association between spanking and intimate partner violence and that spanking is related to engaging in sexual coercion, and that this association remains after controlling for a wide variety of variables, including a history of childhood sexual abuse;*

- *data analyses are also presented showing that spanking predicts other adult criminal behaviour (Straus, et al., 2014).*

In England and Wales, s58 (CA 2004) permits parents and carers to raise the defence of reasonable punishment for common assault on a child. This legal defence is not available for injuries to children which cause actual bodily harm. Anyone acting in loco parentis may use the defence of reasonable punishment, regardless of parents' wishes, as long as they are not specifically prohibited from doing so – as are teachers, foster carers, residential care workers, child minders, staff in Early Years provision and those in custodial and secure settings. Those legally entitled to use this defence include private foster carers, teachers providing under 12.5 hours a week education such as sports coaches, faith teachers, music and home tutors, youth and play workers, hospital staff, lodgers, nannies and relatives.

The Crown Prosecution Service advises that trivial and transitory injuries to a child (in the main not including assaults involving implements) should be treated as common assault while any more serious injury should be charged as actual bodily harm for which the 'reasonable punishment' defence is not available. This approach is criticised by campaign groups:

> this does not deal with punishments which cause pain but not injuries ... Also, assaults ... like blows to the head, ears, kidneys or genitals, are common assaults, as are assaults that cause intense humiliation or emotional damage but no injury. Frequency of smacking is also not a consideration for determining the difference between common assault and actual bodily harm, so children can be smacked many times a day with impunity ... as an attempt to draw a line between acceptable and unacceptable forms of physical punishment, section 58 plainly fails.
>
> (www.childrenareunbeatable.org.uk/the-case-for-reform/flaws-in-section-58.html)

Section 58 (CA 2004) undermines effective child protection because it does not protect children from painful, dangerous, humiliating or frequent assault and deters reporting by children and adults, giving a confused message about the legitimacy of hurting children. Also, the physical punishment of children is not addressed in *Working Together to Safeguard Children* guidance (DfE, 2015).

ACTIVITY 5.4

How is a judgement made about the child being at immediate risk of harm from physical punishment? Think of some questions to help inform your thinking.

COMMENT

Your questions might have included:

- *What is the nature of the injuries? Does the child require urgent medical attention?*
- *What is the child's account and has the child been seen alone?*
- *Are there inconsistent explanations from the child, parents or witnesses?*
- *How can you check the validity of the explanation?*
- *Is there a history of family violence or information about alleged perpetrators?*
- *Is there knowledge about the family's culture and practices that are harmful to children?*
- *How does the family define acceptable parenting methods?*
- *Are there witnesses such as siblings, friends or neighbours?*
- *Is there material or forensic evidence such as texts, photographs, computer images, weapons, implements or damage to property which corroborate a child's statement?*

RESEARCH SUMMARY

Four UK studies, based on the views of 1,500 children aged between 4 and 15 years, about physical punishment, found the following.

Smacking is hitting:

When someone hits you very hard.

They call it a smack, instead of a hit.

Smacking hurts physically and emotionally:

It hurts and it's painful inside.

Sad – feel that mummy and daddy don't love me.

Smacking is wrong:

They are big, the child is small it's not fair.

It hurts and you could break a bone or something.

Smacking sometimes makes them want to smack someone else:

Sad, hurt, feel ill, it stings, inside it hurts, upset, angry.

Grumpy, cross, afraid, feel bad or naughty, feel embarrassed, ashamed.

Adults regret smacking:

They are a bit sorry but don't want to say.

They feel upset, bad.

Adults hit children because of how the adult is feeling:

They just keep doing what they do.

They turn beetroot when they are mad.

Children often get smacked indoors; the bedroom was the most common place followed by when out shopping. They were hit on their bottom, arm or head:

Somewhere no one can see – they know that it's bad.

Somewhere on their own – and nobody's watching.

Children don't hit adults because they are scared they will get hit again:

No-one should smack anyone.

Because grown-ups are bigger and they slap you back even harder.

Half said they wouldn't smack their children when they were adults:

(Continued)

We know what it feels like.

Because it's mean and it hurts the child and they'll just learn to smack.
(Crowley and Vulliamy, 2000; Cutting, 2001; Horgan, 2002;
Willow and Hyder, 2004)

ACTIVITY **5.5**

How might a social worker's personal experience of being hit as a child be a barrier to protecting children from physical punishment?

COMMENT

As with other aspects of child protection work social workers need to reflect on their values and beliefs about the rights of children based on personal experience of parenting and being parented. The widespread acceptance of physical violence towards children may lead social workers to avoid the issue and collude with abusive parenting behaviour. Parental motivation for physical violence to a child may be claimed to be protective even though the action is unreasonable, abusive and requires challenge. Parents may refer to the punishment using euphemisms such as six of the best; a good hiding; a tap; a licking, *leading the child to define the actions as being done for 'good' reasons. Children may also blame themselves for causing the abuse. Children must never be held responsible because children have the right to grow up free from physical violence. This principle is enshrined in international and national legislation.*

When first confronted with evidence or suspicion about a child's injury it is not unusual for parents to respond with shock or disbelief and to be unhelpful to the investigation. The abused child needs support from a non-abusive carer and the social worker will need to take time to create a trusting relationship and assess whether the parent is protective. This process must never be at the expense of a child's safety. This complex work takes place within child protection procedures and is constantly reviewed by a multi-agency team.

Investigating allegations about physical harm to a child – deciding the threshold for intervention

The following case diagrams are designed to promote a questioning approach as they progress from no ongoing concerns to immediate protective action. You should be informed by the list in the Introductory Chapter. Continue to add your own questions and consider the implications and barriers to safe practice in each case.

Case diagram 5.1

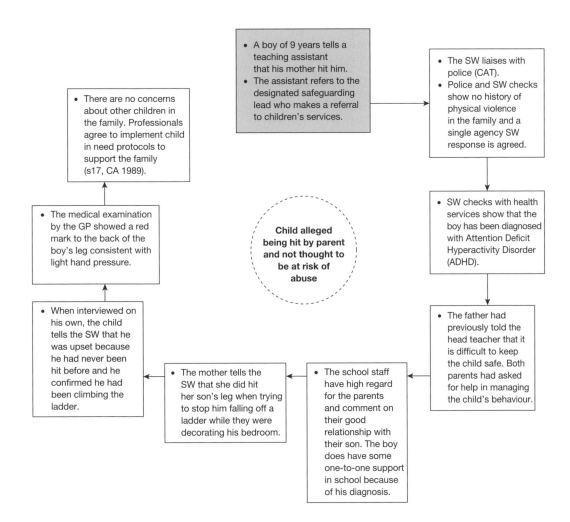

- A boy of 9 years tells a teaching assistant that his mother hit him.
- The assistant refers to the designated safeguarding lead who makes a referral to children's services.

- The SW liaises with police (CAT).
- Police and SW checks show no history of physical violence in the family and a single agency SW response is agreed.

- SW checks with health services show that the boy has been diagnosed with Attention Deficit Hyperactivity Disorder (ADHD).

Child alleged being hit by parent and not thought to be at risk of abuse

- There are no concerns about other children in the family. Professionals agree to implement child in need protocols to support the family (s17, CA 1989).

- The medical examination by the GP showed a red mark to the back of the boy's leg consistent with light hand pressure.

- When interviewed on his own, the child tells the SW that he was upset because he had never been hit before and he confirmed he had been climbing the ladder.

- The mother tells the SW that she did hit her son's leg when trying to stop him falling off a ladder while they were decorating his bedroom.

- The school staff have high regard for the parents and comment on their good relationship with their son. The boy does have some one-to-one support in school because of his diagnosis.

- The father had previously told the head teacher that it is difficult to keep the child safe. Both parents had asked for help in managing the child's behaviour.

Case diagram 5.2

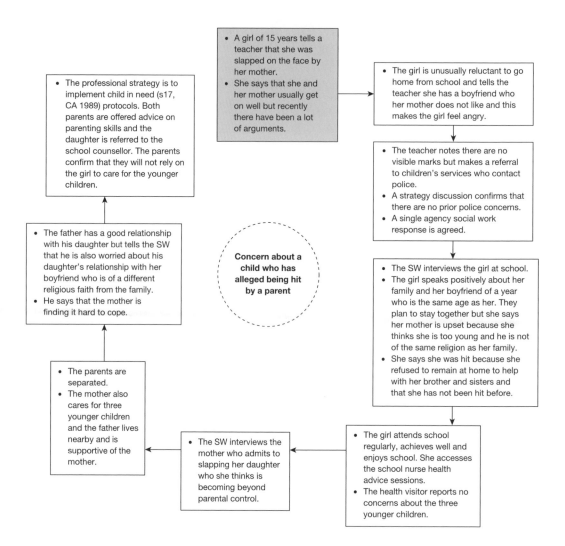

A girl of 15 years tells a teacher that she was slapped on the face by her mother.
- She says that she and her mother usually get on well but recently there have been a lot of arguments.

- The girl is unusually reluctant to go home from school and tells the teacher she has a boyfriend who her mother does not like and this makes the girl feel angry.

- The teacher notes there are no visible marks but makes a referral to children's services who contact police.
- A strategy discussion confirms that there are no prior police concerns.
- A single agency social work response is agreed.

- The SW interviews the girl at school.
- The girl speaks positively about her family and her boyfriend of a year who is the same age as her. They plan to stay together but she says her mother is upset because she thinks she is too young and he is not of the same religion as her family.
- She says she was hit because she refused to remain at home to help with her brother and sisters and that she has not been hit before.

Concern about a child who has alleged being hit by a parent

- The girl attends school regularly, achieves well and enjoys school. She accesses the school nurse health advice sessions.
- The health visitor reports no concerns about the three younger children.

- The SW interviews the mother who admits to slapping her daughter who she thinks is becoming beyond parental control.

- The parents are separated.
- The mother also cares for three younger children and the father lives nearby and is supportive of the mother.

- The father has a good relationship with his daughter but tells the SW that he is also worried about his daughter's relationship with her boyfriend who is of a different religious faith from the family.
- He says that the mother is finding it hard to cope.

- The professional strategy is to implement child in need (s17, CA 1989) protocols. Both parents are offered advice on parenting skills and the daughter is referred to the school counsellor. The parents confirm that they will not rely on the girl to care for the younger children.

Case diagram 5.3

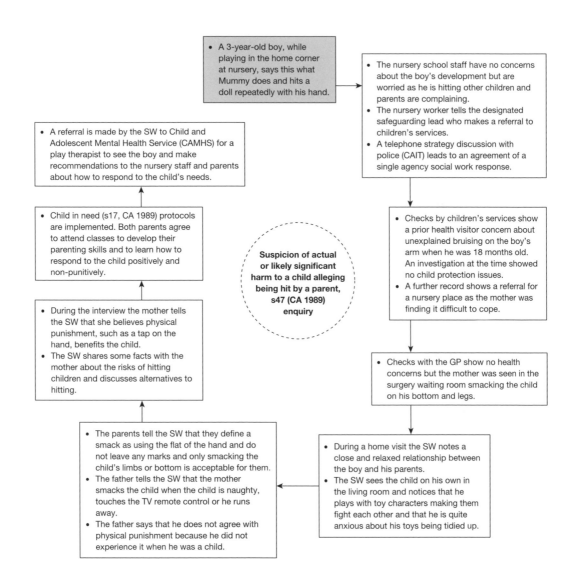

- A 3-year-old boy, while playing in the home corner at nursery, says this what Mummy does and hits a doll repeatedly with his hand.

- The nursery school staff have no concerns about the boy's development but are worried as he is hitting other children and parents are complaining.
- The nursery worker tells the designated safeguarding lead who makes a referral to children's services.
- A telephone strategy discussion with police (CAIT) leads to an agreement of a single agency social work response.

- A referral is made by the SW to Child and Adolescent Mental Health Service (CAMHS) for a play therapist to see the boy and make recommendations to the nursery staff and parents about how to respond to the child's needs.

- Child in need (s17, CA 1989) protocols are implemented. Both parents agree to attend classes to develop their parenting skills and to learn how to respond to the child positively and non-punitively.

Suspicion of actual or likely significant harm to a child alleging being hit by a parent, s47 (CA 1989) enquiry

- Checks by children's services show a prior health visitor concern about unexplained bruising on the boy's arm when he was 18 months old. An investigation at the time showed no child protection issues.
- A further record shows a referral for a nursery place as the mother was finding it difficult to cope.

- During the interview the mother tells the SW that she believes physical punishment, such as a tap on the hand, benefits the child.
- The SW shares some facts with the mother about the risks of hitting children and discusses alternatives to hitting.

- Checks with the GP show no health concerns but the mother was seen in the surgery waiting room smacking the child on his bottom and legs.

- The parents tell the SW that they define a smack as using the flat of the hand and do not leave any marks and only smacking the child's limbs or bottom is acceptable for them.
- The father tells the SW that the mother smacks the child when the child is naughty, touches the TV remote control or he runs away.
- The father says that he does not agree with physical punishment because he did not experience it when he was a child.

- During a home visit the SW notes a close and relaxed relationship between the boy and his parents.
- The SW sees the child on his own in the living room and notices that he plays with toy characters making them fight each other and that he is quite anxious about his toys being tidied up.

Case diagram 5.4

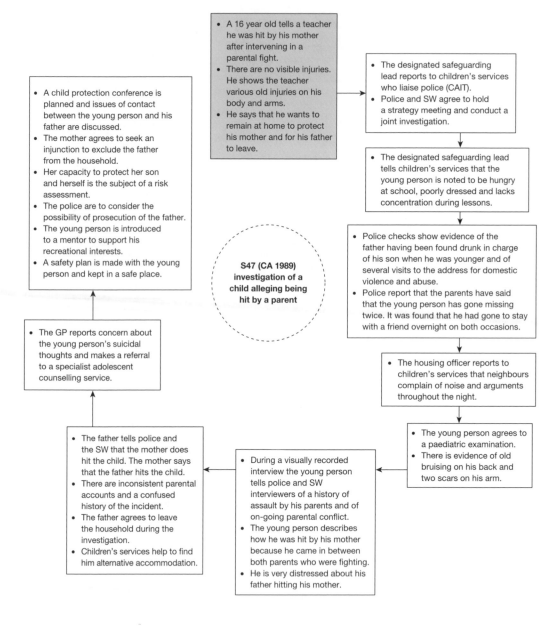

- A 16 year old tells a teacher he was hit by his mother after intervening in a parental fight.
- There are no visible injuries. He shows the teacher various old injuries on his body and arms.
- He says that he wants to remain at home to protect his mother and for his father to leave.

- The designated safeguarding lead reports to children's services who liaise police (CAIT).
- Police and SW agree to hold a strategy meeting and conduct a joint investigation.

- The designated safeguarding lead tells children's services that the young person is noted to be hungry at school, poorly dressed and lacks concentration during lessons.

- Police checks show evidence of the father having been found drunk in charge of his son when he was younger and of several visits to the address for domestic violence and abuse.
- Police report that the parents have said that the young person has gone missing twice. It was found that he had gone to stay with a friend overnight on both occasions.

- The housing officer reports to children's services that neighbours complain of noise and arguments throughout the night.

S47 (CA 1989) investigation of a child alleging being hit by a parent

- A child protection conference is planned and issues of contact between the young person and his father are discussed.
- The mother agrees to seek an injunction to exclude the father from the household.
- Her capacity to protect her son and herself is the subject of a risk assessment.
- The police are to consider the possibility of prosecution of the father.
- The young person is introduced to a mentor to support his recreational interests.
- A safety plan is made with the young person and kept in a safe place.

- The GP reports concern about the young person's suicidal thoughts and makes a referral to a specialist adolescent counselling service.

- The father tells police and the SW that the mother does hit the child. The mother says that the father hits the child.
- There are inconsistent parental accounts and a confused history of the incident.
- The father agrees to leave the household during the investigation.
- Children's services help to find him alternative accommodation.

- During a visually recorded interview the young person tells police and SW interviewers of a history of assault by his parents and of on-going parental conflict.
- The young person describes how he was hit by his mother because he came in between both parents who were fighting.
- He is very distressed about his father hitting his mother.

- The young person agrees to a paediatric examination.
- There is evidence of old bruising on his back and two scars on his arm.

Case diagram 5.5

- A girl of 12 years tells her paternal aunt that her father hit her with a wire coat hanger across the back and that it hurts a lot.
- She has a 6-month-old sister.
- Both children are subject to a child protection plan under the category of physical abuse.

- The aunt calls children's services and wishes to remain anonymous.
- The SW liaises with police (CAIT) and they hold a strategy discussion.
- A joint investigation is agreed.

- Both children are placed with foster carers pending assessment of the paternal aunt and of the mother's capacity to protect.
- The child protection review conference is brought forward.
- Police charge the father with Actual Bodily Harm (ABH).

- SW checks show that the health visitor is concerned about the 6-month-old baby who was noted, when seen a week ago, to be unsettled and miserable. Otherwise there have been no concerns.

- After a medical examination, to which the child consented, the paediatrician confirms that the injuries are consistent with the child's account.
- The paediatrician, after an examination, confirms that there is no current evidence of injury towards the baby.

Immediate action to protect a child/children from physical abuse

- Police checks show that the father has a conviction for grievous bodily harm (GBH) which occurred during an incident at a football match. The mother has two convictions for assaults on neighbours.
- There have been numerous previous referrals to children's services for a range of issues.

- On arrest, the father does not comment. The mother, on interview by police and SW, says she does not know what happened as she wasn't at home at the time.
- Both parents agree to both children being accommodated under s20 (CA 1989) and to supervised contact arrangements.

- The SW and police interview the girl on her own at the child's home and she says she wants to live with her paternal aunt.
- She provides a full account of the incident. She is frightened and worried her father might hit her again and is also concerned for the safety of the baby as she says her mother cannot stop her dad's violence.
- She shows them the coat hanger which is kept as evidence by the police.
- A visually recorded interview is arranged (MoJ, 2011)

- The SW is frightened of the parents and learns of threats to previous SWs.
- The SW discusses the implications of this with the SW manager in supervision.

- The school nurse informs the designated safeguarding lead of the girl's frequent visits to her office with sickness and stomach pains and that she sometimes wets herself.
- The designated safeguarding lead at the school reports continued concerns about the girl being withdrawn and not wanting to participate in physical education activities.

A wide range of forms and contexts of physical harm to children are included in this chapter in response to findings from serious case reviews that gaps in social work knowledge exist of the indicators of physical abuse. A chronology, as a systematic collation of information, is included as a tool for use in practice and to further analytical skills. The abuse of children through a belief in spirit possession and through FGM are highlighted because of a known lack of intervention to protect children in these situations. Case diagrams enable deep learning about the rights of children who are physically punished and about protection procedures in this context.

FURTHER READING

Humphreys, C and Stanley, N (2015) *Domestic violence and protecting children.* London: Jessica Kingsley.
Provides a research-based contemporary analysis.

Willow, C (2014) *Children behind bars. Why the abuse of child imprisonment must end.* Bristol: Policy Press.
A unique exposé of child abuse in secure and custodial settings.

WEBSITES

www.childrenareunbeatable.org.uk
A coalition of organisations opposed to physical punishment of children.

www.respect.uk.net
Confidential information and advice to help perpetrators stop their violence and change their abusive behaviours. They also run a helpline for male survivors of domestic violence.

Conclusion

The Human Rights Council (2014), in *a global call to make the invisible visible*, called for an end to all violence against children stating that *the human dignity of children and their right to protection from violence must be at the heart of a global effort.* This global call is at the heart of this book.

Making the invisible visible is a recurring theme of this book as case study after case study, fact after fact, testifies to children who remained unheard, unseen and unprotected. Despite numerous policies, legislation, systems, extensive knowledge of child abuse evident from survivor and child accounts, inquiries and research literature, something has gone very wrong. The prevalence rates for all forms of abuse are evident in this book and yet only a small percentage of abused children gain protection (OCC, 2015, p8). As more knowledge becomes available about the extent and nature of abuse, the statutory and voluntary services are fast shrinking and expertise is being lost. Social workers are overwhelmed and new staff unfamiliar with the skills of child protection investigation are steered by policies and structures entrenched in the concept of assessment. There is a need for more child-friendly environments with staff skilled in recognising and responding to children's disclosures and indicators of abuse, as part of protective systems which do not rely on a child telling. This approach is referred to variably as proactive enquiry, professional curiosity and problem profiling. It suggests methodologies of multi-agency working which promote trusting relationships across professional boundaries and include co-location, shared resources and joint training. These messages signal the need for strong, clear guidance as provided in *Working Together to Safeguard Children* (DCSF, 2010a), which must be revisited, including an emphasis on both police and social workers conducting ABE (MoJ, 2011) interviews of children, and investigating significant harm. Social work specialist child protection posts need to be created and these social workers specifically trained to work jointly with the police and other agencies. This book has been unsparing in detail and determination to push a powerful message that abused children and survivors deserve so much more than is currently provided. If the *Barnahus* model, tried and tested in Scandinavia, as recommended by the Children's Commissioner for England (OCC, 2015) is implemented, this will introduce a sea-change in approach so desperately needed (Davies, 2011).

This book has aimed to make the invisible visible by including many case studies about children who were not seen by protective systems. In Rotherham it was said that *the extreme nature of the signs required concerns to be escalated to top managers but this did not happen. Ultimately it was the efforts of staff on the ground [listening to children's voices] and their observations and persistence which was the main driver in the eventual identification of CSE* (OSCB, 2015, p9). There is no doubt that high quality social work is carried out by dedicated, committed professionals.

This book was written to enable social workers and other professionals on the ground to be knowledgeable about all areas of abuse covered, and to recognise where there are major gaps highlighted by research, reviews, inquiries and, significantly for this book, the voices of children and survivors. Social workers need to be courageous and persistent in their commitment to social work ethical codes, striving to protect children and acting proactively to keep them safe. Persistence includes obtaining senior management support and responsibility, sufficient resources and effective multi-agency working. Where structures, policies, management styles and cuts in resources do not facilitate the work, then there is a need for persistent campaigning, through trade unions, professional bodies and working with service user groups, and for taking appropriate political measures, as is everyone's right in a democracy, to achieve what you know to be right for your profession and for the children you are struggling to protect.

Alinsky, a community activist, stated that:

> it is as though as an artist he is painting a tiny leaf. It is inevitable that sooner or later he will react with 'What am I doing spending my whole life just painting one little leaf? The hell with it, I quit.' What keeps him going is a blurred vision of a great mural where other artists – organizers – are painting their bits, and each piece is essential to the total

(1971, p75)

Appendix 1

Professional Capabilities Framework

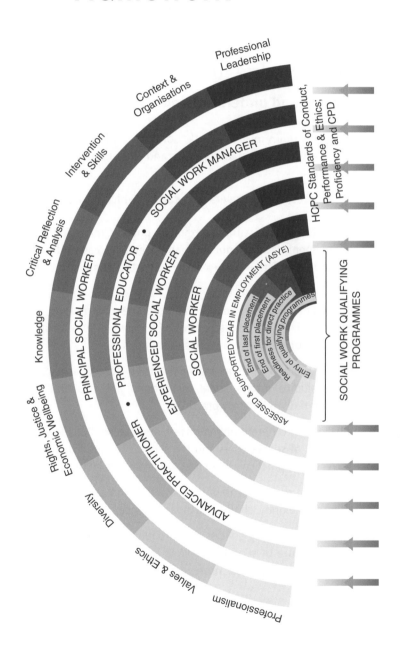

Appendix 2
Subject benchmark for social work

5 Subject knowledge, understanding and skills
Subject knowledge and understanding

5.1 During their degree studies in social work, honours graduates should acquire, critically evaluate, apply and integrate knowledge and understanding in the following five core areas of study.

5.1.1 **Social work services, service users and carers**, which include:

- the social processes (associated with, for example, poverty, migration, unemployment, poor health, disablement, lack of education and other sources of disadvantage) that lead to marginalisation, isolation and exclusion, and their impact on the demand for social work services

- explanations of the links between definitional processes contributing to social differences (for example, social class, gender, ethnic differences, age, sexuality and religious belief) to the problems of inequality and differential need faced by service users

- the nature of social work services in a diverse society (with particular reference to concepts such as prejudice, interpersonal, institutional and structural discrimination, empowerment and anti-discriminatory practices)

- the nature and validity of different definitions of, and explanations for, the characteristics and circumstances of service users and the services required by them, drawing on knowledge from research, practice experience, and from service users and carers

- the focus on outcomes, such as promoting the well-being of young people and their families, and promoting dignity, choice and independence for adults receiving services

- the relationship between agency policies, legal requirements and professional boundaries in shaping the nature of services provided in interdisciplinary contexts and the issues associated with working across professional boundaries and within different disciplinary groups.

5.1.2 **The service delivery context**, which includes:

- the location of contemporary social work within historical, comparative and global perspectives, including European and international contexts

- the changing demography and cultures of communities in which social workers will be practising

- the complex relationships between public, social and political philosophies, policies and priorities and the organisation and practice of social work, including the contested nature of these

- the issues and trends in modern public and social policy and their relationship to contemporary practice and service delivery in social work

- the significance of legislative and legal frameworks and service delivery standards (including the nature of legal authority, the application of legislation in practice, statutory accountability and tensions between statute, policy and practice)

- the current range and appropriateness of statutory, voluntary and private agencies providing community-based, day-care, residential and other services and the organisational systems inherent within these

- the significance of interrelationships with other related services, including housing, health, income maintenance and criminal justice (where not an integral social service)

- the contribution of different approaches to management, leadership and quality in public and independent human services

- the development of personalised services, individual budgets and direct payments

- the implications of modern information and communications technology (ICT) for both the provision and receipt of services.

5.1.3 **Values and ethics**, which include:

- the nature, historical evolution and application of social work values

- the moral concepts of rights, responsibility, freedom, authority and power inherent in the practice of social workers as moral and statutory agents

- the complex relationships between justice, care and control in social welfare and the practical and ethical implications of these, including roles as statutory agents and in upholding the law in respect of discrimination

- aspects of philosophical ethics relevant to the understanding and resolution of value dilemmas and conflicts in both interpersonal and professional contexts

- the conceptual links between codes defining ethical practice, the regulation of professional conduct and the management of potential conflicts generated by the codes held by different professional groups.

5.1.4 **Social work theory**, which includes:

- research-based concepts and critical explanations from social work theory and other disciplines that contribute to the knowledge base of social work, including their distinctive epistemological status and application to practice

- the relevance of sociological perspectives to understanding societal and structural influences on human behaviour at individual, group and community levels

- the relevance of psychological, physical and physiological perspectives to understanding personal and social development and functioning

- social science theories explaining group and organisational behaviour, adaptation and change

- models and methods of assessment, including factors underpinning the selection and testing of relevant information, the nature of professional judgement and the processes of risk assessment and decision-making

- approaches and methods of intervention in a range of settings, including factors guiding the choice and evaluation of these

- user-led perspectives

- knowledge and critical appraisal of relevant social research and evaluation methodologies, and the evidence base for social work.

5.1.5 **The nature of social work practice**, which includes:

- the characteristics of practice in a range of community-based and organisational settings within statutory, voluntary and private sectors, and the factors influencing changes and developments in practice within these contexts

- the nature and characteristics of skills associated with effective practice, both direct and indirect, with a range of service-users and in a variety of settings

- the processes that facilitate and support service user choice and independence

- the factors and processes that facilitate effective interdisciplinary, interprofessional and interagency collaboration and partnership

- the place of theoretical perspectives and evidence from international research in assessment and decision-making processes in social work practice

- the integration of theoretical perspectives and evidence from international research into the design and implementation of effective social work intervention, with a wide range of service users, carers and others

- the processes of reflection and evaluation, including familiarity with the range of approaches for evaluating service and welfare outcomes, and their significance for the development of practice and the practitioner.

Problem-solving skills

5.5 These are sub-divided into four areas.

5.5.1 **Managing problem-solving activities:** honours graduates in social work should be able to plan problem-solving activities, i.e. to:

- think logically, systematically, critically and reflectively

- apply ethical principles and practices critically in planning problem-solving activities

- plan a sequence of actions to achieve specified objectives, making use of research, theory and other forms of evidence

- manage processes of change, drawing on research, theory and other forms of evidence.

5.5.2 **Gathering information:** honours graduates in social work should be able to:

- gather information from a wide range of sources and by a variety of methods, for a range of purposes. These methods should include electronic searches, reviews of relevant literature, policy and procedures, face-to-face interviews, written and telephone contact with individuals and groups

- take into account differences of viewpoint in gathering information and critically assess the reliability and relevance of the information gathered

- assimilate and disseminate relevant information in reports and case records.

5.5.3 **Analysis and synthesis:** honours graduates in social work should be able to analyse and synthesise knowledge gathered for problem-solving purposes, i.e. to:

- assess human situations, taking into account a variety of factors (including the views of participants, theoretical concepts, research evidence, legislation and organisational policies and procedures)

- analyse information gathered, weighing competing evidence and modifying their viewpoint in light of new information, then relate this information to a particular task, situation or problem

- consider specific factors relevant to social work practice (such as risk, rights, cultural differences and linguistic sensitivities, responsibilities to protect vulnerable individuals and legal obligations)

- assess the merits of contrasting theories, explanations, research, policies and procedures

- synthesise knowledge and sustain reasoned argument

- employ a critical understanding of human agency at the macro (societal), mezzo (organisational and community) and micro (inter and intrapersonal) levels

- critically analyse and take account of the impact of inequality and discrimination in work with people in particular contexts and problem situations.

5.5.4 **Intervention and evaluation:** honours graduates in social work should be able to use their knowledge of a range of interventions and evaluation processes selectively to:

- build and sustain purposeful relationships with people and organisations in community-based, and interprofessional contexts

- make decisions, set goals and construct specific plans to achieve these, taking into account relevant factors including ethical guidelines

- negotiate goals and plans with others, analysing and addressing in a creative manner human, organisational and structural impediments to change

- implement plans through a variety of systematic processes that include working in partnership

- undertake practice in a manner that promotes the well-being and protects the safety of all parties

- engage effectively in conflict resolution

- support service users to take decisions and access services, with the social worker as navigator, advocate and supporter

- manage the complex dynamics of dependency and, in some settings, provide direct care and personal support in everyday living situations

- meet deadlines and comply with external definitions of a task

- plan, implement and critically review processes and outcomes

- bring work to an effective conclusion, taking into account the implications for all involved

- monitor situations, review processes and evaluate outcomes

- use and evaluate methods of intervention critically and reflectively.

Communication skills

5.6 Honours graduates in social work should be able to communicate clearly, accurately and precisely (in an appropriate medium) with individuals and groups in a range of formal and informal situations, i.e. to:

- make effective contact with individuals and organisations for a range of objectives, by verbal, paper-based and electronic means

- clarify and negotiate the purpose of such contacts and the boundaries of their involvement

- listen actively to others, engage appropriately with the life experiences of service users, understand accurately their viewpoint and overcome personal prejudices to respond appropriately to a range of complex personal and interpersonal situations

- use both verbal and non-verbal cues to guide interpretation

- identify and use opportunities for purposeful and supportive communication with service users within their everyday living situations

- follow and develop an argument and evaluate the viewpoints of, and evidence presented by, others

- write accurately and clearly in styles adapted to the audience, purpose and context of the communication

- use advocacy skills to promote others' rights, interests and needs

- present conclusions verbally and on paper, in a structured form, appropriate to the audience for which these have been prepared

- make effective preparation for, and lead meetings in a productive way

- communicate effectively across potential barriers resulting from differences

- (for example, in culture, language and age).

Skills in working with others

5.7 Honours graduates in social work should be able to work effectively with others, i.e. to:

- involve users of social work services in ways that increase their resources, capacity and power to influence factors affecting their lives

- consult actively with others, including service users and carers, who hold relevant information or expertise

- act cooperatively with others, liaising and negotiating across differences such as organisational and professional boundaries and differences of identity or language

- develop effective helping relationships and partnerships with other individuals, groups and organisations that facilitate change

- act with others to increase social justice by identifying and responding to prejudice, institutional discrimination and structural inequality

- act within a framework of multiple accountability (for example, to agencies, the public, service users, carers and others)

- challenge others when necessary, in ways that are most likely to produce positive outcomes.

Skills in personal and professional development

5.8 Honours graduates in social work should be able to:

- advance their own learning and understanding with a degree of independence

- reflect on and modify their behaviour in the light of experience

- identify and keep under review their own personal and professional boundaries

- manage uncertainty, change and stress in work situations

- handle inter and intrapersonal conflict constructively

- understand and manage changing situations and respond in a flexible manner

- challenge unacceptable practices in a responsible manner

- take responsibility for their own further and continuing acquisition and use of knowledge and skills

- use research critically and effectively to sustain and develop their practice.

7 Benchmark standards

7.1 Given the essentially applied nature of social work and the co-terminosity of the degree and the professional award, students must demonstrate that they have met the standards specified in relation to **both** academic and practice capabilities. These standards relate to subject-specific knowledge, understanding and skills (including key skills inherent in the concept of 'graduateness'). Qualifying students will be expected to meet each of these standards in accordance with the specific standards set by the relevant country (see section 2).

Typical graduate

7.2 Levels of attainment will vary along a continuum from the threshold to excellence. This level represents that of typical students graduating with an honours degree in social work.

Knowledge and understanding

7.3 On graduating with an honours degree in social work, students should be able to demonstrate:

- a sound understanding of the five core areas of knowledge and understanding relevant to social work, as detailed in paragraph 5.1, including their application to practice and service delivery

- an ability to use this knowledge and understanding in an integrated way, in specific practice contexts

- an ability to use this knowledge and understanding to engage in effective relationships with service users and carers appraisal of previous learning and experience and ability to incorporate this into their future learning and practice

- acknowledgement and understanding of the potential and limitations of social work as a practice-based discipline to effect individual and social change

- an ability to use research and enquiry techniques with reflective awareness, to collect, analyse and interpret relevant information

- a developed capacity for the critical evaluation of knowledge and evidence from a range of sources.

Subject-specific and other skills

7.4 On graduating with an honours degree in social work, students should be able to demonstrate a developed capacity to:

- apply creatively a repertoire of core skills as detailed in section 5

- communicate effectively with service users and carers, and with other professionals

- integrate clear understanding of ethical issues and codes of values, and practice with their interventions in specific situations

- consistently exercise an appropriate level of autonomy and initiative in individual decision-making within the context of supervisory, collaborative, ethical and organisational requirements

- demonstrate habits of critical reflection on their performance and take responsibility for modifying action in light of this.

References

A National Voice (2006) *Brothers and sisters: siblings matter to children in care*. Manchester: ANV.

ACMD (Advisory Council on Misuse of Drugs) (2011) *Hidden harm. Responding to the needs of children of problem drug users*. London: ACMD.

Action for Children (2013) *The state of child neglect in the UK*. Watford: Action for Children and the University of Stirling.

ADASS (Association of Directors of Adult Social Services) and ADCS (Association of Directors of Children's Services) (2011) *See me, hear me, talk to me – talk to my family as well*. London: ADASS and ADCS.

Adfam (Families drugs and alcohol) (2013) *Parental substance misuse through the eyes of the worker*. London: Adfam.

Adler, D (2012) Frontline won't address problematic perceptions about the profession. *Guardian*, 9 November.

AFRUCA (Africans Unite Against Child Abuse) (2009) *What is witchcraft abuse?* London: AFRUCA.

Aiden, H and McCarthy, A (2014) *Current attitudes towards disabled people*. London: Scope.

Ainsworth, M and Bell, S (1970) Attachment, exploration, and separation: Illustrated by the behavior of one-year-olds in a strange situation. *Child Development*, 41, 49–67.

Alinsky, S (1971) *Rules for radicals*. USA: Random House.

Allison, E and Hattenstone, S (2012) A true horror story: The abuse of teenage boys in a detention centre. *Guardian*. 13 April.

Allison, E and Hattenstone, S (2014) Durham police uncover paedophile ring with more than 500 potential victims. *Guardian*, 28 March.

Allnock, D, Bunting, L, Price, A, Morgan-Klein, N, Ellis, J, Radford, L and Stafford, A (2009) *Sexual abuse and therapeutic services for children and young people*. London: NSPCC.

Allnock, D and Miller, P (2013) *No one noticed. No one heard*. London: NSPCC.

APPG (All Party Parliamentary Group) (2012) *Report form the joint inquiry into children who go missing from care*. London: APPG.

Bamburgh, S, Shaw, M and Kershaw, S (2014) The Family Drug and Alcohol Court Service in London: a new way of doing care proceedings. *Journal of Social Work Practice*, 28(3), 357–70.

Barlow, J and Schrader McMillan, A (2010) *Safeguarding children from emotional maltreatment*. London: Jessica Kingsley.

Barn, R. and Das, C (2015) Family Group Conferences and Cultural Competence in Social Work. British *Journal of Social Work*, BCU 105.

Barnardo's (2006) *Past abuse suffered by children in custody*. London: Howard League for Penal Reform.

Barnardo's (2014) *On the outside, identifying and supporting children with a parent in prison*. www. Barnardos.org.uk/on-the-outside.pdf

Barnet, A (2005) Deaf victims end 40-year silence on child sex abuse. *Guardian*, 20 March.

Barter, C, McCarry, M, Berridge, D and Evans, K (2009) *Partner exploitation and violence in teenage intimate relationships*. London: NSPCC/University of Bristol.

BASW (British Association of Social Workers) (2012a) *Code of ethics for social work*. http://cdn.basw.co.uk/upload/basw_112315-7.pdf

BASW (British Association of Social Workers) (2012b) *The state of social work*. http://cdn.basw.co.uk/upload/basw_23651-3.pdf

BASW (British Association of Social Workers) (2013) *Inquiry into the state of social work report*. http://cdn.basw.co.uk/upload/basw_90352-5.pdf

BASW (British Association of Social Workers) (2015) *Historic social work meeting agrees joint approach to safeguard and promote a valuable profession*. www.basw.co.uk/news/article/?id=1000

Batty, D (2008) Jersey police enter new secret chamber in children's home abuse inquiry. *Guardian*, 10 March.

BBC (2005) Today programme interview with Sita Kisanga, 15 June. www.bbc.co.uk/radio4/today/newsletter/newsletter_20050615.shtml

BBC (2006a) *Mother allowed baby son's murder*. 2 November. http://news.bbc.co.uk/1/hi/wales/south_west/6107138.stm

BBC (2006b) *Saving Becky. Real story documentary*. 29 August.

BBC (2009a) *Nursery paedophile Vanessa George jailed indefinitely.* 15 December. http://news.bbc.co.uk/1/hi/england/8345756.stm

BBC (2009b) *Baby Peter: Trio who caused his death.* http://news.bbc.co.uk/1/hi/england/7727641.stm

BBC (2010a) *Young carers are four times the official UK number.* 16 November. www.bbc.co.uk/newsbeat/11758368

BBC (2010b) *Milton mother who killed baby detained indefinitely.* 16 June. http://www.bbc.co.uk/news/10327455

BBC (2010c) *'Rise in female genital mutilation' in London*. 22 August. www.bbc.co.uk/news/uk-england-london-11053375?print=true

BBC (2012) *Witchcraft murder: Couple jailed for Kristy Bamu killing*. 5 March. www.bbc.co.uk/news/uk-england-london-17255470

BBC (2015a) *Victims of historic sexual abuse at deaf school speak about their ordeal*. 5 November. www.bbc.co.uk/news/disability-34639080

BBC (2015b) *Child abuse cases delayed by police backlog*. 5 November. www.bbc.co.uk/news/uk-34713745

BBC (2015c) *Sexting boy's naked selfie recorded as crime by police*. 3 September. www.bbc.co.uk/news/uk-34136388

BBC (2015d) *Marie Black gets life term for child abuse*. 28 September. www.bbc.co.uk/news/uk-england-norfolk-34377382

BBC (2015e) *Historic child abuse: Key investigations*. 17 August. http://www.bbc.co.uk/news/uk-28194271

BBC (2015f) *Homelessness figures: Nearly 100,000 children in England 'homeless'*. 24 September. www.bbc.co.uk/news/uk-34346908

BBC (2015g) *Children missing from Devon and Cornwall care 356 times.* 5 May. www.bbc.co.uk/news/uk-england-devon-31154294

BBC (2015h) *Witchcraft abuse cases on the rise.* 11 October. www.bbc.co.uk/news/uk-34475424

BBC (2015i) *'Fifty girls' taken from UK to Somalia for FGM.* 17 July. www.bbc.co.uk/news/uk-33572428

BBC (2016) New 'sexting' guidance to avoid criminalising children. 15 February. www.bbc.co.uk. news/technology-35577506

Bean, P and Melville, J (1989) *Lost children of the empire.* London: Unwin.

Beckett, C (2007) *Child protection: An introduction.* London: Sage.

Bee, H (1992) *The developing child.* New York: HarperCollins.

Bell, M and Wilson, K (2006) Children's views of family group conferences. *British Journal of Social Work*, 36, 671–81.

Benton, T (2011) *An analysis of reported bullying at school within NFER attitude surveys.* Berkshire: National Foundation for Educational Research.

Berelowitz, S, Clifton, J, Firmin, C, Gulyurtlu, S, Edwards, G (2013) *'If only someone had listened'. Final report inquiry into child sexual exploitation in gangs and groups.* London: OCC.

Berelowitz, S, Firmin, C, Edwards, G and Gulyurtlu, S (2012) *'I thought I was the only one in the world'. Interim Report Inquiry into Child Sexual Exploitation in Gangs and Groups.* London: OCC.

Beresford, B and Rhodes, D (2012) *Housing and disabled children.* York: Joseph Rowntree Foundation.

Biehal, N, Cusworth, L, Wade, J and Clarke, S (2014) *Keeping children safe: allegations concerning the abuse or neglect of children in care.* Final report. London: NSPCC.

Birmingham Safeguarding Children Board (BSCB) (2010) *Serious case review in respect of the death of a child Case 14.* Birmingham: BSCB.

Blackpool Safeguarding Children Board (BSCB) (2015) *Serious case review of Child BT. Overview report.* Blackpool: BSCB.

Blake, N (2006) *The Deepcut review report.* London: The Stationery Office.

BMA (British Medical Association) (2014) *Young lives behind bars.* London: BMA.

Bokhari, F (2008) Removing barriers, protecting children in tourist destinations. *ChildRight*, May Colchester: Children's Legal Centre.

Bowcott, O (2015) Children to be given a voice in Family Law proceedings. *Guardian.* 19 February.

Bowlby, J (1969) *Attachment and loss, Vol. 1: Attachment.* New York: Basic Books.

Brady, M, Kwhali, G, Brown, S, Crowe, S and Matouskova, G (2014) *Social worker's knowledge and confidence with cases of child sexual abuse.* London: NSPCC and University of Coventry.

Brandon, M, Bailey, S, Belderson, P and Larsson, B (2013) *Neglect and serious case reviews. A report by the University of East Anglia.* London: NSPCC.

Brandon, M, Belderson, P, Warren, C, Howe, D, Gardner, R, Dodsworth, J and Black, J (2008) *Analysing child deaths and serious injury through abuse and neglect: What can we learn? A biennial analysis of serious case reviews 2003–5.* London: DCSF.

Brandon, M, Sidebotham, P, Bailey, S and Belderson, P (2011) *A study of recommendations arising from serious case reviews 2009–10.* London: DfE.

Brandon, M, Sidebotham, P, Belderson, P, Hawley, C, Ellis, C and Megson, M (2012a) *New learning from serious case reviews: a two year report for 2009–11.* London: Department for Education.

Brandon, M, Sidebotham, P, Ellis, C, Bailey, S and Belderson, P (2012b) *Child and family practitioners' understanding of child development:* London: Department for Education.

BRAP (2011) Child Protection and BME communities www.brap.org.uk/our-ideas/child-protection

Bridge Child Care Consultancy (1991) *Report on the death of Sukina*. London: The Bridge.

Bridge Child Care Consultancy Service (1995) *Paul: Death from neglect*. London: Islington Area Child Protection Committee.

Bruer, J (1999) *The myth of the first three years*. New York: Free Press.

Bunting, L (2005) *Females who sexually offend against children*. London: NSPCC.

Butler-Sloss, Lord Justice E (1988) *Report of the inquiry into child abuse in Cleveland 1987*. Cmnd 412. London: HMSO.

Caada (Coordinated Action Against Domestic Abuse) (2014) *In plain sight: Effective help for children exposed to domestic abuse*. Bristol: Caada.

CAFCASS (Children and Family Court Advisory and Support Services) (2012) *Three weeks in November, three years on*. London: CAFCASS.

Calder, M (2008a) Professional dangerousness: causes and contemporary features. In Calder, M (ed.) *Contemporary risk assessment in safeguarding children*. Lyme Regis: Russell House.

Calder, M (2008b) Organisational dangerousness: causes, consequences and correctives. In Calder, M (ed.) *Contemporary risk assessment in safeguarding children*. Lyme Regis: Russell House.

Calder, M (2008c) *Contemporary risk assessment in safeguarding children*. Lyme Regis: Russell House.

Calder, M and Hackett, S (eds) (2013) *Assessment in child care*. 2nd edition. Lyme Regis: Russell House.

Campbell, B (1997) *Unofficial secrets. Child sexual abuse. The Cleveland case*. London: Virago.

Carers Trust (2015) *New rights for young carers, young adult carers, and their families: an overview*. London: Carers Trust. https://professionals.carers.org/sites/default/files/new_rights_for_young_carers_young_adult_carers_and_their_families.pdf

Carlile, Lord (2006) *An independent inquiry by Lord Carlile of Berriew QC*. London: Howard League.

CEOP (Child Exploitation and Online Protection Centre) (2013) *Threat assessment of child sexual exploitation and abuse*. http://ceop.police.uk/Documents/ceopdocs/CEOP_TACSEA2013_240613%20FINAL.pdf

CESCB (Cheshire East Safeguarding Children's Board) (2011) *Serious case review CE001: Child B, C and D. Executive summary*. Cheshire: CESCB.

Chaika, A (2013) *Invisible England*. Charleston US: Chalk Circle Press.

Chamba, R, Ahmad, W, Hirst, M, Lawton, D and Beresford, B (1999) *On the edge*. Bristol: Policy Press.

Chamberlain, T, George, N, Golden, S, Walker, F and Benton, T (2010) *Tellus4 National Report*. London: DCSF.

Cherti, M and Bradley, L (2011) *Inside Madrassas*. London: Institute for Public Policy Research.

ChildLine (2012) *Caught in a trap. The impact of grooming in 2012*. www.nspcc.org.uk/globalassets/documents/research-reports/caught-trap-study.pdf

Child Rights International Network (2007) *UK: Bid to end smacking in shops*. http://crinarchive.org/violence/search/closeup.asp?infoID=13028

Clarke-Billings, L (2015) Mary Stroman: Council at centre of Baby P scandal again accused of 'serious failings'. *Telegraph*, 19 October.

Clayton, S (2011) *Hamedullah: The road home*. DVD. London: Eastwest productions.

Clyde, Lord (1992) *Report of the inquiry into the removal of children from Orkney in February 1991*, H0C195. London: HMSO.

Coles, D (2015) *'Could have been saved': failing the mentally ill in prison.* 23 February 2015. www.channel4.com/news/mental-health-deaths-custody-detention-prisons-alex-kelly

Colton, M, Vanstone, M and Walby, C (2002) Victimisation, care and justice. *British Journal of Social Work,* 32, 541–51.

Committee against Torture (2013) Concluding observations on the fifth periodic report on the United Kingdom para 26. www.justice.gov.uk/downloads/human-rights/cat-concluding-observations-may-2013.pdf.

Contact a Family (2011) *Forgotten families.* London: Contact a Family.

Cooper, C (2013) 'To whistleblow is like a death sentence': five people who risked everything to speak out. *Independent,* 23 March.

Cooper, J (2011) Most social workers threatened in past 6 months. *Community Care,* 16 November.

Cooper, T (2007) *Trust no one.* London: Orion.

Cossar, A, Brandon, M and Jordan, P (2011) *'Don't make assumptions'.* London: Office of the Children's Commissioner.

CPS (Crown Prosecution Service) (2013) *Honour based violence and forced marriage.* www.cps.gov.uk/legal/h_to_k/honour_based_violence_and_forced_marriage/

CRAE (Children's Rights Alliance for England) (2014) *State of children's rights in England.* London: CRAE.

CRAE (Children's Rights Alliance for England) (2002) *Rethinking child imprisonment.* London: CRAE. www.crae.org.uk/media/26398/RethinkingChildImprisonment.pdf

Crawford, A (2013) Thames torso case boy 'identified'. *Kenya. Africa Review.* 8 February.

Crawley, H (2012) *Working with children and young people subject to immigration control.* 2nd edition. London: Immigration Law Practitioners' Association.

Crowley, A and Vulliamy, C (2000) *Listen up! Children talk about smacking.* Cardiff: Save the Children.

CSCB (Cambridgeshire Safeguarding Children Board) (2010) *Serious case review of F.* Cambridge. CSCB.

CSCB (Coventry Safeguarding Children Board) (2013) *Serious case review re Daniel Pelka born 15th July 2008 died 3rd March 2012.* Coventry: CSCB.

CSEYHP (Combating social exclusion among young homeless populations) (2008–11*) A comparative investigation of homeless paths.* www.movisie.com/combating-youth-homelessness

CSJ (Centre for Social Justice) (2013) *It happens here: Equipping the United Kingdom to fight modern slavery.* London: The Centre for Social Justice.

CSJ (Centre for Social Justice) (2015) *Finding their feet. Equipping care leavers to reach their potential.* London: Centre for Social Justice.

Cunningham, F (2015) *A modern response to modern slavery.* London: Centre for Social Justice.

Cuthbert, C, Rayns, G and Stanley, K (2011) *All babies count: Prevention and protection for vulnerable babies.* London: NSPCC.

Cutting, E (2001) *It doesn't sort anything.* Edinburgh: Save the Children.

Dale, P, Green, R and Fellows, R (2002) Babies in danger. *Community Care,* 7–13 March.

Danczuk, S (2015) *Smile for the camera. The double life of Cyril Smith.* London: Biteback Books.

D'Arcy, M and Gosling, P (1998) *Abuse of trust. Frank Beck and the Leicestershire children's homes scandal.* London: Bowerdean.

Davies, D (2015) *In plain sight. The life and lies of Jimmy Savile.* London: Quercus.

Davies, L (2004) The difference between child abuse and child protection could be you: Creating a community network of protective adults. *Child Abuse Review*, 13, 426–32.

Davies, L (2007) Responding to the protection needs of traumatized and sexually abused children. In Hosin, A (ed.) *Responses to traumatized children*. Basingstoke: Palgrave.

Davies, L (2008a) Reclaiming the language of child protection. In Calder, M (ed.) *Contemporary risk assessment in safeguarding children*. Lyme Regis: Russell House.

Davies, L (2008b) *In the shadow of a tragedy*. www.guardian.co.uk/society/2008/jan/28/climbie.childprotection

Davies, L (2008c) Where next for social work. *Professional Social Work*, December. Birmingham: BASW.

Davies, L (2009b) Safeguarding children. In Adams, R (ed.) (2011) *Working with children and families*. Basingstoke: Palgrave Macmillan.

Davies, L (2010) A ten-year struggle. *Professional Social Work*. May. Birmingham: BASW.

Davies, L (2011) Interviewing children – good practice in Sweden. *Community Care*, 8 September.

Davies, L (2014) Working positively with the media to protect children, *Journal of Social Welfare and Family Law*, 36:1, 47–58.

Davies, L (2015) Focus must be on needs AND risks or we will fail to protect children from abuse. *Professional Social Work*, October. Birmingham: BASW.

Davies, L and Kerrigan Lebloch, E (2011) *Communicating with children and their families*. Maidenhead: Open University Press.

Davies, L and Townsend, D (2008a) *Working together, training together. Achieving best evidence*. Lyme Regis: Russell House.

Davies, L and Townsend, D (2008b) *Working together. Joint investigation in child protection*. Lyme Regis: Russell House.

Davies, M. (2012) (ed.) *Social work with children and families*. Basingstoke: Palgrave Macmillan.

Davies, N (1998) Lives that were beyond belief. *Guardian*, 1 August.

Davis, N (1999) *Once upon a time. Therapeutic stories to heal abused children*. Charleston, SC: Bibliobazaar.

Dawe, S and Harnett, P (2007) Reducing potential for child abuse among methodone-maintained parents. *Journal of Substance Abuse*, 32(4), 381–90.

DCSF (Department for Children, Schools and Families) (2008) *Safeguarding children in whom illness is fabricated or induced*. London: DCSF.

DCSF (Department for Children, Schools and Families) (2009a) *Incredibly caring. A training resource for professionals in fabricated or induced illness (FII) in children*. Oxford: Radcliffe Publishing Limited.

DCSF (Department for Children, Schools and Families) (2009b) *Safeguarding children from sexual exploitation. Supplementary guidance*. London: DCSF.

DCSF (Department for Children, Schools and Families) (2010a) *Working together to safeguard children: A guide to inter-agency working to safeguard and promote the welfare of children*. London: The Stationery Office.

DCSF (Department for Children, Schools and Families) and Home Office (2010b) *Safeguarding children and young people who may be affected by gang activity*. London: DCSF.

Deakin, J (2006) Dangerous people, dangerous places. *Children and Society*, 20, 376–90.

Department of Health (2016) *Health risks from alcohol: new guidelines.* www.gov.uk/government/consultations/health-risks-from-alcohol-new-guidelines

DfE (Department for Education) (2011a) *The protection of children online: a brief scoping review to identify vulnerable groups.* London: DfE.

DfE (Department for Education) (2011b) *Preventing and tackling bullying. Advice for school leaders, staff and governing bodies.* London: DfE.

DfE (Department for Education) and Home Office (2011c) *Safeguarding children who may have been trafficked. Practice guidance.* London: The Stationery Office.

DfE (Department for Education) (2012a) *The CAF process.* www.education.gov.uk/childrenandyoungpeople/strategy/integratedworking/caf/a0068957/the-caf-process

DfE (Department for Education) (2012b) *National action plan to tackle child abuse linked to faith or belief. Executive summary.* London: DfE. http://media.education.gov.uk/assets/files/doc/c/common%20assessment%20framework%20form.doc

DfE (Department for Education) (2013) *Working together to safeguard children. A guide for inter-agency working to safeguard and promote the welfare of children.* London: The Stationery Office.

DfE (Department for Education) (2014a) *Knowledge and skills for child and family social work.* London: DfE.

DfE (Department for Education) (2014b) *Characteristics of children in need in England, 2013–p14.* www.gov.uk/government/uploads/system/uploads/attachment_data/file/367877/SFR43_2014_Main_Text.pdf

DfE (Department for Education) (2014c) *Outcomes for children looked after by local authorities. Table 4.* London: DfE.

DfE (Department for Education) (2014d) *Care of unaccompanied and trafficked children: Statutory guidance for local authorities.* London: DfE.

DfE (Department for Education) (2014e) *Statutory guidance on children who run away or go missing from home or care.* London: DfE.

DfE (Department for Education) (2015) *Working together to safeguard children: A guide for inter-agency working to safeguard and promote the welfare of children.* London: The Stationery Office.

DfES (Department for Education and Skills) (2006a) *Working together to safeguard children: A guide for inter-agency working to safeguard and promote the welfare of children.* London: The Stationery Office.

DfES (Department for Education and Skills) (2006b) *Safeguarding disabled children: A resource for Local Safeguarding Children Boards.* London: DfES.

Dimmer, S (2013) Schoolboy murder trial: How I fought to save my brother Daniel. *Coventry Telegraph,* 4 July. www.coventrytelegraph.net/news/coventry-news/daniel-pelka-murder-trial-how-4866501

Dirie, W (2001) *Desert flower.* London: Virago.

Doyle, C (2013) A framework for assessing emotional abuse. In Calder, M and Hackett, S (eds) (2013) *Assessment in child care.* Lyme Regis: Russell House.

Dustin, D and Davies, L (2006) Female Genital Cutting (FGC), anti-oppressive practice and children's rights: implications for social work practice. *Child Care in Practice,* 13(1), 3–16.

Ecpat (2008) *Combatting child sex tourism.* www.ecpat.net/sites/default/files/cst_faq_eng.pdf

Ecpat (2011) *Off the radar, protecting children from child sex offenders who travel.* London: Ecpat.

Engelbrecht, G (2014) Medomsley Detention Centre: the 'unpleasant experience' which grew into brutality and sexual abuse. *Northern Echo*, 12 April.

Fairweather, E (2008) Baby P council falsely accused me of abusing a child. *Daily Mail*, 16 November.

Falkov, A (1995) *Study of working together part 8 reports. Fatal child abuse and parental psychiatric disorder. An analysis of 100 case reviews.* London: Department of Health.

Falkov, A (ed.) (1998) *Crossing bridges.* Brighton: Pavilion Publishing.

Fergusson, D and Mullen, P (1999) *Childhood sexual abuse: An evidence based perspective.* London: Sage.

Fitzgerald, J (1999) *Child protection and the computer age.* London: The Bridge Publishing House Ltd.

Fogg, A (2012) Male circumcision. Let there be no more tragedies like baby Goodluck. *Guardian*, 17 December.

Ford, H (2006) *Women who sexually abuse.* Chichester: Wiley.

Forrester, D and Harwin, J (2006) Parental substance misuse and child care social work. *Child and Family Social Work*, 11(4), 325–35.

Foster, C, Garber, J and Durlak, J (2008) Current and past maternal depression, maternal interaction behaviours and children's externalising and internalising symptoms. *Journal of Applied Child Psychology*, 36(4), 527–37.

Frampton, P (2004) *The golly in the cupboard.* Manchester: Tamic Publications.

Franklin, A and Knight, A (2012) *Someone on our side.* London: The Children's Society.

Fyfe, M (2007) *Survivors' stories.* Hitchin: 11th Commandment Publishing.

Gallagher, B, Bradford, M and Pease, K (2008) Attempted and completed incidents of stranger-perpetrated child sexual abuse and abduction. *Child Abuse and Neglect*, 32:517–28.

Garrett, P (2006) Protecting children in a globalised world, 'Race' and 'Place' in the Laming report on the death of Victoria Climbié. *Journal of Social Work*, 6(3), 315–36.

Gilbert, R, Kemp, A, Thoburn, J, Sidebotham, P, Radford, L, Glaser, D and Macmillan, H (2009) Recognising and responding to child maltreatment. *Lancet.* 373, 9658, 167–80.

Gill, A (1984) *Martin Allen is missing.* London: Corgi.

GLA (Greater London Assembly) (2014) *Keeping London's children safe.* London: GLA.

GLA (Greater London Authority) (2003) *Young people, big issues.* London: GLA.

Glaser, D (2002) Emotional abuse and neglect (psychological maltreatment): a conceptual framework. *Child Abuse and Neglect,* 26: 697–714

Global Initiative to End All Corporal Punishment of Children (2006) *Ending legalised violence against children.* www.endcorporalpunishment.org

Goodwin, J (2001) Black magic, the butchered body of a five year old thrown in the Thames. *Daily Mail*, 8 December.

Gorin, S (2004) *Understanding what children say about living with domestic violence, parental substance misuse or parental mental health problems.* York: Joseph Rowntree Trust.

Gower, M (2014) *Ending child immigration detention.* House of Commons briefing paper. SN/HA/5591 http://researchbriefings.parliament.uk/ResearchBriefing/Summary/SN05591#fullreport

Gray, D and Watt, P (2012) *Giving victims a voice. Joint report into sexual allegations made against Jimmy Savile.* London: NSPCC and Metropolitan Police.

Greenshields, M (2009) Baby bled to death after circumcision. *Slough and Langley Observer*, 20 February.

Guardian (2003) He threatened to rape me. *Guardian*, 9 October. www.guardian.co.uk/uk/2003/oct/09/politics.children

Guardian (2015) The scale of child abuse images online is shocking says NSPCC. *Guardian*, 22 July.

Guasp, A (2012) *The school report. The experiences of gay young people in Britain's schools in 2012.* London: Stonewall.

Gyateng, T, Moretti, A, May, T and Turnbull, P (2013) *Young people and the secure estate.* London: Youth Justice Board for England and Wales.

Hackett, S, Phillips, J, Masson, H and Balfe, M (2013) Individual, family and abuse characteristics of 700 British child and adolescent sexual abusers. *Child Abuse Review*, 22(4): 232–45.

Hackett, S and Uprichard, E (2007) *Animal abuse and child maltreatment.* London: NSPCC.

Hamer, M (2007) *Kids need cards.* London: Jessica Kingsley.

Hames, M (2000) *The dirty squad.* London: Little Brown.

Hamilton, C (2007) Would you leave your child alone? http://women.timesonline.co.uk/tol/life_and_style/women/families/articles

Hardwick, L and Hardwick, T (2015) Do we meet the needs of children in asylum-seeking families? *Critical and Radical Social Work*, 3(2), 281–89.

Haskett, M, Scott, S, Grant, R, Ward, C and Robinson, C (2003) Child-related cognitions and affective functioning of physically abusive and comparison parents. *Child Abuse and Neglect*, 27, 663–86.

HC 137: 1 (House of Commons Education Committee) (2012–13) *Children first: the child protection system in England. Fourth Report of session 2012–13.* Volume 1. London: The Stationery Office.

HC 137: 2 (House of Commons Education Committee) (2012–13) *Children first: the child protection system in England. Fourth Report of session 2012–13.* Volume 2. London: The Stationery Office.

HC 107 (House of Commons Internal Development Committee) (2013–14) *Violence against women and girls.* London: The Stationery Office.

HCPC (Health and Social Care Professionals Council) (2015) *Whistleblowing.* www.hpc-uk.org/registrants/raisingconcerns/whistleblowing/

HCPC (2016) Standards of conduct, performance and ethics. www.hpc.uk.org/aboutregistration/standards/standardsofconductperformanceandethics

Health and Social Care Information Centre (2015) *Female Genital Mutilation (FGM), April 2015 to June 2015.* www.hscic.gov.uk/article/2021/Website-Search?productid=18864&q=fgm&sort=Most+recent&size=10&page=1&area=both

Hellen, N (2015) UK soldiers of 16 'too young'. *The Times*, 11 January. www.thesundaytimes.co.uk/sto/news/uk_news/Defence/article1505677.ece

Hershkowitz, I, Lamb, M and Horowitz, D (2007) Victimisation of children with disabilities. *American Journal of Orthopsychiatry*, 77(44), 629–33.

Hessel, S (2011) *Time for outrage (Indignez-vous!)* London: Quartet.

Hicks, L and Stein, M (2010) *Neglect matters. A multi-agency guide for professionals working together on behalf of teenagers.* London: Department for Children, Schools and Families.

Higgins, M and Swain, J (2010) *Disability and child sexual abuse.* London: Jessica Kingsley.

Hill, A (2015a) Child sexual exploitation is in the back of our minds all the time. *Guardian*, 3 March.

Hill, A (2015b) Ofsted reports 36% rise in children missing from foster care. *Guardian,* 15 January.

HM Government (2006) *Working together to safeguard children: A guide to inter-agency working to safeguard and promote the welfare of children.* London: The Stationery Office.

HM Government (2011) *Multi agency practice guidelines. Female genital mutilation.* London: HM Government.

HM Government, Forced Marriage Unit (2014a) *The right to choose. Multi-agency statutory guidance for dealing with forced marriage.* London: Home Office and Foreign and Commonwealth Office.

HM Government, Forced Marriage Unit (2014b) *Statistics on forced marriage 2014.* London: Home Office and Foreign and Commonwealth Office.

HM Government (2014) *The fifth periodic report to the UN Committee on the Rights of the Child. United Kingdom.* www.equalityhumanrights.com/sites/default/files/uploads/Pdfs/The%20UK's%20 Fifth%20Periodic%20Review%20Report%20on%20the%20UNCRC.pdf

HM Government (2015a*) Information sharing advice for practitioners providing safeguarding services to children, young people, parents and carers.* London: The Stationery Office.

HM Government (2015b*) PM announces new taskforce to transform child protection.* 24 June. www. gov.uk/government/news/pm-announces-new-taskforce-to-transform-child-protection

HMIP (Her Majesty's Inspector of Prisons) (2011) *Three reports on unannounced inspections of short term holding facility at Heathrow Airport Terminal 1, 3, and 4.* London: HMIP.

HMIP (Her Majesty's Inspector of Prisons) (2013) *Report on an unannounced inspection of HMP/YOI Feltham.* London: HMIP.

HMIP (Her Majesty's Inspector of Prisons) (2014) *Report on an unannounced inspection of HMYOI Werrington 23 September–4 October.* London: HMIP.

Hobday, A and Ollier, K (1998) *Creative therapy.* Oxford: Wiley-Blackwell.

Home Office (2012) *Statement opposing female genital mutilation.* www.gov.uk/government/ publications/statement-opposing-female-genital-mutilation

Home Office (2013) *Multi-agency working and information sharing project.* London: Home Office.

Home Office (2014) *Female genital mutilation: resource pack.* London: HM Government.

Home Office (2015a) *Revised prevent duty guidance for England and Wales.* London: Home Office.

Home Office (2015b) *Guidance: Domestic violence and abuse.* London: Home Office.

Home Office (2015c) *Mandatory reporting of female genital mutilation.* London: Home Office.

Home Office, Department of Health, Department of Education and Science, Welsh Office (1991) *Working Together: A guide to arrangements for inter-agency co-operation for the protection of children from abuse.* London: HMSO.

Horgan, G (2002) *It's a hit not a 'smack'.* Belfast: Save the Children.

Hoskins, R (2012) *The boy in the river.* London: Pan Macmillan.

Howard League (2007) *Press release. UK government flouting United Nations Convention on the Rights of the Child.* 21 June. London: The Howard League.

Howe, D (1987) *An introduction to social work theory.* Surrey: Ashgate.

HSCB (Haringey Safeguarding Children Board) (2009) *Serious case review child A.* London: DfE.

HSCB (Haringey Safeguarding Children Board) (2012) *Serious case review family Z.* London: HSCB.

HSCB (Haringey Safeguarding Children Board) (2015) *Child O. Overview report. October 2015.* London: HSCB.

Hughes S (2014) *Children will be seen and heard in family courts. Press Release. London:* Ministry of Justice Press Release.

Human Rights Council (2014) *Ending violence against children: a global call to make the invisible visible.* www.ohchr.org/EN/HRBodies/HRC/RegularSessions/Session27/Documents/Endingviolenceagainstchildren_conceptnote.pdf

Humphreys, C and Stanley, N (2015) *Domestic violence and protecting children.* London: Jessica Kingsley.

Humphreys, M (1996) *Empty cradles.* London: Corgi.

IFSW (International Federation of Social Work) (2012) *Statement of ethical principles.* http://ifsw.org/policies/statement-of-ethical-principles/

IFSW (International Federation of Social Work) (2014) *Global definition of the social work profession.* http://ifsw.org/get-involved/global-definition-of-social-work/

Jones, L, Bellis, M, Wood, S, Hughes, K, McCoy, E, Eckley, L, Bates, G, Mikton, C, Shakespeare, T and Officer, A (2012) Prevalence and risk of violence against children with disabilities: a systematic review and meta-analysis of observational studies. *Lancet,* July 2012.

Jones, R (2015a) The stealth privatisation of children's services. *Community Care.* 7 January.

Jones, R (2015b) Hedge funds have no place in children's services. *Guardian,* 17 September.

Jütte, S, Bentley, H, Tallis, D, Mayes, J, Jetha, N, O'Hagan, O, Brookes, H and McConnell, N (2015) *How safe are our children?* London: NSPCC.

Kane, J (1998) *Sold for sex.* Bury St Edmunds: Arena.

Keeble, H and Hollington, K (2010) *Baby X. Britain's child abusers brought to justice.* London: Simon and Schuster.

Keeble, H and Hollington, K (2011) *Hidden victims. The real story of Britain's vulnerable children and the people who rescue them.* London: Simon and Schuster.

Keeble H and Hollington K (2012) *Hurting too much. Shocking stories from the frontline of child protection.* London: Simon and Schuster.

Kelly, A and McNamara, M (2015) 3000 children enslaved in Britain after being trafficked from Vietnam. *Guardian,* 23 May.

Kelly, Sir Christopher (2004) *Serious case review 'Ian Huntley'.* North Lincolnshire: North Lincolnshire Area Child Protection Committee.

Kennedy, M (1996) Sexual abuse and disabled children. In Morris, J (ed.) *Encounters with strangers: Feminism and disability.* London: Women's Press, pp116–34.

Kerrigan Lebloch, E and King, S (2006) Child sexual exploitation: A partnership response and model intervention. *Child Abuse Review,* 15, 362–72.

Kline, R and Preston-Shoot, M (2012*) Professional accountability in social care and health.* London: Learning Matters.

Kothari, P, Witham, G and Quinn, T (2014) *A fair start in life for every child.* London: Save the Children.

Kovic, Y, Lucas-Hancock, J and Miller, D (2009) *Safe: Personal safety skills for deaf children.* London: NSPCC.

Krugman, S, Lantz, E, Sinal, S, De Jong, A and Coffman, K (2007) Forced suffocation of infants with baby wipes. *Child Abuse and Neglect*, 31(6), 615–21.

Laggay, M and Courtney, L (2013) *Time to listen: Independent advocacy within the child protection process.* London: National Children's Bureau.

Laming, H (2003) *The Victoria Climbié inquiry report.* London: The Stationery Office.

Lazenblatt, A and Taylor, J (2011) *Fabricated or induced illness in children: a rare form of child abuse?* London: NSPCC.

Levitas, R (2012) *There may be trouble ahead? Poverty Response series 3.* Bristol. Poverty and Social Exclusion in the UK.

Levy, A and Scott-Clark, C (2010) Tiffany Wright starved to death in this room on a urine-soaked bed surrounded by soiled nappies. *Guardian Weekend*, 6 February.

Longinotto, K (2002) *The day I will never forget.* Women Make Movies Film and Video Department. www.wmm.com/filmcatalog/pages/c604.shtml

Lovejoy, M, Graczyk, P, O'Hare, E and Neuman, G (2000) Maternal depression and parenting behaviour: a meta-analytic review. *Clinical Psychology Review*, 20(5), 561–92.

LSCB (London Safeguarding Children Board) (2015) *London child protection procedures.* London: Association of London Government.

Lyon, C (2000) *Loving smack or lawful assault?* London: Institute for Public Policy Research.

Main, E (2013) *Young carers talking.* London: Carers Trust.

Mallard, C (2008) Ritual abuse – a personal account and the unpublished police guidelines. In Noblitt, R and Noblitt, R (eds) *Ritual abuse in the twenty-first century.* Oregon: Robert D Reed Publishers.

Mann, J (2015) *Wanless review and the Dickens files.* Debate in House of Commons. 4 November. www.theyworkforyou.com/whall/?id=2015-11-04a.371.0&s=speaker%3A11093#g371.3

Mariathasan, J and Hutchinson, D (2010) *Children talk to ChildLine about parental drug and alcohol misuse.* London: NSPCC.

McClenaghan, M (2015) *Schooled in Britain, deported to danger.* www.thebureauinvestigates. com/2015/07/16/600-unaccompanied-child-asylum-seekers-deported-uk-afghanistan/

McSherry, D (2004) Which came first, the chicken or the egg? Examining the relationship between child neglect and poverty. *British Journal of Social Work*, 34(5), 727–33.

Meadows, S (1997) *ABC of child abuse.* 3rd edition. London: British Medical Journal Publishing.

Meghji, S (2007) Children's homes left in limbo. *Children and Young People Now*, 3–9 October 2007.

Mencap (2005) *They won't believe me.* London: Mencap.

Mencap (2013) *Short breaks support is failing family carers.* London: Mencap.

Mepham, S (2010) Disabled children: The right to feel safe. *Child Care in Practice*, 16(1), 19–34.

Miller, D and Brown, J (2014) *We have the right to be safe: Protecting disabled children from abuse.* London: NSPCC.

Milotte, M (1997) *Banished babies.* Dublin, Ireland: New Ireland Books.

MoJ (Ministry of Justice) (2008) *The public law outline.* London: Ministry of Justice.

MoJ (Ministry of Justice) (2011) *Achieving best evidence in criminal proceedings: Guidance on interviewing victims and witnesses and using special measures.* London: Ministry of Justice.

Momoh, C (Ed) (2005) *Female genital mutilation.* Oxford: Radcliffe Publishing.

Morgan, R (2014) *Children's care monitor 2013/4.* London: Ofsted.

Morris, S (2011) Colin Batley, leader of sex cult preying on children, could spend life in jail. *Guardian*, 11 March.

Morris, S (2013) Daniel Pelka: professionals failed 'invisible' murdered boy, report says. *Guardian*, 17 September. www.theguardian.com/society/2013/sep/17/professionals-failed-report-daniel-pelka

Morrison, T (1998) Partnership, collaboration and change under The Children Act. In Adcock, M and White, R (eds) *Significant harm: its management and outcome.* London: Significant Publications.

Mullender, A, Burton, S, Hague, G, Imam, U, Kelly, L, Malos, E and Regan, L (2003a) *Stop hitting mum.* East Molesey: Young Voice.

Mullender, A, Regan, L and Malos, E (2003b) *Children's perspectives on domestic violence.* London. Sage.

Mullender, A and Morley, R (1994) *Children living with domestic violence.* London: Whiting and Birch.

Munro, E (2002) *Effective child protection.* London: Sage.

Munro, E (2011) Munro review of child protection final report – a child centred system. London: DfE.

Munro, E and Calder, M (2005) Where has child protection gone? *The Political Quarterly,* 76(3), 439–45.

Munro, E and Musholt, K (2013) Neuroscience and the risks of maltreatment. *Children and Youth Services Review.* http://dx.doi.org/10.1016/j.childyouth.2013.11.002

Murray, M and Osborne, C (2009) *Safeguarding disabled children practice guidance.* London: DCSF.

Nazer, M and Lewis, D (2004) *Slave. The true story of a girl's lost childhood and her fight for survival.* London: Virago.

NCA (National Crime Agency) (2015) *National strategic assessment of serious and organised abuse.* www.nationalcrimeagency.gov.uk/publications/560-national-strategic-assessment-of-serious-and-organised-crime-2015/file

Nelson, S (2001) *Beyond trauma. Mental health care needs of women who survived childhood sexual abuse.* Edinburgh: Health in Mind (EAMH).

Nelson, S (2002) Physical symptoms in sexually abused women: Somatisation or undetected injury? *Child Abuse Review,* 11(1), 51–64.

Nelson, S (2004) *Neighbourhood mapping for children's safety.* Edinburgh: Womanzone.

Nelson, S (2008a) *See us – hear us. Schools working with sexually abused young people.* Dundee: Violence is Preventable.

Nelson, S (2008b) The Orkney 'Satanic abuse case'. Who cared about the children? In Noblitt, R and Perskin P (eds) *Ritual abuse in the twenty-first century. Psychological, forensic, social and political considerations.* 337–354 Brandon, Oregon USA: Robert D Reed Publishers.

Nelson, S and Baldwin, N (2002) Comprehensive neighbourhood mapping: Developing a powerful tool for child protection. *Child Abuse Review,* 11, 214–29.

Newcastle Local Safeguarding Children Board (2006) *Serious case review executive summary, Baby O.* Newcastle: Newcastle LSCB.

Newiss, G and Traynor, M (2013) *Taken. A study of child abduction in the UK.* London: CEOP.

Newton, J (2013) *Preventing Mental Ill Health.* London: Routledge.

Norfolk Constabulary (2015) *Sex offenders sentenced to over 70 years in jail.* 28 September. www.norfolk.police.uk/newsandevents/newsstories/2015/september/sexoffenderssentenced.aspx

Norman, A (2013) *Human rights have disappeared from 'Working Together'*. http://ukhumanrightsblog.com/2013/04/09/human-rights-have-disappeared-from-working-together-allan-norman/

NPCC (National Police Chiefs' Council) (2015*) Over 1400 suspects investigated for child sexual abuse by people of public prominence, or within institutions*. 20 May. http://news.npcc.police.uk/releases/over-1400-suspects-investigated-for-child-sexual-abuse-by-people-of-public-prominence-or-within-institutions

NSPCC (2007) *NSPCC looks to work with retailers to create smack free shopping*. www.nspcc.org.uk/whatwedo/mediacentre/pressreleases/2007_10_april_nspcc_looks_to_work_with

NSPCC (2008) *ChildLine Casenotes: Children talking to ChildLine about bullying*. London: NSPCC.

NSPCC (2010) *ChildLine Casenotes: Children talking to ChildLine about parental alcohol and drug misuse*. London: NSPCC. www.drugsandalcohol.ie/13691/1/NSPCC_clcasenoteparentalalcoholdrugabuse.pdf

NSPCC (2012a) *Core-info: Oral injuries and bite marks on children*. London: NSPCC.

NSPCC (2012b) *Core-info: Fractures on children*. London: NSPCC.

NSPCC (2012c) *Core-info: Thermal injuries on children*. London: NSPCC.

NSPCC (2012d) *Core-info: Bruises on children*. London: NSPCC.

NSPCC (2012e) *FOI request*. www.nspcc.org.uk/preventing-abuse/child-abuse-and-neglect/child-sexual-abuse/sexual-abuse-facts-statistics/

NSPCC (2013a) *Core-info: Head and spinal injuries*. London: NSPCC.

NSPCC (2013b) *Female genital mutilation. NSPCC Factsheet*. www.nspcc.org.uk/inform/resourcesforprofessionals/minorityethnic/female-genital-mutilation_wda96841.html

NSPCC (2015) *'Always there when I need you'. ChildLine Review 2014–15*. www.nspcc.org.uk/globalassets/documents/annual-reports/childline-annual-review-always-there-2014-2015.pdf

NTA (National Treatment Agency for Substance Misuse) (2012) *Parents with drug problems: How treatment helps families*. www.nta.nhs.uk/uploads/families2012vfinali.pdf.

OCC (Office of the Children's Commissioner) (2006) *Bullying today*. London: OCC.

OCC (Office of the Children's Commissioner) (2011) *'I think I must have been born bad'*. London: OCC.

OCC (Office of the Children's Commissioner) (2012) *Nobody made the connection*. London: OCC.

OCC (Office of the Children's Commissioner) (2013) *A child rights impact assessment of budget decisions*. London: OCC.

OCC (Office of the Children's Commissioner) (2014) *'What's going to happen tomorrow?'* London: OCC.

OCC (Office of the Children's Commissioner) (2015) *Protecting children from harm*. London: OCC.

Ofsted (2009) *Supporting young carers*. London: Ofsted.

Ofsted (2011a) *The voice of the child*. London: Ofsted.

Ofsted (2011b) *Ages of concern: Learning lessons from serious case reviews*. London: Ofsted.

Ofsted (2012a) *No place for bullying*. London: Ofsted.

Ofsted (2012b) *Protecting disabled children. A thematic inspection*. London: Ofsted.

Ofsted (2013) *What about the children? Joint working between adult and children's services when parents or carers have mental ill health and/or drug and alcohol problems*. London: Ofsted.

Ofsted (2014a) *The report of Her Majesty's Chief Inspector of Education, Children's Services and Skills 2013–14.* Manchester: Ofsted.

Ofsted (2014b) *It's the child's time: professional responses to neglect.* London: Ofsted.

Ofsted (2015) *Children looked after placements by English local authorities.* London: Ofsted.

O'Hagan, K (2006) *Identifying emotional and psychological abuse, a guide for childcare professionals.* Buckingham: Open University Press.

Olofintuade, A (2010) *Eno's story.* https://geosireads.wordpress.com/2011/08/31/enos-story-by-ayodele-olofintuade/

ONS (Office for National Statistics) (2011) Census 2011. www.ons.gov.uk/ons/rel/census/2011-census/detailed-characteristics-for-local-authorities-in-england -and-ales/index.html

ONS (Office for National Statistics) (2013) *Focus on: violent crime and sexual offences, 2011/12.* Newport: ONS.

ONS (Office for National Statistics) (2015) *Crime survey England and Wales 2013–14.* London: ONS.

Oranges and Sunshine (2010) London: See Saw Films.

OSCB (Oxfordshire Safeguarding Children Board) (2015) *Serious case review into child sexual exploitation in Oxfordshire: from the experiences of Children A, B, C, D, E and F.* Oxford: OSCB.

Owen, J (2014a) UK under fire for recruiting an army of children. *Independent,* 25 May.

Owen, J (2014b) Shaken babies. Parents to see 'life saving' film. *Independent,* 4 May.

Parker, A (2015) Boy left at home alone. *Sun,* 4 August. www.thesun.co.uk/sol/homepage/news/6674073/Derby-parents-leave-kid-home-alone-to-go-boozing.html

Parton, N (2006) *Safeguarding childhood.* Basingstoke: Palgrave Macmillan.

Parton, N (2012) The Munro Review of child protection: an appraisal. *Children And Society,* 26(2), 150–62.

Peake, A (1997) *Strong mothers: A resource for mothers and children who have been sexually assaulted.* Lyme Regis: Russell House.

Peake, A and Rouf, K (1989) *My book, my body.* London: Children's Society.

Pearce, J, Hynes, P and Bovarnick, S (2009) *Breaking the wall of silence.* London: NSPCC and University of Bedfordshire.

Peckover, S (2009) Domestic abuse and safeguarding children. In Hughes, L and Owen, H (eds) *Good practice in safeguarding children.* London: Jessica Kingsley.

Pemberton, C (2013) Survey exposes rising thresholds leaving children in danger. *Community Care.* 19 November.

Philomena (2013) Los Angeles USA: 20th Century Fox.

Pinter, I (2015) *Cut off from justice.* London: The Children's Society.

Plotnikoff, J and Woolfson, R (2008) *The go between. Evaluation of intermediary pathfinder projects.* http://lexiconlimited.co.uk/wp-content/uploads/2013/01/Intermediaries_study_report.pdf

Pona, I, Royston, S, Bracey, C and Gibbs, A (2015) *Seriously awkward. How vulnerable 16 and 17 year olds are falling through the cracks.* London: The Children's Society.

Pople, L, Rodrigues, L and Royston, S (2013) *Through young eyes.* London: The Children's Society.

Prime, R (2014) *Children in custody 2013–14.* London: HMIP and Youth Justice Board.

Prince, J, Austin, J, Shewring, L, Birdsey, N, McInnes, K and Roderique-Davies, G (2014) *Attitudes to parenting practices and child discipline.* Cardiff: Welsh Government Social Research.

Radford, L, Corral, L, Bradley, C, Fisher, H, Bassett, C, Howat, N and Collishaw, S (2011) *Child abuse and neglect in the UK today*. London: NSPCC.

Rayns, G, Dawe, S and Cuthbert, C (2011) *All babies count. Spotlight on drugs and alcohol*. London: NSPCC.

Reder, P and Duncan, S (1999) *Lost innocents. A follow up study of fatal child abuse*. Abingdon: Routledge.

Reder, P and Duncan, S (2004) Making the most of the Victoria Climbié inquiry report. *Child Abuse Review*, 13, 95–114.

Reder, P, Duncan, S and Gray, M (1993) *Beyond blame. Child abuse tragedies revisited. A summary of 35 inquiries since 1973*. Abingdon: Routledge.

Reed, H (2012) *In the eye of the storm. Britain's forgotten children and families*. London: Action for Children, NSPCC, The Children's Society.

Rees, G (2011) *Still running 3: Early findings from our third national survey of young runaways*. London: The Children's Society.

Refugee Council (2014) *Unlawful detention must end*. www.refugeecouncil.org.uk/latest/news/3905_unlawful_child_detention_must_end

Refugee Council (2015) *The children's section*. www.refugeecouncil.org.uk/what_we_do/childrens_services

Rhodes, G (2015) Britain's child migrants. *Guardian*, 24 October. www.theguardian.com/lifeandstyle/2015/oct/24/britains-child-migrants-i-was-told-i-was-going-on-a-picnic

Richardson, C (2006) *The truth about self harm*. London: Mental Health and Camelot Foundations.

Ring, E (2003) State investigation into vaccine trials under threat. Cork: *Irish Examiner*, 2 August.

Rogers, C (2011) *African children trafficked to the UK for blood rituals*. BBC News. 12 October. www.bbc.co.uk/news/uk-15280776

Roth, D, Lindley, B and Ashley, C (2011) *Big bruv, little sis*. London: Family Rights Group.

Royal College of Paediatricians and Child Health (2009) *Fabricated or induced illness by carers*. London: The Royal College of Paediatricians and Child Health.

RSCB (Rotherham Safeguarding Children Board) (2012) *Executive summary of serious case review Child S*. Rotherham: RSCB.

RSCB (Rotherham Safeguarding Children Board) (2014) *Independent inquiry into child sexual exploitation in Rotherham.1997–2013*. Rotherham: RSCB.

SafeLives (2015) *Getting it right first time: policy report*. Bristol: SafeLives.

Salter, M (2014) *Organised sexual abuse*. London: Routledge.

Salter, D, McMillan, D, Richards, M, Talbot, T, Hodges, J, Bentovim, A, Hastings, R, Stevenson, J and Skuse, D (2003) Development of sexually abusive behaviour in sexually victimised males. *Lancet*, 361 (9356), 471–76.

Saradjian, J (1997) *Women who sexually abuse children*. Chichester: Wiley.

Saunders, B and Goddard, C (2010) *Physical punishment in childhood*. Chichester: Wiley.

SCIE (2011) *Think child, think parent, think family: a guide to parental mental health and child welfare*. www.scie.org.uk/publications/guides/guide30/

Scorer, R (2015) *The English Catholic Church and the sex abuse crisis*. London: Biteback Books.

Secretary of State Home Department (2016) Response to written question 13206 on 23 October 2015. www.parliament.uk

Shakespeare, T, Priestley, M and Barnes, S (1999) *Life as a disabled child*. Leeds: University of Leeds. http://disability-studies.leeds.ac.uk/research/life-as-a-disabled-child/

Shelter (2013) *Nowhere to go. The scandal of homeless children in B and Bs. Policy briefing*. London: Shelter.

Shepherd, J and Sampson, A (2000) Don't shake the baby: Towards a preventive strategy. *British Journal of Social Work*, 30, 721–35.

Sheridan, M (1992) *From birth to five years. Children's developmental progress*. Abingdon: Routledge.

Sixsmith, M (2010) *The lost child of Philomena Lee. A mother, her son and a fifty-year search*. London: Pan Macmillan.

Smith, C, Bradbury-Jones, C, Lazenbatt, A and Taylor, J (2013) *Provision for young people who have displayed harmful sexual behaviour*. Edinburgh: The University of Edinburgh and the NSPCC.

Smith, D and Meadows, S (2000) Maternal understanding of the toxicity of substances used in non-accidental poisoning. *Child Abuse Review*, 9, 257–63.

Smith, J, Duckett, N and Menezes, F (2015) Running to the future: 'youth inequalities, homelessness and points of reinsertion'. In Kelly, P and Kamp, A (eds) *A critical youth studies for the 21st century*. Leiden, NL: Brill.

Staffordshire County Council (1991) *The experience and the protection of children. The report of the Staffordshire child care inquiry 1990*. Stafford: Staffordshire County Council.

Stalker K, Green Lister, P, Lerpiniere, J and McArthur, K (2010) *Child protection and the needs and rights of disabled children and young people*. Glasgow: University of Strathclyde.

Stanley, N and Cox, P (2008) *Parental mental health and child welfare*. London: SCIE.

Stanley, N, Manthorpe, J and Penhale, B (1999) *Institutional abuse*. Abingdon: Routledge.

Stanley, N, Miller, P, Richardson Foster, H and Thomson, G (2010) *Children and families experiencing domestic violence: Police and children's social services' responses*. London: NSPCC.

Stanley, N, Penhale, B, Riordan, D, Barbour, R and Holden, S (2003) *Child protection and mental health services. Inter-professional responses to the needs of mothers*. Bristol: Policy Press.

Stevenson, L (2015a) Should social workers fear David Cameron's plans to intervene in children's services? *Community Care*, 17 September.

Stevenson, L (2015b) 15 quotes from social workers that shouldn't be ignored. *Community Care*, 2 September.

Stickler, A (2005) *Angola witchcraft's child victims. BBC News report and film*. 13 July. http://news.bbc.co.uk/1/hi/world/africa/4677969.stm

Stobart, E (2006) *Child abuse linked to accusations of 'possession and witchcraft'*. Research Report 750. London: DfES.

Straus, A, Douglas, E and Mederios, R (2014) *Primordial violence: spanking children, psychological development, violence and crime*. New York: Routledge.

Striker, S and Kimmel, E (2012) *The anti-colouring book*. London: Scholastic Press.

Summit, R (1983) The child sexual abuse accommodation syndrome. *Child Abuse and Neglect*, 7, 177–93.

Sunderland, M (2001) *Using story telling as a therapeutic tool with children*. London: Speechmark.

Swansea Local Safeguarding Children Board (LSCB) (2006) *Executive summary, Aaron Gilbert*. Swansea: Swansea LSCB.

Talwar, D (2012) *Daily torment of racism in the classroom.* London: BBC. www.bbc.co.uk/news/education-18150650

Tarapdar, S and Kellett, M (2011) *Young people's voices on cyber-bullying: what can age comparisons tell us?* London: The Diana Award.

Taylor, J (2010) Mother of Khyra Ishaq who starved to death cleared of murder. *Independent*, 25 February. www.independent.co.uk/news/uk/crime/mother-of-khyra-ishaq-who-starved-to-death-cleared-of-murder-1910607.html

Taylor, J, Cameron, A, Jones, C, Franklin, A, Stalker, K and Fry, D (2015) *Deaf and disabled children talking about child protection.* Edinburgh: University of Edinburgh and NSPCC.

Taylor, J, Rahilly, and Hunter, H (2012) *Children who go missing from care.* London: NSPCC.

Teather, S (2013) *Report of the parliamentary inquiry into asylum support for children and young people.* London: The Children's Society.

The Children's Society (2013) *Hidden from view: the experiences of young carers in England.* London: The Children's Society.

The Children's Society (2011) *4 in every 10 disabled children living in poverty.* London: The Children's Society.

THSCB (Tower Hamlets Safeguarding Children's Board) (2013) *Serious case review executive summary: Services provided for Child F June 2004–January 2012.* London: THSCB.

Townsend, M (2008) Babies the new target. Met warns as paedophile threat spirals. *Guardian,* 24 August.

Turner, C (2015) Arrests for leaving kids alone at home made every day. *Telegraph,* 31 October.

Turning Point (2011) *Bottling it up: the next generation.* London: Turning Point.

UN (United Nations) (1989) *Convention on the Rights of the Child* (UNCRC). Geneva: United Nations.

UN (United Nations) (2006) *Convention on the Rights of Persons with Disabilities.* www.un.org/disabilities/documents/convention/convoptprot-e.pdf

UN (United Nations) Human Rights Committee (2015) *Concluding observations on the seventh periodic report of the United Kingdom of Great Britain and Northern Ireland.* www.equalityhumanrights.com/sites/default/files/uploads/documents/humanrights/UN/CCPRC%20GB%20concluding%20observations%20(1).pdf

UN (United Nations) General Assembly (2000) *Protocol to prevent, suppress and punish trafficking in persons, especially women and children.*15 November. www.refworld.org/docid/4720706c0.html

Ureche, H and Franks, M (2007) *This is who we are. A study of the views and identities of Roma, Gypsy and Traveller young people in England*. London: The Children's Society.

Utting, W (2005) *Progress on safeguards for children living away from home.* York: Joseph Rowntree Trust.

Veeken, J (2012) *The bear cards. Feelings.* Victoria, Australia: Q cards.

Vine, J (2013) *An inspection into the Home Office's handling of asylum applications made by unaccompanied children: Feb–June 2013.* London: Independent Chief Inspector of Borders and Immigration.

Vizard, E (2006) Sexually abusive behaviour by children and adolescents. *Child and Adolescent Mental Health*, 11(1), 2–8.

Wales Online (2011) *Kidwelly sex cult victim breaks silence to tell of childhood horrors.* 13 March. www.walesonline.co.uk/news/wales-news/kidwelly-sex-cult-victim-breaks-1845707

Walker, A (1993) *Possessing the secret of joy*. London: Vintage.

Ward, J and Patel, N (2006) Broadening the discussion on sexual exploitation: ethnicity, sexual exploitation and young people. *Child Abuse Review*, 15, 341–50.

Wardale, L (2007) *Keeping the family in mind. Resource pack*. London: Barnardo's.

Wastell, D and White, S (2012) Blinded by neuroscience: social policy, the family and the infant brain. *Families, Relationships and Societies*, 1(3), 397–414.

Watson, T (2012a) *Ten days that shook my world*. www.tom-watson.co.uk/2012/11/10-days-that-shook-my-world/

Watson, T (2012b) *Prime Minister's questions*. www.youtube.com/watch?v=e6sTCIJLEKI

WFSCB (London Borough of Waltham Forest Safeguarding Children Board) (2011) *Serious case review executive summary Child W*. London: WFSCB.

White, S (2009) Arguing the case in safeguarding. In Broadhurst, K, Grover, C and Jamieson, J (eds) *Critical perspectives in safeguarding children*. Oxford: Wiley-Blackwell.

Whitham, G (2012) *Poverty in 2012. It shouldn't happen here*. London: Save the Children.

WHO (World Health Organisation) (1995) *Female genital mutilation: Report of a WHO technical working group*. Geneva: World Health Organisation.

Wilkinson, R and Pickett, K (2009) *The spirit level*. London: Penguin.

Williams, A (1943) *Barnardo of Stepney*. London: George Allen and Unwin.

Williams, R (2011) 'Honour' crimes against women in UK rising rapidly, figures show. *Guardian*, 3 December. Available at www.theguardian.com/uk/2011/dec/03/honour-crimes-uk-rising

Williams-Garcia, R (2004) *No laughter here*. New York: HarperCollins.

Willow, C (2014) *Children behind bars. Why the abuse of child imprisonment must end*. Bristol: Policy Press.

Willow, C and Hyder, T (2004) *It hurts you inside. Young children talk about smacking*. London: CRAE and Save the Children.

Wolfe, I, MacFarlane, A, Donkin, A, Marmot, M and Viner, R (2014) *Why children die: death in infants, children and young people in the UK*. London: RCPCH (Royal College of Paediatrics and Child Health).

Women's Aid (2014) *Annual survey: A moment in time*. Bristol: Women's Aid.

Wonnacott, J, Patmore, A and Kennedy, M (2013) Assessing the needs of disabled children, in Calder, M and Hackett, S (eds) *Assessment in child care*. 2nd edition. Lyme Regis: Russell House. pp185–201.

Wood, D, Barter, C and Berridge, M (2011) *Disadvantaged teenagers, intimate partner violence and coercive control*. London: NSPCC.

Wood, Z (2007) Should profit come before children? *Observer*, 21 October.

WSCB (Worcestershire Safeguarding Children Board) (2013) *Serious case review executive summary in respect of the death of FW*. Worcestershire: WSCB.

Young, A, Hunt, R, Oram, R and Smith, C (2009) *The impact of integrated children's services on the scope, delivery and quality of social care services for deaf children and their families*. London: National Deaf Children's Society.

Index